THE FLEMMINGS

THE AMERICAN CATHOLIC TRADITION

Advisory Editor
Jay P. Dolan

Editorial Board
Paul Messbarger
Michael Novak

THE FLEMMINGS

A TRUE STORY

ANNA H. DORSEY

ARNO PRESS
A New York Times Company
New York • 1978

**Publisher's Note: This book has been reproduced
from the best available copies.**

Editorial Supervision: JOSEPH CELLINI

———•———

Reprint Edition 1978 by Arno Press Inc.

THE AMERICAN CATHOLIC TRADITION
ISBN for complete set: 0-405-10810-9
See last pages of this volume for titles.

Manufactured in the United States of America

———•———

Library of Congress Cataloging in Publication Data

Dorsey, Anna Hanson McKenney, 1815-1896.
    The Flemmings.

    (The American Catholic tradition)
    Reprint of the ed. published by P. O'Shea,
New York, which was issued in the Notre Dame series
of Catholic novels.
    I. Title. II. Series. III. Series: The
Notre Dame series of Catholic novels.
PZ3.D738Fl 1978   [PS1549.D3]   813'.3
ISBN 0-405-10817-6   77-11280

The Notre Dame Series of Catholic Novels.

THE FLEMMINGS;

A TRUE STORY.

BY

MRS. ANNA H. DORSEY,

AUTHORESS OF COAINA, THE OLD GRAY ROSARY, ETC., ETC.

NEW YORK:

P. O'SHEA, 37 BARCLAY STREET.

PREFACE.

THE following story is founded upon facts related to us a year or two ago by a saintly Religious, who was well acquainted with all the circumstances which led to the conversion of the good Puritan family whom we have introduced to the reader as "The Flemmings." We have simply made use of events and incidents as narrated to us, and described the *dramatis personæ* only as those events presented themselves to our imagination.

We have not had the happiness to know personally any member of this pious family of converts, but had the gratification to read, during the progress of the story, two letters from "Eva Flemming," the daughter who, soon after their conversion, left all to devote herself to Almighty God in a religious life, where she yet toils, faithful to her vows in His divine service. In the first she says : "I recognized our history even before I received your letter. As to my Father, his character could not have been better described had the author known him all her life." In the next letter she relates some little traits of his great devotion to the Blessed Virgin, speaks of his age, his constant cheerfulness, his saintly life ; and concludes by alluding to an illness under which he was then patiently suffering, in these words : "But my dear father's beautiful and holy life is, I fear, passing away. I am prepared to hear in the next letter from home that he is gone to his eternal reward."

We have not heard that he passed away, then, but
if he did, we do know that the example of such a life
must go on bearing good fruits until the end of time.
It is said by philosophers that "nothing is ever lost,"
but we have the assurance of Eternal Truth that "the
righteous are held in everlasting remembrance."

There are a few characters, and some incidents
gleaned here and there from more southern regions,
which, being true and illustrative of the ways of Divine Providence, we introduced them into the narrative as being in harmony with it.

The trials of Wolfert Flemming's mind, and the
conversion of himself and family in the manner related, may appear either miraculous or improbable to
Catholics who know little or nothing of Protestants,
and are accustomed to regard them as knowingly
blind and irreconcilably embittered against the Catholic Church. This is, no doubt, true in many cases,
but if. the word and experience of one who, born Protestant, has been intimately associated with them all
her life, may be trusted, the most of them are earnestly sincere in religion, and are only prevented from
finding the truth by the circumstances of their birth,
a false system of education, and prejudices which have
grown with their growth, erroneous and illogical, of
course, but which, according to *their* enlightenment,
are reasonable and just. But, notwithstanding all
this, we venture to affirm there is not one Protestant
in a thousand who is not more or less disturbed and
bewildered by doubts, and perplexed by mysterious
fears resulting from a study of the Scriptures, which
cannot be solved by anything in their creed. Minds,
like faces, bear a strong resemblance to one another,

and where we find two or three having the same thoughts, doubts, perplexities and misgivings, it is natural to conclude that, under the same influences and circumstances, there may be many others disturbed in a like manner. Where there is no firm, unshaken belief in a Divine authority, no strong, impregnable faith to sustain the soul, it is natural for it to be "driven to and fro by every wind of doctrine," even while it clings tenaciously to the rule of faith received on the authority of its teachers from the Bible; it clings to doctrine and formula although fully aware that there are hundreds of other sects all differing from, and opposed to, one another, who derive their peculiar belief from the same source. This soul can do nothing better for it knows of no better way.

We have conversed often with Protestant friends, cultivated, intelligent people, who were well informed on every subject, except that of the Catholic religion, and we have listened to their discussions, so full of doubt and uncertainty, until our heart has yearned over them with an unspeakable pity, and we have never failed to hear the oft-repeated, concluding refrain: "We cannot understand it altogether, there are many contradictions; there seems to be something wanting, whatever it may, and we do not feel altogether satisfied, but we have been taught to believe so and so; and, as we have the Bible for our rule of faith, the fault is probably in ourselves, for you know that what the Bible teaches must be true." As ignorant of the Catholic religion as it really is, as if born in heathen lands—an ignorance partly the result of education—they sometimes ask questions about Catholic doctrine and precepts which would be absurd enough to provoke a laugh, if they did not evince such a lamentable and utter want of a knowledge of the truth, and such depths of prejudice, as to make one's soul sick and sad together. But this prejudice, mark you, is, in most instances, without a grain of malice, and we have watched them while they listened to simple explanations of what Catholics really do believe, and seen the look of incredulity and scorn melt from their countenances as their false impressions were removed, giving place to an expression of the deepest interest in the subject presented to them in so new a light. The zeal and good dispositions, and pure intention of pious Protestants, put to shame many of us who, belonging to the True Fold, and having all the Divine help it offers through the Sacraments, live cold and barren lives ; we have known many among them who spend their time and means in the exercise of Christian virtues and good works, who, if the right opportunity presented itself of knowing the True Faith, would embrace it with joy, as did the Flemmings.

Protestants are generally attracted to Catholic Churches by the music, and the beauty and solemnity of the ceremonies, and some by a feeling which they cannot define, but describe as a sentiment of devotion and awe which they never experienced before, and feel nowhere else. We have heard this said repeatedly by Protestants ; but when, with softened hearts, such as these, enter into our holy temples, ready and longing to receive "Bread," and yet a "stone," in the shape of a sermon, loaded with stern invective and harsh expressions against a system which they have been taught to regard as sacred, and in whose precepts they have been brought up, the result can easily be imagined, and is to be deplored. We have known this to happen—not often, it is true—but often enough to send angrily and sorrowfully away souls which otherwise might have been lured by more gentle means into the ONE True Fold.

We once knew a distinguished Prelate of a Southern Diocese * who, long since, went to his eternal reward, whose sermons always impressed, and won Protestants more by the Christian spirit which animated them than by his eloquence and gifts of oratory, both of which were of the highest order, and under whose preaching quite a multitude of converts were gathered into the Church. We have seen the (then) largest Cathedral in the country literally packed with people of all sects, classes, and grades of intelligence, who listened enthralled to the majestic simplicity of his arguments in defence and explanation of the Faith for three hours at a time without exhibiting the least fatigue, and why? Because the Faith which he so eloquently explained, and whose doctrines he so grandly defended, gave such unction and such ample scope to his gifted mind and saintly heart, and inspired thoughts and arguments of an import too sublime and holy to give him either time or desire to descend to a harsh denunciation of those of his hearers who, whatever their views of belief, were animated by a sincere desire to serve God in spirit and in truth, as far as their limited doctrines enlightened them. The words "heretic," "schismatic," and other yet more objectionable expressions were never heard in these famous discourses ; for, while the good Prelate demolished the "houses built upon the sands" by his grand

* Bishop England.

arguments in justification of Catholic Faith which, like
a tidal wave, swept them away, he never spoke of Protestants but as our "separated brethren," and while
he did not spare erroneous doctrines, he was tender
not to wound or insult the feelings of those so unfortunate as to believe them.

Because Catholics are abused and persecuted by
coarse and ignorant minds, minds, in most cases,
blinded by the errors of education, it is no reason
why Catholics, who are blessed in the possession of a
Divine Faith, which supplies every need of their souls,
leaving nothing wanting in life or in death, should as-
sail them with the same weapons ; having the Truth
they can afford to be charitable, magnanimous and
christianly.

When Protestants enter a Catholic church they feel
a natural curiosity to know what Catholics really do
believe ; and, if it can be made plain to them that,
while they claim —with secret misgivings—the Bible
alone as their rule of belief, it is to Catholics, truly,
the corner-stone of their holy Faith, which alone holds
the key to its wonderful mysteries ; a great step will
have been gained, and the way opened for them to
listen with deeper interest to all that may be said of
the dogmas and about the Divine consolations of this
saving Faith, of the practices and obligations of Catholics, and of the tender care the Church has for her
children, living and dead. They will be ready to receive impressions of the true meaning of the SPIRIT of
the Catholic religion, the faithful practice of which
transforms men into saints, in contra-distinction to
that spirit of the world which makes devils of men,
who, with the sign of Faith set upon their foreheads

by the indelible waters of Baptism, only wear the garb of Christianity as a cover for their misdeeds, and bring endless reproach, scandals and crucifixions upon the fair Spouse of Christ.

Let us be forgiven if we have said too much, and of a sort which seems irrelevant, and carries us outside our sphere. Knowing them as we do, our heart is ever full of a great and tender charity for our "separated brethren," and we feel for them as we should if standing upon the safe deck of a staunch and stately ship we saw friends whom we love drifting over the open sea without rudder, compass, or sails, at the mercy of wind and waves, in crafts already leaking and disabled. We do not like to see them driven, wounded and angry, from our temples when we *know* they come to learn something of that Faith whose garments, and the garniture of whose house, appear so fair and beautiful to their eyes. This, we are glad to know, is the exception, not the rule ; there is often gross provocation to excite retaliation from all sides, but the truth and the vantage-ground we hold upon the Rock of Peter is more than sufficient for shield, buckler and defence, against all the powers of evil combined.

The history of the "Flemmings" is very suggestive. Wolfert Flemming represents a large class in our land, and let us hope that at least some few of them may be led by his example to seek the Truth where alone it can be found ; and, like him, rejoice in the solace and rest it affords after all their doubts and toils.

AUTHOR.

CONTENTS.

THE FLEMMINGS.

CHAPTER I.

THE OLD "HOMESTEAD," AND ITS OCCUPANTS.

IT was a wild and bitter night even for that region, where the Ossipee mountains dip their feet into the waters of that beautiful Lake, which the red man, with his higher appreciation of nature, called *Winnipiseogee*, the smile of the Great Spirit; a night so stormy and cold that not a living thing was unhoused, far or near, either on the broad farm-steads which lay upon the sloping lands between the mountains, or around the rude log huts perched like eyries on their rugged sides. Only the wild creatures driven down from the pathless forests of the mountain ranges beyond, by cold and hunger, nearer towards the habitations of men, were abroad; and perhaps some luckless traveller who, belated on his journey, had lost his way among the drifts. Since the day before, snow had been steadily falling, until not even the bleached head of Chocorua could be seen as the day faded into the whiteness of the storm, and both were wrapped together in the black-

ness of the wild night. Gusts of wind swept down
through the mountain gorges with a blending of
fierce, shrill sounds, as if the spirits of ten thousand Indian warriors were abroad, mingling their
savage war-whoops and death-songs together,
while like mounds of the mighty slain, the snow-
drifts rose higher and higher, until every by-way
and road became impassable.

But there, inside Wolfert Flemming's great ram-
bling farm-house, there was ruddy light, warmth and
good cheer. That quaint old room where he and
his family sat grouped about in the warm glow of
the fire-light would have charmed the eye of a
Flemish painter; and I will describe it—not with
an idle purpose—with its depths of shadow, its dancing lights and glowing warmth. It was a large,
low-raftered room, at the north end of which was a
fire-place of enormous breadth and depth, whose
sides and high mantlepiece were set with pictured
tiles representing goodly scenes from the Old Testament, while upon the brightly painted hearth a
pair of massive andirons, crowned with great globes
of burnished brass, were piled up with blazing logs
of hickory and resinous pine which flamed and crackled with a merry din, while the smoke, ruddy with
fire, went curling with a soft roaring sound into the
deep chimney as if the thousand of sparks that it
carried into the dark recesses aloft were golden bees,

humming and swarming home to their hives. On
the broad shelves arranged on one side of the wall
there was a great array of white china, and plat-
ters and tankards of pewter, scoured to the brightness of silver, over which the fire-light leaped and
played in many a line of crinkled gold; upon the
oaken floor, dark and polished by the feet of the
generations who had trodden it, it danced and glim-
mered; upon the glass of the small deep-set win
dows, it flashed and glittered until they looked like
the jewelled windows of Alladeen's palace; up
among the dark rafters, it lit up the old Continental
muskets and swords; the deer's head with its broad
antlers; the Indian bows and arrows; and the fes-
toons of sweet-smelling herbs, which were in various ways secured to them, until one might have
thought–watching it flashing in and out–that birds
with wings of flame were flitting through the shadows under the roof. But still more brightly it dashed
itself into the antique beaufét set in an angle of the
wall, and broke into a thousand sparkles on the old-
fashioned pieces of silver, and the odds and ends of
rare burnished china—the precious heirlooms of the
Flemmings—which were ranged in state behind the
glass door, as if this spot above all others were most
worthy of being glorified. And right bravely they
gleamed in the red dancing fire-light, those antique
pieces of silver and those scraps of marvellous china,

brought from the ends of the earth by the ancestral
Flemmings, some of whom had sailed their stout
ships with the first explorers amongst the ice floes
of the Arctic seas; while others had fought the
Spaniard and burnt his forts among the spice
islands of the Orient. Somewhere about the time
that the imperishable "May Flower" landed that
"goodlie companie,"—who afterwards proved how
well they had learnt the science of intolerance from
the persecutions and oppressions they had themselves endured—on Plymouth Rock, a Flemming.
the last of the European line, found his way with
his wife and household chattels to the American
wilderness, and pitched his tent on the spot where
we find his descendants. In the course of time he
built his modest homestead, which consisted of this
low-raftered, oaken-floored room, and a smaller
sleeping apartment. Those were the times when
the Indians, taxation and intolerance—sometimes
one, sometimes another, and sometimes all together
—made the lines hard for dwellers in the land; but
he and his brave sons, and their descendants after
them, defended their home against savage violence
and destruction, and afterwards through the fire
and blood of seven years revolutionary war spared
no sacrifice to serve their country, shrunk from no
toil to raise their children to a better condition than
their own, and fill their home with every. domestic

comfort within their reach. In that corner the old
beaufét had been built when the walls of the "homestead" were raised, and upon its shelves the first
American Flemmings had arranged their treasures
of silver and china; always hidden away in times
of danger, again taken out and burnished and set in
goodly array by fingers long since crumbled to dust.
And here Wolfert Flemming decreed they should
remain, although his wife and daughters with womanly vanity and many soft persuasions showed
reasons why they should be displayed in the "best
room" of the large and new addition he had made
to his house; but their special pleading availed
nothing, the old heirlooms were to stay where his
forefathers had placed them, and here, with the
old oak settles and the clumsy old oak chairs,
and the clumsier old oak tables, they were still
shining and glistening in the red cheery fire-light.
This room was very dear to the man's true honest
heart, for its old associations as well as its new—
and to the hearts of his household; indeed they
never used the "new house," as they called it, except on extraordinary occasions, such as the instal-
lation of a new minister or a "Forefather's Day,"
or a grand quilting or apple paring, or something
of that sort, when all the young folk, far and wide,
were invited to work, feast and frolic. There was
a subtle attraction in this quaint old room for all

the Flemmings, old and young, a something which
made them feel nearer and dearer to each other, for
here each one uttered his thoughts without restraint, and with that sweet confidence in one
another which left but small occasion for any un-
charitableness or heart-burning. Here also, in plain
and genuine sincerity, they admonished and reproved each other with christianly spirit, holding
up one another's hands, warming one another's
hearts, until the bonds that bound them together
were stronger than death. Here the weak sought
the strong, the sad of heart clung to the hopeful,
and the desponding came to bask in the cheerful
and wholesome mirth of the happy; here, from
their earliest recollection, they had gathered together, morning and evening, around their father
and mother, to worship God according to their
teachings and with the genuine simplicity of honest
hearts hear read the word of God, which, full of far-
off mysteries to them, impressed their minds with a
noble love of truth, high spiritual aspirations, and a
solemn reverence for religious things. Simple in
mind and heart, they accepted as true what they were
taught, and lived justly according to the lights they
had. But the Flemmings took no thought of ana-
lyzing their lives, and if any one had said *to* them,
what *I* have written *of* them, they would have set
him down as a shiftless sort of dreamer, and unfit

for a useful work-a-day life; such an one as they feared their golden-haired Reuben would be. They were a matter-of-fact, clear-headed people; and if a thought once got into their heads, and this thought had fair play—which it generally got in their well-balanced brains—and lifted like a lever some tangible principle into existence, there was not a Flemming of them all who would not have suffered martyrdom in its defence.

There they all sat, that stormy winter's night, their comely, honest faces fairly glorified by the golden radiance of the fire, almost inclining one to believe in the old Saxon superstition that angels are always basking in the light of a wood fire.

Eva and Hope Flemming sat together, their young faces bent over wonderful blocks of patchwork, a brillant geometrical problem known as "Job's trouble," which they were uniting with much taste, while they chattered together in an undertone of the quilting bee they would have when it was finished. Very fair and comely were these two daughters of the house, in the first flush of a healthy and pure womanhood: their forms well developed and symmetrically rounded; their features well cut and handsome; their teeth showing like pearls between their red lips, and their beauty crowned by thick suits of soft golden brown hair, which was pushed back loose and curling from Eva's rounded forehead, but which fell in smooth, heavy bands on each side of Hope's more intellectual brow, and was twisted together in a heavy coil at the back of her finely formed head. Their father, Wolfert Flemming, sat a little apart from them, at a table upon which was outspread the large family Bible, a relic of early English printing, for which the *savans* and literary people who sometimes came to spend their holidays amongst the romantic scenery of the neighborhood, had time and again offered him large sums; but no money could have purchased it, and no inducement persuade him to part with it. He liked the looks of it, the obsolete spelling, the quaint letters, the rude line engravings; and above all, the family record of his house for generations back. The book was opened at the sixth chapter of St. John's Gospel, and he was reading to himself, with a reverent but troubled look upon his countenance. He was a tall, muscular man, broadshouldered and well formed, his lower jaw square and firmly set, with a cleft in the chin just redeeming his countenance from grimness; his eyebrows were dark and heavy, and overhung a pair of large intelligent gray eyes; his forehead broad and moderately high, crowned with a full crop of soft black hair, thickly sprinkled with white. Dressed in a ⁀uit of brown homespun, which hung loosely upon

him without anything to relieve its homeliness of
color or style, except the exquisite whiteness of his
coarse linen collar, turned well back from his throat,
and the spotless cuffs fastened around his sinewy
wrists by a pair of old-fashioned gold sleeve-buttons,
there was yet in the appearance and attitude of the
man a dignity and power as remarkable as it is difficult to describe. There was a vacant chair near—
one of those prim, low-seated high-backed chairs,
rich in beading and grotesque carving, all filled in
with fine cane-work which people who own them
declare, with due solemnity, were brought over in
the "May Flower;" but the Flemmings had no such
tradition of this one, and yet they never doubted
but that it was brought in the old Puritan days from
England by some of the early settlers; and wished
sometimes that it might speak its own history, for
it may have belonged to Miles Standish himself.
Its origin, however, gave them small anxiety; it was
so well filled that their eyes, hearts and minds were
fully satisfied when its usual occupant, their little
mother, was throned upon it; and had she by any
inexorable event been forced to vacate it, it would
never have been used again, but put aside as a precious relic of the best wife and mother who ever
lived. They had all of them a very good idea of
relics in a limited sense, and would only have regarded them as superstitious if religion had invested

them with a sacred or spiritual meaning. **Mrs.**
Flemming had just flitted from her chair, knitting
in hand, to see after the welfare of a calf which was
so unfortunate as to be born in the middle of a New
England winter, and about which all her motherly
instincts were aroused. There was yet another of
the family group present, who sat leaning against
an angle of the fire-place, poring over the pages of
a well worn book, while the glow of the yellow
flames fell round and upon him with a radiance
that brought him out from the dark back-ground
like one of those celestial figures one sees in the
pictures of Domenichino and Velasquez. He was
slight and delicately formed, his forehead broad and
serene; his eyes large, blue and tender; while his
pale golden hair, parted in the middle, fell in soft
waving masses over his cheeks and neck. This was
Reuben Flemming, the youngest of the children, a
puzzle and sweet torment as well as mystery to the
strong. practical, wholesome minds of his kindred,
who were utterly at a loss to know what he was
good for, because hard, energetic, ceaseless work
did not agree with him, but set him to faint if he
attempted to do what his sturdy brother Nicolas
did, or turn white and trembling with a strange
sickness which neither he nor they could understand. But Reuben Flemming had a marvellous
energy for books; indeed all of them were fond of

books, and read intelligently, but with him it was a
passion in whose sweet trances he would lose himself with utter forgetfulness of his surroundings:
and Hope, who often watched him in those moods,
declared that it was equal to seeing the rich glory
of sunset reflected on the haze of the distant mountains, to mark the changeful emotions of his heart
pictured on his lovely countenance.

Mrs. Flemming came in now and brought good
news of the calf, and also a wholesome breath of pure
chilly air as she fluttered around, and passing her
hand lightly and tenderly over her husband's head,
leaned over his shoulder and with a little sigh whispered: "Still troubled over the text;" and getting
no answer, left him and took her seat upon her
throne. A little body was Martha Flemming, neat,
tidy and alert, with a quick, shrewd intelligence in
her fine black eyes, and an expression of benevolence on her forehead which almost belied the
rather suspicious and vindictive mouth whose thin
lips and narrow chin made strangers think she was
a hard one to deal with, as she was, until to her
clear thinking all that seemed doubtful in principle
or fact was made clear to her.

"I am thankful," she said, as she settled herself
and began turning the heel of her sock; "that the
last chore is finished. The poor silly calf is as comfortable as can be; but I do wish Nick was at home

It is still snowing ; indeed it falls thicker than ever

"I told you so, Hope—I knew yesterday by the white mists over the mountains that we should have a good old-fashioned snow before long. I am so glad," said Eva with a little laugh.

"So am I, "said Hope ; " the ground is well frozen, and the sleighing will be perfectly splendid. I do admire to see a great heavy fall of snow that covers up fences and walls, and blocks one up until one has to be dug out." Just then a gust of wind was hurled down from the mountains with such a roar and commotion that the house trembled at the shock, while the sleet lashed the windows and walls with a shrill whistling sound that rose and fell with the wind like despairing shrieks. The women, although accustomed to the wintry storms of that region, had never heard the like of this before, and let fall their work and looked at each other, startled and pale. The boy Reuben did not hear the din ; he stood beside Uriel in the sun, listening to the cherub who sought knowledge of Eden, his soul thrilling with horror, as at the angel's touch the beautiful heaven-clad thing faded into the swart, defiant, scowling image of Lucifer.

Wolfert Flemming lifted his head from the inspired page, and with an exalted look exclaimed: "O ye cold and heat, bless the Lord! O ye dews and hoar frost, bless the Lord! O ye frost and cold, bless the Lord. O ye ice and snow, bless the Lord; O ye nights and days, bless the Lord. O let the earth bless the Lord ; let it praise and exalt Him above all, forever." With another man, this might have seemed like a dramatic display, but in him it was the spontaneous outflowing of a soul whose thoughts dwelt habitually on the infinite attributes of the Supreme Being, and who searched the Scriptures daily, hoping to find in them—nay, believing that he had—the words of eternal life.

"I guess father," said Mrs. Flemming after a little pause, "that we ought to be thankful that everything is housed. There's no such apples, potatoes, or pumpkins either, around as ours. I'm glad to know they are safe; but, deary me! I do wonder where Nick can be this wild night?"

CHAPTER II.

WHAT CAME OUT OF THE STORM TO THE FLEMMINGS.

"Nicholas is safe, depend upon that, mother," said the Elder, as he arose and stretched himself; then grasping the heavy tongs, he turned over the fire, heaped up the coals, and poked and punched between the crevices of the logs, with an infinite relish in the din and sparkle that he raised. "I suppose he is up to Deacon Sneath-en's."

"Yes," said Eva, laughing slyly, "he promised to tell Huldah how to manage her hydrangers."

"So. It is early to begin spring gardening," said the Elder, with a grim smile, not displeased at the hint.

"Huldah is a natty, industrious girl," said Mrs. Flemming, knitting vigorously; "and raises the finest chickens and spins the evenest yarn of any one from here to Alton Bay."

Wolfert Flemming—or "the Elder," as he was called by the people of his sect—turned, and looked fondly at the little figure of his wife, smoothed her hair with his great, brown hand very gently, and said: "Martha! Martha! thou art troubled about many things."

"Yes, I know it," she replied, with a merry little laugh. "I don't know what in the land's name would become of you all if I were not."

"I don't like that word trouble, 'little mammy;' it sounds reproachful, and I am sure that you are very proud of us all," said Eva.

"Trouble's trouble, my dear. It was no fun to have raised the family I have—"

"And the husband—"

"Nonsense, father, you were raised before I was

born, but land sakes! just listen at the storm. I do wish that Nick had not gone away this morning."

"Mother, you forget that Nicholas has spent the last four years of his life in Franconia, where he's learned to take care of himself. Trust in God for your boy's safety, and in his own sagacity," said the Elder gravely, for he could not bear to have her troubled or anxious.

"Well, I'll try my best; but it would be frightful for any living thing to be exposed to the fury of this storm." Then, after a little while, she said: "What do the people down at —— say about the new-fangled meeting house?"

"They are greatly excited over it, and guards are stationed around it every night to prevent its being torn down," said the Elder, sternly.

"What in the world sort of sect is it? Is it Romish?"

"Well, about as bad; it's one of the Church of England tabernacles, and their preacher or priest, or whatever he is, is as ignorant of the simplicity of the Gospel as the Pope of Rome himself."

"It's enough to rouse the Pilgrim Fathers from their graves, to have such doings on the soil of New England. Time was, when the lines would not have been quite so easy for them as now. I heard my grandmother tell of one that was kept in the pillory a day and night, and branded, for preaching strange doctrines in our borders. What's that?" exclaimed Mrs. Flemming, with a start.

" Mother, I hear nothing but the wind," said her husband.

" Land sakes! I certainly heard a knocking somewhere ; I hope it is not Indians. The house don't overget their filthy ways for a week when we have to harbor them. There it is again—"

" Yes, some one was knocking at the side-door of the new part of the house ; there was a momentary lull in the storm, and they all heard it—a low, quick knocking, a smothered cry and sudden silence. The Elder took up the candle and went out, followed by Eva. Mrs. Flemming sat still, and knit with nervous rapidity, not overmuch pleased at the prospect of entertaining Indians. The Elder strode through the room adjoining the ' old homestead,' and turned down a long narrow passage, at the extremity of which was the door whence the sounds came. He gave the candle to Eva, who stood shading it with her hand, and unlocked the door ; then, turning the latch, quickly opened it, and was almost thrown off his feet by a man falling heavily on him. The wind rushed in with a wild shriek, driving in sleet and snow, and extinguished the light. Eva screamed with terror, but her father's voice, clear and distinct, yet slightly tremulous with excitement, rose out of the darkness, bidding her close the door: 'I am not hurt,' he cried; 'but here is a man frozen, or dead, in my arms. Courage, child, and close the door quickly.' The wind was blowing with tremendous force, but the strong healthy girl threw herself against the door, and after a struggle which quickened her breath, she succeeded in closing and locking it. By this time Mrs. Flemming and Hope, uneasy at their long absence, joined them—all in the dark together, asking and answering questions, as they groped their way back to the sitting-room, moving slowly, for the weight of the frozen man was heavy even to the Elder."

"I knew that I heard a knocking," said Mrs. Flemming; "and now, suppose he should be frozen to death through our not going at first."

"I don't think he's frozen to death, mother," he replied. "God forbid such a thing should happen at our door. I think he is only benumbed with the cold and fatigue together."

They were now in the room next to their sitting-room, and through the open door a stream of light and warmth entered, and the Elder laid his unbidden guest very gently down on a broad chintz-covered lounge, while the others ran to get restoratives, blankets, and pillows. He unfastened the man's wrappings, unbuttoned his vest and shirt, and laid his hand anxiously over his heart; for there was no pulsation in the big brawny wrists, no life in the blue frozen hands so helpless and cold. "It beats," he said at last; "beats very faintly. Open the door wide; that will let in heat enough for him now, poor fellow," said the Elder, while he rubbed the stranger's chest vigorously. "A few drops of brandy, mother—now a little more—he swallows it—rub his wrists; bring in warm flannels—" And they rubbed him and ministered to him long and patiently, and hopefully, until the signs of life grew more frequent and distinct, and finally his stagnant blood flowed slowly and warmly through his veins. He opened his eyes, and looked with a dreamy wonder about him and into the strange faces around him.

"You are all right now, friend," said the Elder; "take a drink of this hot coffee;" and he held the steaming cup to the stranger's lips, while he put his arm under him, lifting his head from the pillow. Who was this waif that the storm had driven into their home? was he a prophet of evil to the happy household, or were they entertaining an angel unaware?" They did not know; they had not even thought of who or what he might be. Mrs. Flemming was only heartily glad that he was not an Indian, and the girls thought him uncommonly hard-featured. There was not the smallest figment of anything in his appearance in which there was a possibility of romance; his features were large and coarse, his head was covered with a shock of grizzled sandy hair, almost red; and the lower part of his face was hidden by a thick tawny beard, grotesquely covered with small icicles, which were melting at their leisure. The sisters thought he was a Jew; but all of them recognized only one fact concerning him, and that was he was their guest, thrown by Providence upon their hospitality. He drank the hot fragrant coffee slowly, and with some difficulty in swallowing; then he began to fumble about his breast, inside his vest, and about his neck, with trembling fingers and perplexed look.

"He misses something," said Mrs. Flemming. "Is it your money that you are looking for?" He shook his head in the negative; the cold had had such an effect upon him that his powers of articulation were not yet restored. It was not his money.

"Perhaps it is his watch. Is it your watch, sir? See, here it is, safe and sound," said the active little woman, holding his old silver watch, as big as a turnip, before his eyes.

No, it was not the watch, which he motioned

away from him; nor was it a "locket" or a "minia-
ture." "Well," exclaimed Mrs. Flemming, "I'm
beat out. Come here, Reuben; this stranger has
lost something, and is fretted about it; see if you
can help me make out what he means." Reuben
had just come in; he had been helping with the
rest to restore the frozen man, but had stepped out
at his mother's bidding to fetch an additional
blanket from an upper room.

"Perhaps it is this. While father was rubbing his
breast, this flew off upon the floor; father must
have broken the string," said Reuben, holding by
a bit of broken cord a brass medallion, upon which
was graven the figure of a woman. Whatever it is,
there is a cross on the other side." A gleam of joy
lit up the homely face of the stranger; he
stretched out his hand to take his treasure, and
pressing it to his lips, murmured, "Blessed Mother;" then, folding it close to his breast, he fell into
a quiet sleep, heaped over with soft fleecy blankets,
his head p   ed on downy pillows, while the storm
howled without as if enraged at losing its prey.

"Poor man, I am glad he found that thing of his
mother's; I guess it is some keepsake she gave
him years ago, and I shouldn't wonder if she is
dead," said Mrs. Flemming, settling herself once
more at her knitting. "I do wish Nick was home
with us—it is an awful night."

Wolfert Flemming's own heart was not altogether easy about his absent son. He might be safely housed at Deacon Sneathen's, or he might be lying cold and stark among the frozen drifts; but he kept his anxiety to himself, and talked of other things, trusting all the while in God for the safety of his first-born. "We have just rescued a stranger from death," he thought to himself; "we have done unto him as a brother; so may our Father in Heaven do unto us;" and somehow he was comforted.

"I tell you what, father," said Mrs. Flemming, after a silence longer than usual; "maybe that man in there is not a safe one to have under our roof. Suppose we move him to the barn; there's plenty of nice sweet straw there, and he can have the blankets and pillows."

"Nonsense. I won't have him disturbed, wife," said the Elder, frowning.

"I shan't sleep a wink to-night," she continued. "Eva, see if the beaufét is locked; but stop. Reuben, you and the girls take the silver out and carry it up stairs to my room."

"Let the silver be," said the Elder, gravely. "Is it seemly for Christians to hold a halter in one hand, when they do a thing for God's sake with the other? Be patient, thrifty, and careful, little wife; and comfort yourself with the thought of those treasures which are laid up where neither moth nor rust doth consume, and where thieves break not through and steal."

Mrs. Flemming had too much respect for the genuine goodness of her husband to argue this point with him; but she felt that, according to her common-sense view of the matter, he was wrong in *fact*, however right he might be in principle; so this managing little woman determined on a piece of strategy, by which she could preserve her treasures from harm, and at the same time avoid disobeying her husband; she would, under some domestic pretence, stay in the sitting-room a little while after the family had retired, and bolt the door between it and the other one occupied by the stranger; and being always the first one down in the morning, she could slip the bolt back, and no one be the wiser. This idea quieted her mind, and she began to narrow the toe of her sock with much complacency, taking part now and then in the cheerful conversation of her daughters; while the Elder walked up and down, with his hands clasped behind him, pondering over that chapter of the Gospel of Saint John, which had for years troubled him secretly, thinking deep thoughts which led him into a mental labyrinth whereof he held no clue, which led him, as the Star did the Eastern kings, until having come to Jerusalem, it disappeared.

The next morning Mrs. Flemming found everything safe—none of her treasures had taken to themselves wings and flown away, and she saw how much anxiety she might have spared herself; but, womanlike, she reasoned: "It is best to be on the safe side; there's no knowing what *may* have happened." Then she bestirred herself to prepare a substantial and delicious breakfast, which was ready to be spread on the snow-white cloth by the time their morning devotions were over. They were all seated around the table when their guest came in. He had a stooping, ungainly figure, and returned their salutations with an awkward obeisance; the Elder made a place for him near himself, and Mrs. Flemming began to pour out a cup of coffee for him, feeling a little guilty as she looked into his honest eyes. The man sat down, then he bowed his head, and lifting his right hand, made the sign of the cross, not in a little twiddle on his breast, as if he were ashamed of it, or in a twirl and flutter of his fingers, as if he were catching flies, but a slow, deliberate, broad-spread sign, in which there was so little to be mistaken that Mrs. Flemming, who had been watching him, exclaimed: "Good gracious!" and gave such a start that the cup and saucer fell from her hand with a clatter upon the tray, spilling its contents into a freshly-filled bowl of her best maple sugar.

The stranger raised his eyes and looked around, unconscious of the excitement he had caused; the Elder asked him how he felt, while he helped him to bacon and eggs, and Mrs. Flemming, with a red flush on her cheeks, poured out another cup of coffee. Before he began to eat, he held his knife awkwardly poised, and with a hesitating bashfulness, said: "I'm heartily obliged to you all for your kindness; God and His saints reward ye for the same, I must have perisht if ye hadn't taken me in. I was almost agone, when of a sudden I saw the light from your windows; after that I couldn't remember anything."

"We are thankful to have saved a fellow-being from such a dreadful death. Where were you go-ing?" said the Elder.

"To Wier's Landing," he replied.

"A long journey, even for a summer day. You must be a stranger to these parts?"

"It hasn't been six months, sir, since I landed in Boston, from Ireland, and I thought I'd come up the counthry with my pack,—I am a peddler;— but I staid longer than I intended, and was on my way back when the snow caught me on the moun-tains, blinding me so that I lost my way entirely."

"You have had a narrow escape—I don't re-member such a storm in many years"—said the Elder, who had not noticed him bless himself.

"You are very welcome to the small service we have rendered you, and also to remain with us until it will be safe for you to travel." A warm, grateful glow suffused the stranger's countenance; his heavy eyes lit up, and, folding his hands together, he leaned towards the Elder and said in fervent tones: " *May the holy Mother of God reward you.*"

There. It was out. It had exploded like a bomb in the very bosom of this good Puritan family, that their guest was neither Indian, thief, or Jew, but a papist, than which they had nothing in greater horror; and here, under their very roof, eating at their table, practicing his superstitious rites and uttering his idolatrous prayers, before their very eyes, he sat in this room of all others, where for generations God had been worshipped according to the orthodox teachings of Luther and Knox. An Irishman his speech betrayed him, a papist his little acts of devotion confessed him; the combination was overwhelming, and the meal was finished in silence, for there was an ominous look on Martha Flemming's face, seldom seen, but when seen they all knew its portent, and respected as well as dreaded it. She followed her husband from the room, her step quick and firm, her head thrown a little back, a sparkle in her handsome black eyes and a red spot on each cheek. Meanwhile the

simple soul, utterly unconscious of offence, drew a
chair up beside Reuben, and told him, with an
effort to be brave and careless over it, that he had
lost his "pack," containing all of his earthly goods,
in the drifts. "He thought, as well as he could
remember, that he had it when he saw the lights
from the windows, and that was the last bit of consciousness he felt; did Reuben think he could get
some one to go a little way with him to look for
it?"

"I'll speak to my father, sir, when he comes in,"
said Reuben, kindly. Then he asked him if he had
travelled much in the "old country." "Yes, the
man had been to France, and Spain, and Algiers!"
Then Reuben, all aglow with enthusiasm, asked
question after question about those beautiful lands
of his poetic dreams, and if he got no poetry and
romance in exchange, he received shrewd, sensible
answers, which made him feel as happy as if he
were reading a new book. The girls were busy
over their morning duties in the household, and
when Mrs. Flemming came back she saw her son,
his arm leaning on the man's shoulder, their heads
so close together that his golden hair and the
other's grizzled locks mingled, the one telling
strange tales of other lands, the other listening
entranced.

"Reuben," she said sharply, "come, get down

some bundles of yarn to reel; I don't see how you can sit around idling, where all are busy."

CHAPTER III.

WHaT THE FLEMMINGS THOUGHT, AND WHAT THEIR GUEST THOUGHT.

It is not as safe to judge by the actions as by the intention and the degree of light which gives expression to the motives in different minds. The confession of faith made by the stranger at the breakfast table of the Flemmings, when he blessed himself in his broad, old-country fashion, and gave vent to his gratitude by invoking the Mother of God to reward his benefactors, produced different effects upon husband and wife. The Elder went away to a quiet little room, where he kept his papers, books, and the farm accounts; a room not fine enough to be called a library, office, or study, but a matter-of-fact sort of a place, where a plain desk, two or three chairs, a tool-chest, some book-shelves, a fowling-piece, and an array of fishing tackle completed the furnishing. The books were sermons, essays, and arguments on Puritanical doctrines; orthodox, quaint and severe—permeated through and through by that

anti-catholic spirit which formed one of the inte-
gral essences of their creed; books written before
the innovation of the newer lights had polished
down its monstrous angularities and sweetened the
bitter waters with something of Christian charity;
books cherished by the Flemmings for the sound
doctrine of them, and for the sort of moral sheet--
anchor they were to their spiritual life. The Elder
closed the door, went to a window, brushed the
frost-work from a pane and looked out at the
snow, which still fell heavily. He drummed softly
on the glass, and his great eyebrows lowered over
his eyes, a sure sign that he was perplexed and
annoyed. But he never acted hastily; it was his
way to look things squarely in the face, to measure
and gauge them in length, breadth and depth, before he undertook to cope with them; and there
he stood, girding his thoughts together for counsel, when Mrs. Flemming, who left the table almost
immediately after him, came in. She did not
speak until she got close to him, then laying her
hand upon his arm, she said: "Elder!" She had,
two or three times before, since their marriage,
when she thought the gravity of the occasion required, or her own sense of dignity of right de-
manded it, called him "Elder;" it was a portent
which he understood, and when he turned and saw
the flushed, and determined countenance lifted to

his, he braced himself for battle, for he knew from his religious point of view that she was terribly exercised, and as much alarmed by the presence of the papist that had dropped into their midst, as if a wolf from the Franconia mountains had got into their sheep-fold; nay, more.

"What is the matter, wife?"

"You may well ask that, Elder Flemming, after seeing and hearing what happened at the breakfast table with that miserable pedler. That man is a papist. I never saw one before, and hoped I never might; but I've read of them to some purpose."

"Yes," said the Elder gravely, "he is a papist; there can be no doubt about it, and I am sorry for it."

"But what are we to do? We cannot have him staying on," she replied, in her quick decided way.

"We must be patient. There is no help for it," he replied in his quiet tones.

"Patience in this case were an offence to God. I can have no patience, not the least grain, with an idolatrous papist; and he certainly must not stay under this roof."

"What would you have me do, wife?" said the Elder, as he turned and faced her, and looked gravely down upon her.

"I would have you go this instant and bid him leave the house."

"Have you looked out to-day?" he asked in the same even tones.

"Yes, I have looked out, and know that it is snowing as fast as ever—but that is not my business; I will not have that man contaminating my house with his idolatrous breath, and if you want peace under your roof you must send him off."

"'Won't' and must' are senseless words under certain circumstances," answered the Elder. "Providence sometimes gives us blind work to do, and it is not for us to gainsay the wisdom of it. God knows that I would suffer even death for the integrity of my faith; but in this case, after looking at it in all its bearings, I can come to but one conclusion. *I* did not make it storm—*I* did not bid this stranger to my door—the storm arose at the bidding of Him who takes into account the falling of a hair from my head; and this, His creature, let us remember—permitted by His providence—was driven by the violence of the storm to the shelter of my roof; let him therefore be what he may, he shall stay. Why, woman! he would perish in an hour!"

"But consider, Elder Flemming," responded the little woman, impressed in spite of herself by his simple practical reasoning, "consider what an offence it is to our simple God-fearing faith, to have him flouting his crosses n our very faces, and say-

ing his idolatrous prayers to the Virgin Mary.
You are not faithful to your christian duty, and
your responsibility as an Elder of the Church, to
to allow it. Those books, full of sound doctrine,
from whose pages we have not only found a safe
guide, but learnt the unction of the word, cry out
against you!" she added, pointing to the book-
shelves.

"I do not hold with superstitious practices, wife,
neither do I love popery," said the Elder, with just
a little quaver in his voice; "but neither one nor
the other can hurt the integrity of my belief in
sound doctrine. But I should feel worthy of condemnation if I turned one of God's creatures from
the shelter of my roof in such a storm as this—and
I will not do it."

"Very well. The responsibility be upon your
head. I have done *my* duty ; and I tell you, Elder,
that there's something lying at my heart which
means trouble, and that man is to bring it upon
us. I never felt so. I am not used to such things,
and it troubles me. You and Reuben can fix up a
place somewhere over the kitchen for him to sleep
—christian men have slept there before him—and
he can take his meals by the kitchen fire whilst we
are at ours," said Mrs. Flemming.

"He shall eat at my table whilst he is my guest.
Now, little wife," he said, laying his broad hand

kindly upon her shoulder, "would you have me, your husband and a Flemming, lose my self-respect, and offend my conscience, by doing unto others that which I would not they should do unto me? I have never done so yet. It would be against my views of christian hospitality and humanity. No, no!—think better of this, and the time will come when you will be thankful that your husband did not do that which would call a blush to his cheek to his dying day."

"You ought to blush to your dying day for eating and drinking with a papistical Irishman," she said, giving her head a little toss.

"Christ ate with publicans and sinners," replied the Elder, in his grave low tones; "and we are but the servants of our Master. In the Book of books He tells us that a cup of cold water given in His name to one of His little ones, and for His sake, is service done unto Himself; He does not say *to whom* we are to give, whether to Jew or Gentile, but places all the value upon *the act done for the love of Him*. I am sorry that you have been ruffled, little wife; I would not for my right hand anger you lightly, but the question between us is one that I must settle according to the precepts of the gospel, and *not* according to the old code, which would have hung that papist for coming within our borders."

"I do not wish to hang the man; though I don't know that it would be far from wrong to hang idolators, that the poison of their doctrines might not imperil the God-fearing," she said, holding her head very erect; then, knowing how useless it would be to argue the matter further, she turned and left the room to go the round of her endless domestic duties, the first act of which was—as we have seen—to rout the dreamy Reuben from his comfortable seat beside the pedler, to go up with her to the weaving-room, among the yarn hanks—rather a prosy thing to come to, after listening to a rudely eloquent account of a battle on the romantic shores of Spain, for the old pedler had fought under Wellington on the peninsula. Poor Reuben! cobwebs for banners, scaling the loom instead of a rampart, the sharp quick tones of his little mother's voice instead of the sound of clarion and trumpet, dust for the smoke of battle, and the great hanks of blue, grey, and white yarn for bastions and forts; the boy's head was full of the fancy, and he pitched over the heavy, twisted hanks—thinking of the Spaniards all the time—with such vim that his mother cried out: "Reuben! my son, you will bury me under the wool if you don't stop,"—while she looked with a tender, puzzled expression at his flushed, beautiful face; "and besides, you are getting everything in a muss up there; come down."

And Reuben came tumbling down through the warp of the loom, breaking about five hundred threads, and to his great astonishment bumping his head as it fell where his feet ought to be, while his feet stuck up helplessly through the broken meshes. "What *is* he good for?" thought his mother, looking with dismay at the broken threads; "what ever shall we do with him? I intended to begin weaving my carpet this very day!" He was very sorry after he had scrambled loose, and putting his arms tenderly around his mother, promised to mend the mischief he had done, and be more careful hereafter; and his mother, always tender of him, kissed him, smoothed the knob raised on the back of his head and told him that he "was as awkward as a young colt," upon which he laughed, and gathering up the yarn he had pitched down, followed her down stairs.

Later in the day, the Elder came into the sitting room—the old homestead where we first saw the Flemmings—and saw his guest standing at a window, looking disconsolately out at the pitiless white storm. It was ironing-day, and Eva and Hope were ironing the family linen; rosy, cheerful and happy, they smoothed and folded the spotless garments, their chatter, and laughter, and scraps of song, filling the room with homely but sweet music as they flitted to and from the fire, and from their broad table to the great rack where they hung the fragrant linen to air. Mrs. Flemming was getting dinner, and Reuben was sitting by the kitchen fire, making strenuous exertions to half-sole his boot, by way of being useful; but his long white fingers were in his way; they tangled the thread, and put things out of line, and got punched with the awl and cracked with the hammer so often that he felt like throwing the whole affair into the fire. And so the waif was left alone to his thoughts. Eva and Hope, in the tender womanly pity of their hearts, had spoken now and then to him, and he had replied with a genuine readiness which showed how much inclined he was to be social and friendly; but there was their work to be done, while the thought of his being a papist and a wholesome dread of their mother acted as a sort of moral check-rein on their kindly natures; so he had dropped into silence, and was brooding over the prospect.

"I am sorry to learn from my son that you have lost your pack," said the Elder kindly.

"Faith, sir, and I have, I'm afeard; and it's no trifle for a poor man like myself to lose," he said, as he turned and took the chair his host offered him.

"It may be lying within arm's length of us, Mr.—"

"McCue, Patrick McCue, sir, at your service."

"We will get shovels presently, Mr. McCue, and turn over the drifts around the door where we found you last night; it may be lying there under the snow. Do you remember having it when you came towards the house?"

"Yes, sir; yes—surely," said Patrick, brightening up. "It is the last thing I remimber, was seeing the lights and feeling to see if my pack was safe; but I niver see such mountains of snow, and it takes the heart out of me to think how it'll iver be found."

"Well, we must hope for the best, Mr. McCue; if it is lost, there is your life to be thankful for."

"That's thrue, sir, thanks be to God and the Blessed Virgin first, thin to yourself, and all of yez," he said fervently. Down dropped the Elder's heavy eyebrows, and his forehead grew red. Must he speak? Would it be a christianly act to rebuke this benighted mortal? Yes, he thought so. Was it not his duty, there before his children, to break a silence that might otherwise seem like pusillanimity, or consent to strange irrational practices? It seemed so to his well balanced judgment; and he asked:

"What religion are you of, Mr. McCue?"

"What religion, sir? I'm none of your religions; I'm a Catholic, God Almighty be thanked," said

the man, opening wide his dull grey eyes and looking full in the Elder's face.

"Are you convinced, and firmly persuaded, that
what you profess is right, and that it is a faith unto
salvation?"

"No, I'm not convinced, nor persuaded, nor any
of that, sir; I KNOW IT; and sorra a bit do I want
of any other. If I ever want to turn haythen I'll
go to Algiers, where I was once before," exclaimed
McCue. "Yes, sir! I'm satisfied for this world,
and the next, with the ould faith."

There was much in this to irritate the Elder's
religious ideas; there was, to his thinking, an arrogance, a profanity, and a something in the Irishman's reply, which came very near calling him a
heathen, that tried his patience; but he was not
one, as we know, to quarrel with a man on his own
hearthstone on account of his religion; but the
crowning paradox of it all was, the man had said
"I'm none of your religions, I'm a Catholic;" ac-
cordingly then, to his views, it was an acknowledgment that he (the man) was without religion, the
Catholic religion or faith being in his opinion beyond the pale of what he (the Elder) knew as
Christianity. What had he then? What *was* being a Catholic? Was *that* a religion? He thought
not, Catholics being idolaters, and where there was
idolatry there could be no religion; then the

thought came up before him with a dark splendor like one of Salvator Rosa's pictures, of one "clothed in scarlet, who was drunk with the blood of the saints." But the Elder said nothing of all this to Patrick McCue, who, ignorant as he was in all worldly lore, could have enlightened him upon many points on which he deemed him ignorant, and might perhaps have used his fists by way of emphasis, as is an Irishman's way when his holy faith is insulted. So the Elder, in his grave and gentle voice, only said:

"The grace of God is sufficient for all men, and I pray that He may open your eyes to the truth as it is in Christ. I mean no offence, friend, but we are a simple, God-fearing family, serving Him in spirit and taking no account of outward observances and signs; and while you tarry with us, which you are heartily welcome to do until the roads are safe, you will be doing us a favor if you will omit making the signs over yourself that you did this morning at the table."

"And is it the sign of the Cross?" cried Patrick McCue, staring with wide open eyes. "Why, man alive! I always blesses myself before and after meat, and I'd be an ill-mannered cur not to, surely."

"It is an offence to us, such practices," said the Elder; "and I do not think it too much to ask you to omit them while under my roof, at least at my table."

"Sir," flamed out Patrick McCue, "and do you think I'd be ashamed of the blessed cross of Christ, if the whole world stood forenent me? I, that was redeemed by it, baptized by it, and expects to make the sign of it with the last life that's left in my fingers. Let the Jews that crucified Him, and them that houlds with them, be offinded, but sorra a bit of a Jew, or a black bitther Protestant, is Patrick McCue; and, sir, with many thanks for your kindness, I'll be off at the risk of my life in the snow, sooner than stay where I daren't make the sign of the Cross."

And Patrick McCue got up, buttoned up his rough coat to the chin, and was about putting on his fur cap, when the Elder laid his hand upon his shoulder and began to speak: "Sit down, sit down. No man ever left my house in a passion or in a storm. There must be sincerity in your error, or you would not be so ready to die for it. Such doings are strange to us, but you are my guest, and hospitality was always something sacred with the Flemmings. I have done my duty before God and my children in protesting against what I consider idolatrous; but while you remain here, the subject shall not be renewed." Then the Elder could not, for the life of him, help wondering if "after all it was a *very* rank error, or even idolatrous for a christian to make upon his body the sign of that cross upon which the Son of God paid such an infinite price for his salvation; but he only said: "I will go and fetch the snow-shovels, and we will search for your pack;" while Patrick McCue thought: "Well, and surely this bates Bannagher! first to find myself somewhere away at the North Pole, and kilt among the snow-drifts, then to be tould that I'm little better than a pagan, and mustn't bless myself; and the man with sich a straight, kind face on him all the time. Sorra a bit if I know whether he's poking fun at me or not, it seems so out-and-out foolish; and if he's in airnest, bedad! but he's the most benighted man I ever met this side the Algerines."

CHAPTER IV.

HOW THE DAY PASSED, AND HOW IT ENDED.

ELDER FLEMMING came in with snow-shovels and gave one to Patrick McCue, and they went out to search among the drifts for the missing pack. Nearly up to their shoulders in snow, they worked with a will, clearing a space around the door and a few rods beyond, without success, until the Irish-

man, much of whose life had been spent in warm,
sunny latitudes, felt disheartened and benumbed,
and would have given up the search and gone back
to the fire; but the sight of Flemming, whose face
was ruddy with exercise, who worked on, plying
his shovel vigorously while he tossed the great
drifts aside as lightly as a ship tosses the white
foam from her track on the seas, made him ashamed,
and he bent his will to his shivering hands, pitching off the snow here and there as well as he could,
seeing that he was cold and nearly out of breath—
when suddenly, just when Flemming himself began
to think the search useless, there lay the pack under
a drift he had finished shovelling off, just where the
broad flagged footway bordered with myrtle turned
in from the road—its leather casing still frozen, but
otherwise uninjured. Patrick McCue was over-
joyed, and would have poured out his thanks on
the spot in voluble eloquence and pious invoca-
tions, but the Elder hurried in to avoid hearing
them. "He had done his duty," he thought, in
helping the man to recover his pack, but that in-
volved no obligation on him to listen to his idle
and superstitious prayers." He told Reuben to
show Patrick McCue his sleeping place to stow his
pack in, and Reuben turned to his mother to know
where it ought to be, who briefly said: "Over
father's work-room;" and thither they went. It

was a good enough nook, furnished with a cot, one
or two chairs, a table on which lay a Bible, and an
old spider-legged washstand, with cracked basin
and pitcher—but comfortless looking and bare.
However, this did not disturb Patrick, who was
thankful to have a place to himself, since with the
quick perception of his nature he had come to feel
himself unwelcome, and his religion abhorred.
Here, at least, he could bless himself in the name
of the Holy Trinity, knowing it to be a sign of his
belief in a crucified God, whose passion and death
it kept him reminded of, and nourished in his soul
the divine virtues of Faith, Hope, and Charity;
Faith, by the belief it signified in the death of the
Son of God for his salvation; Hope, nourished and
increased by this belief; Charity, or the love of
God, excited by the sacred sign which represented
to him the love which God showed mankind by
dying on the cross for him. No wonder Patrick
McCue made much of the sign of the cross, and
was ready to brave peril and death for its sake; no
wonder he was glad to be where he could bless
himself to his heart's content, and ask the intercession of the Blessed Virgin and the saints, and say
his beads, and pray after his own fashion for the
benighted souls who had taken him in from perishing in the snow, without let or hindrance; and
pray for their conversion he would to the day of

his death, " for," he reasoned, "they've done more
than give me a cup of cold water for the love of
God, though mebbe they don't know it; and it is
unknownst that He ever let sich like actions fall to
the ground unnoticed. Any way, I'll say my rosary for them, morn and night, though faith! it
does seem like thrying to move a mountain to pray
for their conversion; but there's nothing like thrying, and if my faith's no bigger than a millet-seed,
I'll trust to the Blessed Virgin and the saints to
make up what I lack." All these thoughts passed
through Patrick McCue's mind while he was un-
strapping his pack, never uttering a word but tug-
ging away at the straps and buckles, and unlock-
ing the padlocks at each end, until finally he opened it, Reuben looking on with all the natural
curiosity of a boy, to see what would come of it.
The pedler thrust his hand into the depths of the
pack and drew out a small crimson-covered book,
blazoned with gilt, and altogether dazzling, which
he gave with a beaming smile to Reuben, saying:
Faith! it's the very one I was looking afther; and
do you take it, my lad, for a bit of a keepsake.
It's the poems of my countryman, Tommy Moore,
and you'll find the beautifullest things in it that'll
do to pray by, to swear by, or love by; for you
must know he's got some sacred songs there that
'ud melt the sowl of you; and some of the stirring-

est ditties about ould Ireland that rouses the
blood agin the Sassenach till it's like to boil over;
and the love songs, honey, bate Bannagher—rale
genuine poetry—take it, my lad, with a hearty welcome." And Patrick McCue thrust it into Reuben's
willing hand, who could have fallen upon his neck
and kissed him out of gratitude for a new book;
but after the first glow there fell a sudden shame
upon him, and he said: "I have never been used
to taking gifts: my father will give me money to
buy it of you if I ask him, but I thank you, sir,
indeed I do."

"There's no money could buy that book my lad,
afther I've offered it as a free gift; and if you don't
take it, I'll make short work of it by putting it into
the hottest place I can find under the logs down
there," said Patrick McCue, buckling up his pack
with an irate sparkle in his dull eyes. "Where I
came from it's not the way, bedad, to slap a man
in the face with a gift offered out of gratitude, as if
he was a beggar, too mean and too poor to be noticed." Then Reuben, so delicate in all his perceptions, felt another sort of shame, for he saw that
he had wounded the heart of one who, under heavy
obligations to them all, had sought in this spontaneous sort of a way to show his gratitude; and he
said: "I am glad to have the book Mr. McCue,
only I was afraid I might be robbing you; but I'll

take it with many thanks, and keep it for your sake." Then Reuben opened the book at "Paradise and the Peri;" his greedy eyes devoured the verses, while his imagination and heart, dazzled and glowing, felt as if under a spell of enchantment; his golden hair fell over his flushed cheeks, his dreamy eyes flashed and his heart swelled with great pulses of delight while he read; indeed he clean forgot Patrick McCue and everything else. until suddenly his vision of delight was dispelled by his mother's voice calling them with rather a sharp accent to come to dinner; then he thanked the pedler again in his warm, boyish fashion, and put the book in his pocket, feeling richer in its possession than if some one had given him a string of diamonds. "I knew you'd like it," said Patrick, with a kindly smile; and they went down to dinner.

Mrs. Flemming felt it to be a fiery ordeal to sit at the table with the Irish pedler; and when he blessed himself, after the Elder's lengthy and sonorous grace, she winced and snapped her eyes as if hot iron had touched her flesh, but said nothing. Then the Elder began to ask him some questions about Boston, which neither he nor any of his family had ever visited, it being a hundred miles distant, and in those days the facilities for travelling were few, and at the best difficult as well as dangerous, so that prudent and timid men were deterred from attempting the journey; but Patrick could give him but little information about this famous New England city, except that he was arrested, fined and put in prison, and not treated too kindly there, "for just taking a suck at his pipe on Sunday evening, coming from Vespers, and was troubling nobody at all wid the smoke of it, being in the open street; 'bating that, it seemed to be a flourishing sort of a town, but it looked small to him just landed from Dublin, where the English sogers, bad as they be, lets a fellow smoke his *dudheen* day in and day out without molesting him.

This was not very satisfactory about Boston to any one except Mrs. Flemming, who, although she did not say so, was delighted that the pedler had been made to suffer for breaking the Sabbath, and thought Boston must be a most godly place. Then some one asked him about his voyage across the seas, and the Elder wanted to know something about the vine-growing in France; and Patrick McCue, who had travelled here and there with his eyes wide open, gave such pleasant accounts of it all, mixed up with strange and perilous adventures, and now and then such racy descriptions of his own blunders, that two or three times a peal of hearty laughter ran around the board; and Mrs. Flemming, even while she knitted her brows to pretend she was neither interested or amused, wished to herself that "Nicholas were there to enjoy it all." Eva and Hope were enchanted; it was all new to them, this free and easy way of telling things they had been dreaming of all their lives, and only thought of as they did of the possibilities of the moon, as mythical and unattainable; and they were sorry when there was no more pumpkin pie to be eaten, for no excuse was sufficient in this systematic puritan family to linger around the table when a meal was finished; so with the glamour of Patrick McCue's adventures, like a new atmosphere around them, they rose from their chairs, standing while their father "returned thanks" and the Irishman made devoutly the blessed sign of the cross upon himself, which gave them all a sensation like the sudden discharge of a pail of cold water in their faces. But he was nothing daunted; it was as natural to the spiritual life of him to make this blessed sign as it was to his natural life to breathe, and he could not for the soul of him understand how any rational being, who was not a heathen, could object to a symbol which meant so much. But he sat down with Mr. Flemming, and smoked with him, and fell back into the conversation which was interrupted by their rising from the table; and later, when the Elder went away to his "workroom," and Mrs. Flemming started to go to look after the calf, and its mother, whose udder over-full made her low complainingly, he began to tell the girls about the dances of the Spanish peasants, and a bull-fight he saw in Seville.

"I say, mother," called the Elder, who saw the little woman flit past his door, "let *me* go; it is very cold. Go back to the fire."

"Tut," she replied, coming in for a moment, "I'm not so old or thin-blooded, father, that I can't attend to my own business, and all under shelter too. I'm warm enough." So she was, for the ferment of her blood over the papistical ways of Patrick McCue had not yet cooled off.

"I spoke to the man about his doings," began Flemming.

"I wonder now!" exclaimed she.

"I did indeed, mother; not offensively, mind you; but I did. I told him that his cross, and praying to the saints, was an offence to the simplicity of our religion, and asked him to refrain from such usage while with us."

"I thought you couldn't stand it, father, any more than I," she said approvingly. "And what did he say?"

"He got up, when he understood what I meant, buttoned up his coat and put on his hat, and was about going out into the storm, 'for,' he said, 'rather than stay under a roof where he dare not make the sign of the cross upon him, he'd try his chances in the snow; and if he perished God would be merciful to him;' and he was going, mother—going, remember, to his death; but I held him back, seeing his sincerity in being ready to perish for what he thought was right, and told him to stay and welcome, that his conscience should not be interfered with again."

"That was manful of him, father, to say the least of it," said Mrs. Flemming after a thoughtful pause. "It beats me, though, that a man should be ready to die for so small a thing as that."

"It seems so at first thought; but as he sees it—mind, mother, as *he* sees it—he would have felt guilty of denying his whole Faith, of which the cross is a symbol, by putting it under foot at any man's bidding. I am ashamed to have asked him.

"Land's sake's, father, what may that be? Listen now! The man must be singing; singing some of his ungodly songs there, where the Word has been read, and the hymns of Zion have been sung for more than a hundred years; and now—I wonder! there's a jingle like sleigh-bells keeping time. Hope and Eva shall come away," exclaimed Mrs. Flemming, a move towards the door to call them; but Flemming laid his hand upon her shoulder and detained her, saying: "Let them be, mother; let them be. The young and unregene-

rate are always fond of novelties, and we must be
wary how we go about pulling up the tares, lest we
pull up good wheat with them. They are good
children, according to the natural law, and a little
harmless amusement won't harm them."

"Ah, father! no wonder that people say you are
wanting in orthodox discipline in your over-indul-
gence of your children. It wasn't so in *my* young
days. But I can't stay here another minute; that
cow is needing me," said Mrs. Flemming, in tones
of reproof.

Yes, it was Patrick McCue, singing. Feeling
more genial after the bull-fight, he began to tell
Hope and Eva about the Spanish muleteers, and
ended by singing a muleteer song while he accompanied himself by softly jingling the tongs against
the brass globe of the andirons, in such good time
and with such light touches that the girls almost
imagined themselves on some romantic slope of
the Sierra Nevada, listening to the bells of the
mules and the songs of their leader as they wound
their way among the mountain passes, far above
the blue waters of the Guadalquiver. It was a
treat to these isolated young things, a novelty so
enjoyable, to hear the music and language of other
lands sung in a clear flexible tenor which was
melody itself, that they forgot everything—even
Bunyan's picture of the Pope sitting at the door of

a cave, with bones and skulls strewn around, watching like an ogre for unwary pilgrims, to devour
them body and soul—and asked for more, and yet
more, until the old black rafters rang again with
the songs of old; they forgot their wholesome
dread of displeasing their little mother; they forgot Patrick McCue's homely face and red head, his
superstitions and idolatries, while his voice, like
one of those exquisitely toned old Straduarius
violins, uncultivated but rarely sweet, melted into
some of the ballads of his own Emerald Isle,
which he sang with such pathos that the sewing
dropped from their fingers moistened with tears.
In the midst of it all, a sudden illumination glorified the room: a sharp bright gleam of sunlight
burst through the western window—the prison-gates
were open, and the golden gleams swept through
broken bars of cloud, fringing the black overhanging edges above with brilliance, and crowning the
snow-clad mountain peaks with diadems of irides-
cent light, and their slopes with a tissue of spangled silver: while the scattered snow-flakes, large
and fleecy, that fell slowly here and there, gemmed
and reddened by the setting sun, floated in the air
like the torn plumage of some tropical bird swept
captive by the storm-winds from her nest in the
nutmeg trees of the Orient. With a joyous cry Eva

and Hope sprang to the window, while Patrick
McCue hailed the sunset splendors as a sign of
promise and home.

The night was cloudless, and the distant ridges
and crests, the far-off peaks and boulders, the nearer slopes of the mountains, all glistening in robes
of crystal as the full moon anointed them with
silvery chrisms, rose silent and beautiful beneath
the spangled heavens, while Orion, glittering in full
armor, seemed to rest his jewelled sandals upon
their heads. There was no human sound to disturb this grand repose, only a low quivering chime
rang out now and then, whenever the wind soughed
through the glittering ice-covered trees of the forest
belts, smiting them like cymbals with a soft clash
together. But presently a confused sound of voices,
full of lusty cheer, intermingled with chorus
and huzza, was heard in the distance, drawing
nearer and nearer towards the "Old Homestead,"
and before long the cause appeared. The young
men of the country-side, led by Nicholas Flemming
and John Wilde, were out with their ox-teams,
their heavy sleighs, and snow-shovels, breaking the
road by moonlight, and when they got in sight of
the lights gleaming through door and window of
the "Old Homestead," their cheers rang out loud
and clear on the night, while the panting oxen and
tired horses, scenting the well-filled racks, put forth

all their sinewy strength to get to them. Mrs.
Flemming was soon clasped in the arms of her
great broad-shouldered son, who, "bearded like a
pard," lifted his little mother up and kissed her
fondly, while she whispered : "Thank God that you
are safe, Nicholas ; I have had an uneasy time
about you."

"And I up there at the Deacon's, having the
best time I ever had in my life," he said laughing,
as he put her down to kiss his sisters, shake hands
with his father, and pull Reuben's golden hair :
then all of a sudden he saw Patrick McCue and he
exclaimed : "Hilloa, *you* here ! I thought the
wolves had eaten you, my friend ;" while he shook
him heartily by the hand.

"And I'm sure, sir, after we crossed each other
up yonder last night, I never expected to see you
alive again ; but you see how things come together.
Almighty God was holding you in safe keeping,
your people here saved my life ; may the Blessed
Mother of God reward them," answered the irre-
pressible Patrick, with beaming countenance.

"Hilloa! The what——? but never mind, it's a
free country. Mother, get us some supper. John
Wilde don't want any ; but I'm hungry enough, I
can tell you." John Wilde and Hope were standing
apart, he still holding the hand she had held out to
welcome him, whispering words to each other that

brought a softer light into their eyes and kindled a warmer glow upon their cheeks, for they were betrothed lovers.

CHAPTER V.

PATRICK McCUE'S KEEPSAKES.

THE table was soon spread with a generous and plentiful meal; for except the salaratus which the New England house-wives will poison their bread and pastries with, there are no people in the world who understand better what the art of cooking and the spreading of a hospitable table means. On this occasion there were two cold roast fowls, a dish of savory flitches of bacon just fried to a turn; there were mince and pumpkin pies, home-made cheese, preserves, pickles, white biscuits, doughnuts, and two or three large loaves of bread, flanked by tankards of cider and plates piled up with great rosy apples and nuts; while the roaring fire cast its ruddy light like a broad smile of welcome over it all; and the young stalwart farmers, with laugh and jest, drew round the board, and after "Thanks" were offered by the Elder, fell to like hungry kites, doing ample justice to the inviting fare, while Mrs. Flemming flitted around, attending with compla-

cent happiness to the needs of all; for the little
woman dearly loved an occasion like this, when
she could demonstrate her domestic superiority by
showing that however sudden the emergency her
well supplied and well-filled larder could bear the
strain. Hope and John Wilde sat beside each
other, quietly happy; and Eva, who was thought
to be something of a flirt in the country-side, enter-
tained two or three of her shy admirers on the opposite side of the table. But Patrick McCue by
little and little became the life of the company.
Some of the youngsters, seeing that he was a dull-
looking fellow, began to chaff him, but the New
Hampshire flints struck such fire out of his Irish
wit that he completely turned the laugh on the
other side, and kept up the fun to the great delight
of them all. It was late when they left the table,
long past the usual bedtime, but they sat in merry
groups around, talking over their bear-hunts and
other adventures, until Mrs. Flemming, assisted by
her daughters, cleared away the fragments of the
feast and placed everything in perfect order, leaving only the Elder's table, upon which lay open the
old family Bible, in the centre of the room. Patrick
McCue was in the corner of the room next to the
fire, in a high chat with Nicholas and Eva; Mrs.
Flemming was seated, at last, in her quaint old
chair; and Hope, with John Wilde and Reuben,

were sitting near her, while a cheerful hum of voices filled the room. Suddenly the Elder cleared his throat, and going to his table, sat down, and a deep silence fell upon them all, which was at last broken by his grave level tones, as he read the fourth chapter of the fourth book of Kings, and Patrick McCue found himself in the midst of family prayers. He would have slipped off to bed if he had known what was coming, and said the dear old comforting prayers of his Faith ; but he was fairly cornered, and listened to the narrative of the miraculous things done by the prophet of God, not as to a far-off tale of dreamland, or cloudland, never to be realized on earth ; for he knew that Almighty God had never ceased working miracles as great as these, by the hands of His saints, down to the present time ; his Faith was a living, deathless faith ; neither torpid or sleeping and full of anxious, fitful dreams ; and it seemed as natural to him to hear the wondeful story of Elisius, and the Sunamitess, as if he had been there and seen it all. He sat and listened, gravely twirling his thumbs over each other, benignly thankful that his entertainers were not the pagans he took them to be ; when the first lines of a familiar hymn being given out, they all sang together, old and young, and Patrick thought it sounded pleasantly, all those full round voices swelling out in devotional harmony to

one of the old quaint puritan airs; and if he had
only been out of it he would have enjoyed it yet
more—for the man had a fine natural ear for music—but he was caught, and couldn't tell fairly
what to do with himself, until they all knelt down,
then he drew out his rosary, composed of large
black beads strung on a brass wire, to which was
suspended a brass crucifix some four inches long;
the jingle as he took the beads from his breast
pocket made Eva start round, and she saw him
bless himself reverently with the crucifix, then kiss
it, after which his lips moved in an earnest fashion
while he slipped bead after bead through his fingers, all to her own distraction and the confusion of
Nicholas, who also saw him and thought him crazy.
The next morning, about ten o'clock, the young men
were to start with the teams and sleds on their
road-breaking mission, to unite with other parties
for the same purpose, and thought they might possibly get as far as Centre Harbor. Patrick McCue
was going with them, and Mrs. Flemming thankful
to him for going; and with a womanly sort of pity
for the lone stranger who had sat on her hearthstone, but without the faintest relenting towards the
superstitious and papistical side of him, packed a
basket with provisions, not forgetting a bottle of
their best cider, which would have put to shame the
brightest Cliquot by its sparkle, and gave it into

the care of Nicholas with the strict charges to give
it to him on the way, for she did not want to be
thanked for it. She shook hands with him; and
"wished him well," the Elder shook hands, so did
Reuben and the girls, to whom he whispered:
"God bless the winsome face of yez; may the
saints hould yez in their keeping, for your kindness
to a homeless stranger. You'll find a picture, and
a little image of the blessed Blessed Lady, up
where I slept; and may she bring yez both into
the fold of her Son." No one heard what he said
except the sisters, and it was like Greek to them,
so far as his meaning went; then the waif of the
storm, the simple-minded, uneducated, unpolished
Irish pedler, with his pack over his round shoul-
deres, went his way, leaving what? Little brown
sparrows sometimes, in flying, drop from their bills
a rare seed, which, falling into the earth, germi-
nates and grows into strength and beauty, covering with vines, blossoms, leaves and fruits some
ruined wall or blasted tree, affording shade and refreshment to the noonday traveller and shelter for
the song-birds at night; the wind goes on its mission wafting earthward the germs of mighty trees,
which in time cast broad shadows on the mountain
sides, or stretch their wide boughs over the peaceful brown homes in the valley; man's mission is
more mighty still, for Almighty God in His own

wise designs sometimes makes use of the ignorant and humble as messengers of His will, as prophets of His coming, to plant the seed of His word in desert places, to make them blossom as the rose.

When the Elder went into his workroom, after the departure of the young men, to see about mending the double sleigh harness, he saw a neatly wrapped package lying on his desk. He took it up and saw that it was addressed to "Mister Flemming, from his grateful friend, Patrick McCue;" then he snapped the string, opened the wrapper, and found a book neatly bound in leather; and turning to the title-page, he read: "The End of Religious Controversy; by a Catholic Divine."* A flush mounted to his face and he closed the book with a snap, and lifting the lid of his desk, threw it in, thinking: "To waste time over the pages of such a book as that would be not only idle, but culpable. He would some day wrap it up, direct it to Patrick McCue, and send it to Boston by the first person he heard of going there." Then he went about his harness-mending and forgot all about it.

Mrs. Flemming, who was busy over her churn, sent Hope and Eva "to take the bedclothes off the cot the Irishman had slept in the night before, to

---

* Millner's End of Controversy.

fold the comforts and blankets and put them in the press, and throw the sheets and pillow-case among the soiled house linen; then lock the door, as she had no use for the room."

Full of curiosity to see what Patrick McCue meant when he bade them good-by, Hope and Eva lost no time but ran up stairs, and on entering the room the first object that greeted their sight, standing upon the Bible where he had placed it, was a plaster cast, about a foot high, of the Blessed Virgin holding in her arms her divine Son, and lying near her feet was a picture of the Crucifixion, in which she was represented standing by His Cross, bearing with Him the bitter passion and pain she could neither soothe or avert. It was a high-colored, badly executed print, but it told the story with a graphic power which could not be mis-understood. This then was the "image" for Hope, and that the "picter" for Eva. They did not then comprehend whom the "image" represented; they thought it might be some poet-sculptor's idea of "Charity," or "Peace," or "Maternal Love," but whatever it might mean, it was beautiful in its holy expression of serene peace. But the picture thrilled them through; it was the first one of the kind they had ever seen, and although they had read and heard of the Crucifixion ever since they could remember, it never seemed to them such a reality as now—while they stood, Eva's head leaning on Hope's shoulder, gazing upon it.

"Only think, Hope," said Eva in a low voice, which had something of her father's tone in it; "only think of her being there, close beside Him, seeing all that was done and not able to give Him a drop of cold water, or even wipe the sweat and blood from His face."

": Whom do you mean, Eva? Who is it do you think?" asked Hope slowly.

"Don't you see, that must be Mary, the Mother of Jesus, standing there, for we read in the Bible that "she stood by the Cross;" but oh, Hope! *how* could she bear it; for was she not human like ourselves?" Ah yes! they could understand this much because it appealed strongly to their womanly sympathies, but the rest was a sealed book to these fair Puritan maidens, and the time not yet at hand when "out of many hearts thoughts should be revealed" to them.

"I think," said Hope at last : that we had better finish up and get back to our sewing. It seems to me that you might keep the picture. I see no harm in it, although I fear that mother, if she knew of them, would think both these were "graven images," and destroy them; but she never comes here, and there's no use in fretting her by letting her know. I will leave the image here; it can hurt no one, and it is certainly very pretty. I should like to put it in the 'best room,' but imagine the excitement that would come of it," said Hope with a little laugh.

"Yes! I can see old Father Ray peering at it over his big horn spectacles, and our little mother on tiptoe with righteous anger, for of course she would take it for granted that it was some idolatrous Romish image, just because Patrick McCue left it here," said Eva laughing, while she and her sister folded the comforts and quilts. "I shall put the picture between the leaves of my Bible; as you say, Hope, it can't hurt me; indeed I think it will do me good whenever I see it, for it brings that sorrowful scene on Calvary so plainly before me, and makes it seem so real, that I can almost imagine I saw it all. I tell you, Hope, that all Father Ray's preaching from now until doomsday could not give me such thoughts as that picture does."

"How strange that a papist should care enough about our Saviour to have a picture like that," said Hope; "for you know, Eva, that in John Bunyan's book he says that the Pope of Rome is Antichrist; but I suppose the man bought it with other things to sell again."

"It is very likely. No, I don't think he knows much about the plan of salvation, for instead of listening to father's solemn prayer last night, he hauled out a great string of black beads and made that sign on himself again, then began whispering to himself while he counted them one by one; indeed he did, Hope, and Nicholas laughed as if it was great fun. Any way, I'm glad he's gone, and more than glad to have the picture. But, Hope, why does mother never come here? I never heard that before."

"I'll tell you, Eva, because you might some day or other ask mother, and that would never do. I never heard her say anything about it; but old Sarah Gill, who used to live here when we were little things, to help, told me all about it one day when I went to read to her. One night an old Indian squaw, who had been in the habit of coming here to beg, was taken in out of a storm, pretty much as the pedler was, only she was ill, and died that night in this room. Mother was leaning over her, doing all she could to soothe and make her more comfortable, when all at once she screamed, and fastening her long bony fingers around mother's throat, sprang out of bed, and they both fell together on the floor. When Sarah Gill, who had gone down for mustard and hot water, was coming up with them, she heard the terrible cry; and hurrying in, found mother nearly suffocated and the squaw stark dead, lying across her, with fingers still clutching her throat. It was some time before she revived, and has never entered this room since. You must take care and never speak of it before her, for Sarah Gill says that it always gave her a dreadful nervous turn whenever father or she referred to it; and she finally told them both never to speak of it in her presence again, or before the children, as she wished it to be entirely forgotten."

"Poor little mother! It was frightful; no wonder she can't bear the sight of an Indian, and avoids this room. Did you ever hear that it was haunted, Hope?" asked Eva.

"What nonsense, Eva! I thought you had more sense than that. Such a question is worthy of Sarah Gill, who hears death-watches, and believes in signs and witches. No! There is nothing to dread here except the thought of the dreadful thing that happened here long years ago, when God was so merciful as to save our mother, alive, out of the deadly clutch of a poor delirious wretch who was not conscious of what she was doing and had always loved her with the fidelity and humbleness of a dog."

"It was dreadful. But I guess we had better go now. I shall be careful never to give a hint to mother about this; but indeed, Hope, it makes me shiver to think of it," said Eva, as they went out, locking the door after them; and having put away the comforts and quilts, they ran lightly down stairs and were soon chatting merrily over their sewing, about the grand sleighride they expected to have as soon as Nicholas and John Wilde came back. They were not conscious of the little seed dropped into the virgin soil of their hearts by the soft wind that had breathed over them; but it was nestling there invisibly, cumbering nothing, so light was it, and giving them no uneasiness by its presence; but by-and-by it would begin to send out its fibres, and spring into beautiful life.

Cold weather now set steadily in; such cold as people who live in southern lands can scarcely imagine. The roads, hard packed with frozen snow, were as smooth as polished marble; and over them from morning until night, from night sometimes until morning, gay cutters and large double sleighs filled with young people rosy with health and life, and old people whose cheeks wore the bloom of a winter apple, and children shouting and laughing with glee, skimmed here and there, up and down the country, to the jingle of numberless bells, which tinkled far and near in scales of sweet-sounding notes. It was the gay season of the sedate puritan neighborhood, and much visiting was done, much tea was drunk, and warm hospitalities exchanged. Of course there was gossip, and scandal, and match-making, and even merry-making, and heart-burn-

ings, and envyings, and petty jealousies; besides a
great deal of solemn talk amongst the old "members" about religious matters; then the stranger
who had been weather-bound at the Flemmings' was
turned over, and much indignation expressed that
a papist should have abode among the godly;
after which followed a discussion on the dangers of
popery; then more than one or two disparaging
hints were thrown out against Elder Flemming for
giving the man hospitality; "if he must needs take
him," said they, "the barn was a good enough
place for such a ch racter, and not the sacred
hearthstone where the righteous have sat for more
than a century; then some of them thought the
Elder cherished " peculiar views," and wondered at
the loose reign he held over his children, at whose
vanities he winked, even allowing them to dance
to the " sound of the viol" in the assemblies of the
wicked; concluding with : " there is something unsound at the core,"—meaning him. And there was
no want of kindness among them; they thought
they were serving God, and vigilant in His service,
when they sat in judgment on their brethren's short-
comings or actual transgressions; they imagined
they knew what self-righteousness meant, without
dreaming that they were clothed in it as with a
garment; and they firmly believed that their first
duty to God and man was to cherish and defend

everything in their religion in the sternest way
against popery, their views of which were as an-
tithetical to the real thing as darkness is to light.
This was the rallying point where all agreed;
the forlorn hope which kept them from wildly scat-
tering, and straying into open infidelity; the enemy
which kept them vigilant, and alert, and concen-
trated; at times, when stranded among the bewild-
ering rocks of the right of "private interpretation,"
each one felt authorized to set up new doctrinal
lights, until there was danger of their being lost in
utter darkness. So when these offshoot sects of the
old Puritan tree disagreed in all things else, they
shook hands over the "downfall of the Pope" and
buried the tomahawk.

Up and down through the wild, glorious scenery
of this region, with the sun sprinkling millions of
lesser suns on ice-crowned peak and snow-draped
mountain, skimmed the fleet sleighs; and many a
poor half-famished family received gifts as they
stopped a moment in front of their brown huts—
such gifts as a fat turkey, or a joint, or a basket of
pies, and other substantial things which fed the
hungry and sent the little ones to bed happy and
warm. They generally looked close at the main
chance, but on the whole were as humane and kindly of heart as most people, fulfilling all the duties
of the natural laws with scrupulous fidelity, but as

ignorant of the truth as revealed to His Church by
Jesus Christ, as are the dwellers in Hindostanee or
Central Africa.

But nothing of this disturbed the sedate carnival-
time of our puritan friends, along the lake shore
and up the mountain slopes stretching back from
its frozen waters.   Eva, Hope, Nicholas, Reuben
and John Wilde, in the double sleigh, drawn by
four horses decorated with fringes and bells; snugly
tucked in with Canadian blankets and covered with
buffalo robes, whirled up with gay clangor to Deacon Snethen's, lifted Huldah, who was expecting
them, into the midst of them, smothering her laughter under the soft furry mantle that Nicholas threw
around her ; then sped, swiftly as any swallow
could fly, along the up-country road, singing chatting and laughing by turns, enjoying the ecstatic
aerial motion, and the prospect of a good supper
at John Wilde's mother's and a quiet home-dance
after it, with such wholesome and delightful anticipations of pleasure as it is the privilege and happiness of the young and innocent to enjoy.

CHAPTER VI.

THE INNER LIFE OF WOLFERT FLEMMING.

NEVER shone the sun on a scene more grand or beautiful! Covered to a depth of four or five feet with snow, which in some places where it had drifted lapped in great folds and ridges, in graceful curves and furrows of unsullied white, the mountains from Ossipee to Belknap, from " Whiteface " to " Red Hill ;" and rising beyond these, the chain stretching northward, whose peaks could be seen like jeweled crests flashing in the sunlight, looked as if fashioned by giants out of alabaster, so transparent and aerial did they appear through the crisp dazzling atmosphere, so gracefully did the long blue shadows sweep down their sides like the folds of royal robes bordered with ermine, so softly waved the green plumes of the pines clustered with ice-gems ; while the beautiful Lake with its romantic indentations, and isles set like jewels on its bosom, lay gleaming in the sunshine, a level sea of crystal, its murmuring waters holding gay revel beneath their roofing of ice.

This region was not thickly settled ; the noisy clangor of modern progress had not yet disturbed its grand solitudes ; the fiery dragon of iron and steam, with his jar, and power, and discordant roar,

had not yet sent the echoes thrilling back with af-
frighted shrieks to their romantic caves, or made
the earth tremble and quiver as with the shock of
the last trumpet; no steamboat had then fretted
the fair waters of Winnipiseogee; no, forty years
ago if any of the old sachems had come from the
"setting sun" to revisit the scenes where they had
roamed at will, the "monarchs of all they sur-
veyed," they would have seen but few changes.
Farm houses with cultivated fields about them, a
small hamlet or two near the borders of the lake,
brown cottages nestling between the slopes, a wind-
mill here and there, and the meeting-house as near
the centre of the scattered neighborhood as it could
be located, were the only changes the swarthy
ghosts would have seen had they come. So insular
was the neighborhood, that a man of it who could
say he had been to Boston, distant a little over
a hundred miles, was considered a great traveller,
whose conversation was listened to with respect.
The meeting-house was open every Sabbath day—
by a sort of compromise these sects call it the Sabbath day, but in reality keep holy the day established by the Catholic Church to celebrate resur-
rection of Christ, little dreaming that they are in-
debted to her authority and tradition for it—and
crowded with a grave and decorous assemblage of
old, middle-aged and young, who met to hear the

words of their well-meaning teacher, an old man who had been nursed in the early cradle of puritanism and who laid down the spiritual law as he understood it, disintegrating the Scriptures blindly and at will with much unction, and had devoted the labors of his life to building upon a sandy foundation, happy in the conceit that it was rock of a safe but soft kind. With the Bible in one hand and the "Articles of the Westminster Assembly" in the other, Father Ray—as he was called—preached total depravity, and regeneration without baptism, and justification by faith without works, until the converted ones felt all the stern dignity of the elect, and the unconverted believed as they were taught —some of them with an amazed sort of wonder that a merciful God should allow His creatures, for whose salvation His own Son had died, to be born and live under such a wrathful ban—that they were children of perdition and bond slaves of the devil; and thus believing, much of their youth was spent in the shadow of severe restraints; the innocent pleasures of life were condemned by the harsh creed of their fathers as sins not to be forgiven, and as they could not all of them get up the state of mind which they called conversion, many of them became indifferent—so indifferent that religion appeared an unattainable myth to their aspirations; and when those who thought much of such

matters got to measuring the morality and purity
of their own lives with the christian character of
the "brethren," they found so little difference that
the balance sometimes seemed in their own favor,
which of course scandalized them and made them
suspect that religion was not, after all, the holy and
divine power they had thought it to be. But on
the "Sabbath" there they all assembled, the elect
and the unregenerate together, looking as if they
had all taken a dose of the waters of Marah and
didn't care to have them sweetened; and old
Father Ray would wind up the saints with his
"pure doctrine" until they felt like marching into
the lightnings of Mount Sinai, while the sinners—
those who cared—looked as if they were going to
be hanged. Then it was all over until the next
meeting, and they went their ways, the members
carrying nothing with them to sanctify and sweeten
the routine and toils of daily life; their souls bris-
tled with the thorns of the Law, upon which they
hung their interpretations of the Holy Scriptures in
good faith; there was nothing done for the sake of
Him who preached the Sermon on the Mount, because they believed He had done all, and anything
that they might do would be idle works of supere-
rogation; so they went on reading the Bible, and
thinking of "Free Grace" and "Predestination,"
and symbolizing the teachings of Christ, and driv-

ing sharp bargains with each other between whiles, never losing sight of their worldly affairs, until another Sabbath rolled round.

Mrs. Flemming was one of the stern disciples of Father Ray; while her husband, although a just man and living a godly life before the world and his brethren, who held him in high esteem, sometimes differed from him, and in their private conversations often startled the old minister by broaching opinions which he denounced as dangerous and devilish errors. The sons and daughters of the house were on the "seat of the sinner;" they had not professed that change known among their people as "conversion," and were consequently the objects of many stern reproofs and warnings from the old minister.

On this bright and lovely day, when amidst the pearly lights resting on the glistening peaks and sharp edges of the snow-covered ridges, one might almost have imagined himself up among the opal-like cirri of a summer sky, the old brown mare of the minister was seen bearing down towards the Flemming homestead. Sitting erect and clothed in a severe suit of black, his black hat pulled down over his ears, his coat collar pulled up to them, he and his old mare would have looked like a sprawling blot on the fair face of nature but that by some chance he had tied a red comforter around his neck, the ends of which streamed over his shoulders, giving to the cold white foreground of the landscape just the little dash of scarlet it needed. Riding with him was a young man wrapped in furs, whose handsome, intelligent face looked brightly out from under his cap of Russian sable, from which escaped a curling fringe of yellow hair. This was Father Ray's grandson and ward, who having graduated at Yale was studying law in Boston. He had come up to the White Mountain country to spend a few days with his grandfather —uncomfortable days, full of sermon and lecture, admonition and prayer, which the young scapegrace, who had adopted while absent the exceedingly comfortable doctrines of "universal salvation," listened to with suppressed yawns—and was now riding over with him to visit his old friends, the Flemmings, and assure himself that Eva Flemming was unchanged ; not that they were lovers, but that he hoped some day to win her if the world went well with him. The young folks were all at home, and he received a warm greeting; their delight on seeing their old playmate taking much of the edge off the reproving salutations of the minister, whom Mrs. Flemming took immediate charge of, helping him off with his wraps and giving him a comfortable seat near the fire, after which she went to the "work-room" to tell her husband he was there ;

then hurried on to send their man-of-all-work in to kindle a great fire in the "best room," for she knew that the two always liked to have a private talk together; after which she plunged into her store-room to consider the possibilities of a feast; while she kept thinking and could not get it out of her head "what a nice match George Merill would be for Eva." The old minister was glad to go away with Elder Flemming to the quiet well-warmed parlor in the new part of the house; for the young people, although they felt the restraint of his presence, and with long faces tried their best to be serious, George Merill, full of delight at seeing them all again in the beautiful quaint old room, broke out in such gushes of talk and fun that for the life of them they could not keep it up, and laughed and talked with the most unprecedented irreverence; while father Ray sat bolt upright, twirling his thumbs over each other and gazing with a displeased countenance into the fire as if he were settling their final doom, So he was as much relieved to go out from among them as they were at his going. When they were comfortably seated, each in a well-cashioned arm-chair, Father Ray said :

" George Merill came down with me. He's going away in a day or two, and wanted to see the young people."

" George is a very fine fellow. I am very glad he came! " said the Elder heartily.

" George is a thorn in my flesh, a reproach to me and my ministry, he has got his head full of strange notions, and disputes with me on the affairs of his salvation. My head is bowed down with shame that he is gone so far astray, for he is the child of many prayers," said Father Ray, sternly.

" What are his notions? " asked the Elder.

" Universal salvation. He argues that our Saviour died for all, and that all men will be saved ; and to fill the climax of his folly he has the audacity to say he has Scripture authority for it. He has read the Bible since he could read at all ; in season, and out of season, I have made him read it ; he is familiar with it, and now wrests it to his own perdition! " cried the old man with indignation.

"I have come to think," said Flemming in his slow level tones, " that there are many things in the sacred writings to confuse the mind of the inexperienced, and it has become a subject of grave import to me why so few of our children walk in the way of our fathers. There seems to be something wanting to hold them from running here and there after strange doctrines. George is only one of many, and it was so even in my young days."

Father Ray placed his hands upon his knees, straightened himself up, and looked with surprised and severe aspect at the Elder, who met it calmly, and continued : " You know that all who differ from us show Scripture to authorize their opinions, even when their doctrines are as much opposed to each other, and as far asunder as the east is from the west."

" I deny their right to do so," replied the minister in a sternly authoritative tone. " It is because of the ungodly and carnal imaginations of such as wrest the Scriptures to their own destruction, that these differences arise ; that the young and unregenerate follow after the idols of this world, and trample in the dust all orthodox meaning and discipline. But when a man like yourself expresses a doubt, a man raised on the very ' milk of the word,' whose head is already whitening in the service of the Lord; then, Wolfert Flemming, I am filled with fearful misgivings as to his state."

" That is exactly the way I feel about myself, until sometimes the light becomes so obscure that I almost despair ; in fact, I have been wishing for some time past to lay before you, as they are laid bare before God, some of the perplexities which have arisen in my mind from reading the Scriptures," said Flemming.

" I am ready to listen. I can tell you nothing on

doctrinal points that you do not already know as well as I; but we will take counsel together, Wolfert, and if the spiritual experience of a man much older than yourself will be any help to you, it is at your service."

Flemming got up and walked to and fro the room two or three times, his head bowed in deep thought, then resumed his seat and began: "I sometimes think that these thoughts are temptations, and put them away from me, until I remember that they are the sayings and the express commands of Him whom I believe to be the very Son of God, equal in all things unto Him: in whom and through whom alone we trust for salvation: then I go over the same ground again, and apply text after text to the articles of belief in which I was raised, and which, on my conversion, I publicly professed and accepted, and lo you! some of them seem to crumble away at the test. I should like to forget all—to bury these doubts in oblivion, and be as I was at first; but how can I, seeing that I believe Jesus Christ to be the Eternal Truth, disbelieve His word?"

"No christian doubts His word," said the minister. "If you receive it in a limited sense, or go beyond its meaning, there is your condemnation. But I do not easily see the drift of your words."

"Well," continued the Elder in his grave quiet

way, " I can explain what I mean—God help me—
on at least one point. We deny that regeneration
takes place in baptism."

" Certainly."

" But when Nicodemus asked Christ ' How can a
man be born again?' He—the Eternal Truth—
replied: ' Except a man be born of water and of
the spirit, he cannot enter the Kingdom of
Heaven ;' and yet we refuse baptism to an adult,
until he is first born of the spirit, or converted. It
is true that we baptize infants, but how ? We give
it to them as a symbol, a pledge or testimony that
we will do our best as sponsors to raise them
christians; for the child, we deny that it has a
saving, a cleansing significance or power, even
when we know that He said *born of water.*"

" Christ spoke figuratively," said Father Ray, in
positive tones ; " for how can a man be born of
water? He meant simply a dedication of themselves by baptism to His service, as an outward
sign that they believed and hoped in Him : but
the new birth of the spirit is the essential thing!
How can water wash the total depravity of man's
nature away? Absurd ! "

"I do not know *how*," said Flemming, with a
troubled expression in his eyes. "I can only set
what we are taught against what HE said, and see
the discrepancy ! Not only what His own words

declare, but what His apostles and disciples preached and insisted on. St. Paul calls baptism the 'laver of regeneration, and renovation of the Holy Ghost.' He baptized 'whole families,' we are told, among whom were doubtless little children and infants ; children must therefore be capable of this regeneration by water, since Christ said ' Suffer little children to come unto Me, for of such is the kingdom of Heaven ;' but *how*, since He declares it, shall even these enter without being 'born of water;' and what becomes of total depravity, which *we* believe can only be eradicated by justification by faith? Throughout the New Testament, baptism is insisted on as an *essential* and not as a figurative thing. St. Paul says : ' Arise and be baptized every one of you, in the name of Jesus Christ, for the remission of your sins, *you shall receive the gifts of the Holy Ghost.*' 'Arise,' said Ananias to Paul, ' and wash away thy sin.' Paul tells us again that ' Christ loved the Church, and gave himself for it, that He might sanctify it cleansing it by the laver of water in the word of Life.' This, and much else, disturbs me ; but while we are thanking God that we are not as other men, we stand blind and naked before Him."

"Wolfert, Wolfert Flemming! that old Bible of yours, in which you take such pride, was printed too near the ancient popish days not to have some corruptions in the text. I have always misdoubted it, and now see with good reason," said the minister earnestly. "Put it away—into the fire, or anywhere—so that you read it no more; and get one translated in more enlightened days."

"No!" said the Elder, while a flush deepened on his face; "I stick to my old Bible. It is an early Lutheran edition; and what is so near its source it is reasonable to think ought to be the purest. As the title-page tells me: 'it was revised and approved by the great 'Reformer' himself."

"Beware then, Wolfert Flemming, how you turn the word of God to your own destruction. The exercises of your mind are not uncommon. Doubts and temptations are the ordeal by which the soul—if faithful and steadfast—reaches sanctification. You know what orthodox doctrine in its purity means, and understand experimentally what justification by faith is. I cannot admonish you on these points, but I do adjure you in the most solemn manner to have recourse to prayer; *that* is the only weapon by which you can victoriously combat these doubts. Pray without ceasing, and may He in whom we both hope deliver you from your perplexities," said Father Ray with an almost imperceptible quaver in his harsh voice.

CHAPTER VII.

MRS. FLEMMING IS THANKFUL FOR THE PROSPERITY
AND HAPPINESS OF HER FAMILY.

" Yes, I will pray on, hoping for light," said
Flemming in his grave, level tones. " So far my
prayers are unanswered; I have knocked but the
door remains closed; and the end of it all is that
my spiritual life is full of discord. In the pages of
the ' word,' where I found only peace, I discover
contradictions which so confound me that I sometimes wonder if I have risked my soul on a lie."

Wolfert Flemming's mental condition is one not
at all uncommon to thinking religious minds outside the One True Fold, though there be only a few
who are honest enough to admit the fact in regard
to their own individual experience; they go stumbling on over their doubts and misgivings, and
search the Scriptures diligently only to find outside of the texts on which their own peculiar doctrines are founded, things hard to be understood,
and an apparent authority for contradictory belief,
with a strange want of harmony which perplexes
and dismays them. How should they—who have
always been taught that it is a false, idolatrous
creed—know that it is only in the Holy Catholic
Church, which acknowledges the eternal and indis-

soluble unity of one Lord, one Faith, one Baptism, that the integrity of the Scriptures is preserved intact, that their unbroken harmony like golden links stretch from the promise, given by almighty God to our first parents, of a Redeemer, down to the birth of Jesus Christ in the stable at Bethlehem ; from the manger to the cross, from the cross unto the end of time, from time into a boundless and infinitely glorious eternity? To the true believer there is no discord in the Holy Scriptures, for his is no ephemeral belief in an amateur religion founded for the glorification and selfish ends of man, but a science of eternal principles coming from God Himself, sealed by the precious blood of His Son, and vivified by the Holy Ghost who abideth with it ; a faith whose commission of authority is divine whose interpretations are infallible, founded upon a rock against which the gates of hell can never prevail ; which—immutable, unchangeable, and unshaken after the tempests and buffeting of nearly nineteen centuries—stands as firm as the everlasting hills, more glorious and beautiful than the sun, her battlements glittering with the souls she has won, her watch-towers enlightening the ends of the earth ; awaiting the consummation of time to ascend in triumph with her spoils and conquests into the eternal heavens.

Our good Puritan knew nothing of this True

Faith; he had heard and read of a monstrous and
devilish system called popery, worse than the creed
of Buddha, more infamous than the priestcraft of
Egypt; a thing so full of the abomination of desolation, so corrupt and antichristian in its tenden-
cies that it sickend his upright soul and made him
wonder at the great patience of almighty God in
bearing with it; but beyond this mistaken view he
knew nothing; he was as ignorant as any pagan in
the jungles of India of the one true Catholic Church
—its Faith, Creed, Dogmas, Precepts and usages.
He was only one of many God-fearing, truth-seek-
ing men who, like Saul of Tarsus, think they are
best serving God when in their blindness they rage
against His Church. He had the Bible for his
guide, but we see how sorely he was confused in a
labyrinth of which he held not the clue.

"These are temptations, Wolfert," said the old
minister, laying his hand upon the bowed head of
the strong man; "but keep them from the knowledge of your family, lest you scandalize the weak
and unregenerate of your own household; pray,
pray without ceasing."

Jacob, overwearied with fatigue in his journey to
Mesopotamia, took a stone and laying it under his
head slept there and had a glorious vision of angels, and when he awaked out of his sleep he said:
"Indeed the Lord is in this place and I knew it

not."* So was it with this man who with earnest purpose rested on the Scriptures, which, now more comfortless than a stone, would by-and-by become the very gate of heaven to him.

Mrs. Flemming came in to invite them out to dinner, and her beaming smile was somewhat checked when she noted the stern and troubled expression on the countenances of her husband and the minister; but she at once imagined in her quick conclusive way that they had been deep in grave religious discussions, which accounted for it very satisfactorily to her mind, for it was utterly impossible for her ever to disassociate religion with a stern gravity; and except that she straightened herself up a little to meet the emergency, she gave herself no trouble about it, and thought they were both saints. The young people were having a cheerful time around the bright hearth of the old room, judging from the hum and laughter that came sounding through the open doors; but it. smote upon Father Ray's ears so gratingly that when he came in his countenance wore a severe and displeased look, which passed over the blithesome and innocent young hearts like a cold wave, chilling them into sudden silence.

"It is all levity," he thought; "they are children of the devil, and what right have they to be laugh-

Genesis xxviii.

ing on the brink of woe." Then he looked around
at the handsome comely young faces, all drawn
down into a serious silence, which was a revolt
against nature and innocence, while in their hearts
they were thinking "how unlovely religiou is;"
then, as if satisfied with this outward seeming, he
folded his hands, and closing his eyes began to
"offer thanks." It was a long grace, more full of
reproof, than of thankfulness for blessings received,
which gave the turkey and other viands time to
cool, while the mouths of the wholesome hungry
young folks watered ; and George Merill wondered
if a Harpy or something would not fly down and
seize the good things before his grandfather got
through. But no ; he finished, and in solemn
silence on their part the dinner was eaten. They
ate, and that was all they could do ; for the Elder,
the minister and Mrs. Flemming got into a talk
about religious affairs in which "justification by
faith " and "free agency" were gravely discussed,
which quite extinguished their spirits. Nicholas
whispered : "I wish that pedler fellow was here.
Wouldn't it be fun ?" at which a contraband giggle
was heared for an instant but as instantly hushed.
The "pedler fellow" had been the subject of their
conversation before dinner, and their hearty laughter had been over the recollection of his pleasant-
ries, blunders and songs ; but the audacity of Nich-

olas snggested a situation too ludicrous for their
gravity even under the awful restraints of Father
Ray's presence. But everything comes to an end,
and so did the dinner ; after which the Elder and
his wife, with their reverend guest, sat round the
broad cheerful hearth of the quaint old room, while
the young people went away into the new part of
the house and took possession of " the best room "
and enjoyed themselves.

George Merill thought Eva more lovely than he
had imagined ; every movement was full of unrestrained grace ; her intelligent mind gave anima-
tion and interest to all she said, and there was over
it all an expression of an innate purity which made
her strangely beautiful, and he resolved that he
would offer himself to her before he went back to
Boston. Father Ray, when he took leave, " admonished each one to give up the vanities of the
world, and declared that it was their own perver-
sity and hard heartedness that kept them from
being converted." Said he : " You harden your
hearts and stiffen your necks, and by-and-by you
will be abandoned by the still small voice, unless
you repent." Mrs. Flemming sighed a genuine
sigh from the depths of her motherly heart over
her children ; the Elder looked on the sweet comely faces of his daughters and the brave handsome
ones of his boys, and the thought that there was

indeed " but one thing needful " to make them perfect; but wished that the stern old preacher would
try and make religion a more winning and lovely
thing to them ; for his heart yearned tenderly over
them that they might become true and faithful servants of God.

That evening the Elder and his wife sat talking
over the fire; the young people having gone off in
a sleigh to the old meeting-house, a mile distant,
to attend the singing class. They were quite alone,
Said Mrs. Flemming :

" I think, father, we ought to feel very thankful.
God has prospered us abundantly, and our home
here is happier than most. Indeed, I often wonder
if many have been as happily matched and mated
as we two."

" I'm afraid there are not many, little wife ; more
is the pity. Yes, as you say, we have reason to be
thankful, and I hope that we are so," said the Elder
smoothing her hair.

" And I will tell you what, father," she went
on. " I think our children will be happy too ; they
are handsome and thrifty, although I say it who
oughtn't ; and they are going to marry so suitably,
and will have none of that rough close struggle that
most young couples have Deacon Sneathen's a
well-to-do man, and Huldah is a good, managing,
natty girl, and will make Nick a good wife ; then,

John Wilde—I don't know a better young man—
you know that he is rich; leastways he's got the
biggest and best stocked farm in these parts, and
will be a good husband to Hope, depend upon that.
And I am sure that George Merill will ask Eva;
I saw it in his eyes to-day if I ever saw anything."

"What a clever little mother it is," said the
Elder, smiling; "and what a proud one you'll be
to sit down among your children and grandchil-
dren some of these Thanksgiving-days. But you
are mistaken, it is likely, about George Merill; he
will want a city wife, and don't you see that he's a
bit of a dandy?"

"He may be that; but if he's not head over ears
in love with Eva, I never was so deceived in all my
life," said Mrs. Flemming, poking up the fire with
the tongs.

"It would be a good match, a very suitable
match," replied her husband complacently. "Only
I should not like Eva to go so far off."

"Neither should I; but such things are to be expected, and it would be selfish to stand in the way
of her happiness and interest if she likes him," answered Mrs. Flemming.

"That is very true. Why, mother, the old home
will be very empty and lonely for us when they all
go. I think we shall have to fetch Huldah and
Nicholas to live with us."

"It is time enough to think of that, father. It *would* be very lonesome; but, to my thinking, young people are best off to themselves, in their own house. Mothers-in-law and daughters-in-law oftener than not get to hate each other, and I shouldn't like Nick's wife to hate me. I'm afraid that your plan won't answer; I've been mistress here too long."

"And shall be to the end, my good faithful little wife and helpmate. As long as you live this house is your kingdom," he said fondly, while a warm glow of happiness passed over her face. softening away every hard line until the beauty of her youth seemed given back to her for a few moments;— then:

"It will be pleasant, I guess, to have them all coming to see us, father; and you know we shall have Reuben all the time."

"Our poor Reuben! I fear that his life will be spent uselessly. I can't imagine what he will do," sighed the Elder, while his heavy eyebrows lowered.

"Ah well! there is no use fretting our hearts to fiddle-strings over Reuben. I dare say something will turn up to suit him," replied she, also sighing. "But I feel pretty well tuckered out, and shall go to bed."

That night, after Hope and Eva got home, they

sat together on the hearth rug, reluctant to leave the warmth and glow of the fire, so grateful to their half-benumbed feet after their cold ride—talking over the evening after the manner of young girls :

" I think," said Hope, " that George Merill is very handsome."

" Yes, George is good-looking. I don't think the city has changed him much," replied Eva in a tone of unconcern.

" You seem very indifferent," said Hope teasingly.

" No, I am not indifferent. I like George—"

" Aha ! so I thought !"

" As a friend. We were playmates at school you know, Hope, and I liked him then just as I did Nick and Reuben ; and I like him so now," answered Eva seriously."

" Well I guess that's something ; but good night, I have to be up betimes in the morning. I should like to sit here all night if it were not for that," said Hope, getting up to begin her preparations for rest—" good night; tell me all about the pictures you find in the coals. Poor Ruby's pictures !" And Hope kissed her sister's fair upturned face ; then with a sudden impulse she placed her hands on each side of her head, and pressed her cheek lightly on her golden hair. Soon Hope's low, soft breathing told she was asleep ; but Eva still sat mo-

tionless on the rug, lost in thought. Presently she
reached out her hand and took her Bible from a
small work-table standing near, opened it and
drew out the picture of " the crucifixion," the keepsake of Patrick McCue,—and gazed, her eyes full
of deep thought, her heart stirring to strange pul-
sations, upon it. The picture and she who stood
beside the Cross ever haunted her. Like the aerial
echoes of Killarney, which continue to float and
repeat in clear sweet musical cadences the notes of
the instrument which evoked them, long after it
has ceased, so through the pure and quiet realms
of this young girl's mind floated ever and ever, no
matter where she was or what she was doing, the
thought of the Virgin Mother; and all of her
thoughts converged to the question : Who was she?
She had never thought of her before, beyond the
natural fact of her being the Mother of Jesus. She
had read of august mothers : the mother of Moses,
the mother of the Gracchi, the mother of Washington, and many other noble and true mothers whose
virtues she admired and revered. She had also
read of mothers whose sorrow could not be thought
of without tears : she had wept over the grief of
Hecuba ; her soul had glowed with a sort of burning ire and pity at the sevenfold martyrdom of the
mother of the Machabees ; she had lamented with
the mothers of Bethlehem over their slaughtered

innocents; but the Mother of Jesus! it actually
seemed something new to her, now she came to
think of it that this holy Mother was not a myth,
but an actual mother, who had lived and suffered.
She had never thought of her before, and had felt
no more veneration for her than for other women;
the mother of Washington had stood far above
this lowly Virgin Mother, who was altogether sub-
ordinate and lost sight of in the life of her Divine
Son; but now she began to have deep thoughts,
which would not let her alone, and being possessed
of a clear analytical brain and keen womanly perceptions, it is not strange that she should want to
study out the problem that haunted her. And
even after she laid her head upon her pillow, instead of dropping off to sleep she got to wondering how this Mother could only stand weeping and
suffering by the Cross upon which her sinless Son
was expiring in cruel torments, when it seemed only
human that she should have died in a sublime endeavor to defend and shield Him; then she
thought over all the mothers she knew, and there
was not one of them, she was morally sure, who if
they could not have rescued their child from his in-
human enemies, but would at least have died in the
effort. But this Mother, unlike any other, accepted
the wrongs and ignominies of her Son with passive
endurance without lifting hand or voice to protest

against the injustice of His persecutors and the
wanton cruelty of His torments. " There must be,"
she thought, " a reason for this, a mystery which
I cannot understand," but she determined to begin the very next morning, at the first chapter
of Genesis, and search carefully through every line
and verse of Holy Writ, down to the last word in
Revelations, to see if she could make it out. Then
it seemed strange to her that she had never felt
the least reverence for her who was the Mother of
Jesus, because she was His Mother. The mother
of Washington was reverenced next to himself in
the American mind ; but here was the Mother of
the Saviour of the world, scarcely known, never
venerated, never spoken of, and held in the lowest
esteem of all the holy women named in the Bible.
Eva could not make it out, but fell asleep murmuring " unlike other mothers."

Unlike other mothers ! Yes ! promised from the
beginning, this Virgin Mother was unlike all others ;
this second Eve, through whom the fault of the
first Eve was to be repaired ; this gate through
which the King of glory was to enter ; this Virgin
expected, and sung, by the patriarchs and prophets,
to whom an archangel was sent with wondrous
message from the Most High ; this Mother to
whom Simeon prophesied that a " sword of grief
should pierce her soul." Yes, truly was she unlike

above want; but an idle man! This was a *lusus naturæ* which she could not endure to think of, and he a Flemming!

George Merill staid on from day to day, from week to week, and spent much of his time at the old homestead; then something happened which gave them all great happiness. John Wilde experienced the "saving evidence," and professed conversion, and was afterwards baptised by old Father Ray, not only with water, but with the old minister's tears that flowed over the furrows of his harsh face without an effort to check them, on the head of the stalwart, handsome young fellow, whom he had held in his arms and blessed, when he was only a few hours old, beside the bed of his dying father. His heart was softened when he thought of this; and he felt in administering this christian rite that he was redeeming a pledge made long ago to a dying man, and he rejoiced that he was spared for the work, no doubt ever crossing his mind as to the method, or his right in performing it. John Wilde was always a good, moral young man; but all of his friends, those who were "members" and those who were not, rejoiced over his conversion because they thought it a safe thing for a young man just starting in life to be religious. Nicholas Flemming grumbled over it a little, and told Hope that he "expected John would get as ugly and sour

as Father Ray himself, and he supposed that he
would think himself too good to shake his foot in a
reel again." No : John Wilde would never dance
again, but Hope was thankful to see that he was
only a shade more serious than usual, and that he
did not grow disagreeable or sour. He only ex-
horted her now and then in such a way that she
got afraid that she was not good enough for him ;
but on the whole he was the same, and they were
all very happy together, except Wolfert Flemming,
whose doubts and perplexities increased   instead
of diminished; and the more he pored over his
old theological books—some full of Lutheranism,
some full of Moravian doctrine, to seek a standing-
place for his feet—the deeper he got into the mire,
for none of them agreed ; each one gave different
interpretations to the texts that disquieted him,
and in his thirst he could find no drop of water in
the broken cisterns they had hewn out, until at last
it became clearer to the man's mind, every day,
that in the administration and government of God's
kingdom upon earth, there must be a unity, a one-
ness and a divine authority worthy of Him, its head
and founder. But here he was obliged to stop
short. He had not found the clue yet, and he went
stumbling on in the shadow of darkness, blindly
groping for the keystone of the arch, which seemed
far beyond his reach. These were not the days of

railroads, telegraph wires, steamships, literary pri-
vateering, and cheap dissemination of philosophy.
Kant and Spinoza had not yet enlightened the
American mind with their transcendental and pan-
theistic effusions. Renan had not written, and one
heard nothing of " Symbolic Christs," of " Spiritual
Christs," of " Representative Christs," and but little
of no Christ at all, or it is just possible that our
good Puritan might have been drawn into an insidi -
ous, cheating and destructive maelstrom of infidel
ideas, and tried to measure an infinite God by the
poor guage of human reason. Happily safe from
such temptations, his whole mind was bent on trying to reconcile the glaring discrepancy between
the literal words and commands and teachings of
Christ, and the doctrines and teachings of the sects
which he believed to be orthodox ; but he could
not make them harmonize either symbolically, prac-
tically or theoretically ; so finding that this perpetual study of what became daily a deeper mystery to him, was beginning to make him morose and
gloomy, he got into his cutter one morning, and
went a day's journey up the country, among the
pines, where his men were felling timber. Here,
with axe in hand, he hewed away at the great trees
from morning until night, with such force in his
sinewy arms, that his six-foot lumbermen felt
ashamed of their more puny blows, and braced

themselves up with a will, for these half wild men
of the mountains did not like to be outdone by one
who followed the plough and pottered about the
lowland valleys ; and there was more timber felled
in those few days than was ever brought down before in so short a time.   Wolfert Flemming's blood
circulated more healthily, and he brought a good
appetite with him to the repast of bear-steaks,
potatoes and brown bread that was daily set before
him, while he found mental occupation in settling
two or three quarrels among the rough fellows
around him ; but none of these expedients quieted
the vexed needs of his souls, and at the end of a
week he went back with a vague yearning and longing after an indefinable something which could
settle the difficulties and exercises of his mind.
Father Ray could not do it, neither could his books,
for they contradicted each other ; and he had prayed
—he thought in vain—for light.   His Bible most
of all disturbed him, for therein were the words of
Divine Truth itself, which meant everything or
nothing.   If they meant everything, why was he in
darkness or doubt ?   If they meant nothing, then
all religion was a lie. 'If Christ was the Eternal
Truth, then were His words the truth ; if He was
not, then His teaching was an imposture.   And
upon this proposition Wolfert Flemming's mental
struggles hinged themselves.   He believed truly,

honestly and with all the strength of his will and understanding, that Christ was the Son of God, the very Redeemer who came upon earth not only to ransom man, but to found a law of Faith in which he could walk without stumbling, and this law of Faith should be something divine and perfect, without contradictions and pitfalls. It became more and more clear to him that this divine code did not belong to any of the contradictory creeds with which he was familiar, because some of them made a dead letter of the literal words of Christ, while others gave them meanings to suit themselves. How could a thorn tree bring forth figs? He opened his Bible one day, and read of the wonderful power given to Peter and the Apostles: "Whose sins ye remit, they are remitted; whatsoever ye loose upon earth shall be loosed in heaven." "As My Father hath sent Me, I also send you!" and to Flemming's mind, even in the ordinary affairs of life, it would have seemed more than absurd to have bestowed such powers and withheld the means of executing them. He inferred, then, that this august power had been given, with the authority and means to execute it, otherwise the words were as meaningless as anything in Joe Smith's Bible. Had this power become a dead letter? He could not be certain. The German Lutherans, he had read, claimed some such power, but the other reformed sects trampled it under foot as one of the abuses of popery. Then, too, Christ had said, " If he will not hear the Church, let him be anathema." He did not say churches ; therefore, if He was to be believed, there was a Church in which was vested a power not only to remit sins, but to ana- athematize those who stubbornly refuse to hear it, if he was to credit the Bible. These were some of the doubts arising from his study of the Scriptures ; but the crowning and most weighty one of all, was in the sixth chapter of St. John, which seemed to be the key-note of his difficulties, the mystery which if he could understand it, would unfold the rest ; the pillar of cloud that led him he knew not whither, only drifting farther and farther away from the dogmas he had been taught from his youth up ; while the Bible, which he had always held as the true rule of Faith, was now his stumbling block· Was he a hypocrite ? This thought reddened his honest face with shame ; but he feared that it was something like it to be outwardly holding with the shallow belief of his sect and doubting all the time. What right had he to set up to be wiser and of deeper penetration than his brethren. Was it not the presumption of a fool to measure his distrac- tions against the sacred wisdom of three centuries ? "There must surely," he sometimes thought, "be a maggot in my brain, or something corrupt in my soul. I *will* shake off these importunate temptations." But he might as well have said that he would not breathe, and expect to live on ; for, do all that he would, he could not silence these demands of his soul ; and he went on plodding the routine of his everyday practical life, wrestling with the strong Angel in the darkness until sometimes he felt almost spent, and wondered if the day would ever dawn. In the outward man there was no change. A close observer would have thought him a shade more reticent, a fact resulting from his mental exercises, which he now confided to no one, not even to Father Ray, with whom he declined any further discussion by telling him one day " that he should try to let things fall back into the old way ; he saw no help for himself otherwise, and he should endeavor to silence his doubts, and serve God according to the lights he had ;" which the old minister thought a very judicious, christian-like course, and rejoiced over him as over a sheep that had been lost in the wilderness and found again. But it did not seem to strike him that on the two last "sacramental Sabbaths" Elder Flemming was not in his usual place in "meeting." He heard that he had gone up among his lumbermen in the pine region ; but when the third one rolled round, and he was not present at the " Table of the Lord's Supper," he called upon him to admonish and re-

buke him, with a heavy heart; for the shortcoming
of a brother so looked up to by other professors as
a " burning and shining light" and example on
which they sought to model their own lives, was no
ordinary grief to the old man; but Flemming heard
all that he had to say patiently, and only replied,
" I was compelled to go away;" which, although
not entirely satisfactory, was worth, coming from
him, a hundred excuses of any other man.

We have seen how happy and prosperous the
Flemmings were, and heard them congratulating
each other, with thankful hearts, for the blessings
which crowned their lives. Of course we leave out
Wolfert Flemming's mental disquiet, because his
family had not the remotest idea that he was thus
exercised. Except that, there was not in all the
broad land a more truly happy and united home
circle, or one bound together by bands of stronger
kindred love. But have you ever in a calm summer day, when there was not a cloud to be seen to
obscure the brightness, noticed a shadow suddenly
sail over your head and flit like a thing of omen
over the waving heads of the golden grain, shadow-
ing the poppies among the corn and the asters in
the meadow, and, on looking up, shading your
eyes with your hand, seen that it was a hawk sail-
ing through the amber hued air? You had no superstitious dread of the hawk or its fleeting

shadow, but it was not pleasant to have an eerie phantom drop out of a cloudless sky on your head, and go creeping and gliding over the beautiful things of earth around you, like an .evil thought, aud a little chill quivered over your flesh, as you watched the broad-winged bird until it went out of sight into the far off depths of the distance. Well, I will tell you that one day such a shadow fell upon the old homestead, a shadow which they thought no more of after it had passed away, but which was the avant-courier of others yet darker for that happy household. It happened in this wise.

One afternoon, George Merill rode down to say good-by to them all. Hope and Nicholas were away at Deacon Sneathen's, but expected back before night. The Elder was busy somewhere in his outbuildings and Reuben was with him, full of the amiable endeavor to be useful, but, as usual, getting himself in the way and throwing well planned things into disorder, much to his own surprise, for he looked chiefly at his motives and aspirations, without paying much attention to his ability to execute; and Mrs. Flemming and Eva were employed in some household sewing in the family room, gossiping cheerily over the little affairs of the neighborhood, but abstaining from all malice or slander; that was one of the moral laws of this family to which they scrupulously adhered

—when George Merill came in, his well-knit, handsome form set off by a plain rich city suit of broadcloth, and his fine face aglow with hopeful, healthy vitality; and both the women thought they had never seen him so noble-looking and attractive. They shook hands; and Mrs. Flemming inquired after his grandfather's health. "He was well," George said; "but my grandfather's religion seems to hurt him all the time like a tight boot. I don't mean any disrespect, Mrs. Flemming; but, except one or two, here and there, people's natures appear to be affected by religion just as a green persimmon does a fellow's mouth; it puckers them up morally, and makes them crabbed. I can't make it out, and shouldn't bother myself over it, only my grandfather and some of his friends are forever preaching to me, and I get heartily sick of it."

"Your grandfather is a faithful minister of God's word, George, and you ought to be ashamed of yourself to try to show off your city smartness at his expense," said Mrs. Flemming.

"Yes, my grandfather *is* a good man, Mrs. Flemming; but he is troubled with spiritual hypochondria, which gives him awful notions of things; in fact, I don't call a thing that makes a man miserable, religion; at least, if it is, it don't suit me. But I don't pretend to make it out; some of these days I'll try to, perhaps. I am going away, to-morrow, and I came down to shake hands with everybody," he said, looking at Eva.

"I guess we shall all miss you, George," she said frankly.

"I am glad to think that I shall be missed," he replied gravely.

"You have taken a good long holiday; but I expect you'll go back and forget your country friends, amid the great city folk," said Mrs. Flemming.

"No," he answered simply; "I shall never forget them. There is nothing in Boston that I like half so well as being here. Where is everybody to-day?"

"Father and Reuben are among the stock, looking after some pigs that need currying. Nick and Hope went up to see Huldah; but I expect them back presently," said Mrs. Flemming. Then it seemed to occur to her that George, here at the last moment, might wish to say something to Eva, and she rose up saying, "she would go and see where father and Ruby were, and bring them in; she knew they would be sorry to hear that he was going away;" and she gathered up her work, dropped it into the work-basket, and fluttered out

George Merill drew his chair closer to Eva's, and said, "It depends upon you, Eva, whether or not I ever come back."

"I hope not, George," she replied, while the roses faded out of her cheek.

"*You hope not!*" he repeated. "It does, I tell you, depend upon the answer you give me now. I love you, Eva. Ever since we were children, you know you were always my little sweetheart when we went to school together. — I have loved you, and the hope of one day winning you for my wife has been the incentive to all my best exertions, and the safeguard of my manhood and honor. What have you to say to me?"

"I am sorry, George;" and the girl's voice was tremulous with pity; "I am sorry to pain you; but—"

"Don't, Eva; don't!" he cried, putting forth his hand with a deprecatory gesture; "don't tell me that all my patient waiting and love goes for nothing. I couldn't stand that; indeed I couldn't."

"You must have courage, George," she said at last, as she lifted her pure, honest eyes, so like her father's, and looked frankly into his. "I cannot return the preference you have honored me with. It is kind of you to think so well of me, and I thank you for it; but I can give you no hope beyond my friendship."

"But why—why, Eva? What is there in me so repulsive and disagreeable that you refuse to allow me at least to hope to win you?" he exclaimed.

"No, there is nothing of that sort, George; on the contrary, I do not know any one who has greater personal advantages, and I have a thorough liking and respect for you, such as I have for my father and brothers——"

"But, perhaps," he interrupted almost rudely, "there is some other person towards whom your liking goes a little farther than this dutiful kindred sentiment!"

"That is none of your business, George Merill!" she answered, while an angry light flashed for a moment in her eyes. Then pitying him for the breaking up of the hopes that had brightened his dreams so long, she added more gently, "There is no other person."

"Then I *will* hope, Eva. Remember, I will not give you up; I will write to you, I will come; I will importune you, and bear with your caprices and wait patiently; but I will not give you up, remember that," he said.

"It will be all useless, George; and you will waste the best years of your life in an idle pursuit. I will not receive your letters. As a friend of the family, I will give you welcome when you come, but nothing more," she said in a grave determined tone.

Just then the Elder and Reuben came in, and there was a great hand-shaking, in the midst of

which Hope and Nicholas arrived. They had heard
at Deacon Sneathen's that George was going, and
went over to Father Ray's to see him; but he was
not at home, and the housekeeper told them he
had gone up to John Wilde's; but here he was, to
their great joy, at their own fireside; and the
pleasant, friendly things that were said to him, and
the sorrow they all expressed at his going away,
should have consoled him, but it did not, and he
felt so hurt and disappointed that he could not
stand it, but got up to take leave and go.

CHAPTER IX.

THE FLOATING SHADOW.

"Don't forget old friends, George," said the
Elder.

"No fear of that, sir," he replied, while they
shook hands; then, with a frank audacity, full,
however, of an honest purpose to fight his battle
out single-handed, he added: "Since I am sure
of your friendship, sir, may I hope for something
nearer?"

"You could not be too near to us, George," said
the Elder, something at a loss how to answer him

but the sincerity of his soul asserted itself, and he merely uttered the simple truth.

"And you, Mrs. Flemming—you know I want Eva for my wife," he blurted out.

"You have my best wishes, George," she replied, while a soft womanly blush stole over her face from the shock of his strange, outspoken wooing, and the sudden fulfilment of her hopes for her child. "But what does Eva say? Of course——-"

"Eva," he interrupted, "gives me no encouragement."

"And," interrupted Eva, as she stood with her arm carelessly thrown over Hope's shoulder, while an angry sparkle flashed in her eyes, "you ask the influence of my parents when I have already answered you, and complain of me. Fie upon you, George Merill."

"Not so, Eva!" he answered bravely "I only do what any other honorable man would. I ask their sanction of my endeavor to win you; for although you have answered me, and pretty decidedly too, remember I do not accept your answer. I told you that; and knowing that you all have no secrets from one another, I speak openly, and tell you again, before them all, that I will not give you up. I intend to persevere in my suit until my faithfulness and constancy shall win you," he added manfully.

"It will be so much time wasted, George. Since you are so very frank in your wooing, I will be equally so ; and I positively decline, before all these witnesses, your offer," said Eva with spirit.

"Do not be too hasty, Eva !" said Mrs. Flemming, whose breath was almost taken away by the scene.

"It is not the result of hastiness or caprice, mother. I like George Merill, and wish him well," she replied ; "but he might as well know, up and down, for good and all, that I will not marry him. It is no use for him to set his mind upon it, and lose chances in Boston which will suit him better. Besides, what is the use of a man throwing his life backwards in such waste ? For myself I don't intend to marry. I am going to be the old maid of the family."

"Well, good-by, Eva. All that you say makes no difference to me. I shall come again, and perhaps you will change your mind. I don't know whatever I have done to make you hate me so;" and George held out his hand towards her to shake hands, but she withheld hers.

"I do not hate you ; you know that I don't ; I only treat you as one honorable person should treat another, by telling you the truth. I have no idea of marrying. It does not seem to me that marrying should be the sole end and aim of a woman's life ; and I am very happy here," she said bravely.

" You are heartless, Eva."

" No, I am not heartless, George, and you have no right to say that. I am sorry to have pained you, for you are like a brother ; and Nick and Reuben were never angry with me in their lives. Surely you would not like a wife who could not love you," she said, pitying the grief and disappointment that she saw surging up in his eyes.

" Yes, Eva, because I know that in time I could win your love," he said quickly, hoping that she would relent.

" There has been enough of this, George. I wish you well with all my heart," said Eva, to whom the scene was becoming more painful and embarrassing. Then she turned abruptly away and left the room, without throwing another word or look towards him. About five minutes later she heard his horse galloping off as if his rider had dug the spurs pretty deeply into his sides.

No one said a word to Eva about George Merill : indeed, no one saw her until supper time, for she had gone straight up to her room, and shut herself in, then had a good womanly cry, for she was both sorry and exasperated : sorry to have brought such a disappointment into her old school-fellow's life, and angry at his presumption in assuming the position he did after she had positively rejected him ; but most of all was she mortified at the scene which had just taken place in the presence of the family. Eva Flemming could not brook being treated like a capricious child, when she knew how perfectly in earnest she was, and how firm her purpose, as George Merrill should find out to his cost. After supper, when they were all gathered around the old hearth, as usual, a casual observer could have detected no change. The fire burned brightly; between the andirons simmered a row of great juicy red apples; a little farther off stood a large stone pitcher of cider, slowly warming; on the other side the cat was curled up asleep at Reuben's feet, as he sat reading. They talked to each other, trying to be cheerful; but there was a restraint; and one after another they dropped into silence, which nothing interrupted except the crackling of the fire, the rustle of paper, as the Elder and Reuben—both reading—turned the pages of their books, and the sharp, rapid click of Mrs. Flemming's knitting needles. At last the Elder closed his book, and looking around at the serious faces, he said, "It seems to me that you are all uncommonly quiet to-night! I scarcely feel at home, mother—what is it all?"

"Don't bother about us, father. I guess we shall overget the trouble, whatever it is," said Mrs. Flemming, in her quick, sharp way. Nicholas thrust his hands down into his pockets, and tilting back his chair, looked up at the black rafters overhead, festooned with sweet-smelling herbs, and whistled to himself. Reuben laid his book down over his knee, and turned his soft, mild eyes inquiringly from one to another. Hope felt her face redden as if she were the guilty one, and stole her hand down and folded her sister's lovingly in it; but she—Eva—a little paler than usual, lifted her handsome eyes, and looked steadily at the unquiet countenances around her, and *felt* intuitively that if they were not displeased with her, she had at least disappointed them all. Her affectionate nature was pained to think that she should be the first to create a discord in the family harmony, always so perfect; but it was a way the Flemmings had, to have no secrets from each other, and to speak out openly of whatever troubled them; so she took heart and said:

"I guess, father, that I am the cause of the quiet that you complain of. I'm afraid that you are all displeased by what I said to George Merill."

"I'm sorry for George, that's a fact," said the Elder; "he's a great favorite of mine, and of all of us; and I should have liked him well for my son-in-law; but when that is said. all is said that is in my heart about it; for, as much as I like him. I value you and your happiness still more. You have not offended me, daughter."

"Thank you, dear father," said Eva, while her voice trembled with emotion. It was much for her to be assured that her father, whom she idolized, was not angry with her; but the rest——

"Well!" said Nicholas, "my opinion is that George is a man that *any* girl might be proud of; and it looks to me like a foolish caprice to throw him over like that."

"It would be a silly caprice, and a wicked one, too, Nick, for Huldah to throw *you* over; but the cases, you know, are entirely different," said Eva, with spirit. Nicholas subsided and held his peace, for this came directly home to him.

"George will be a very rich man. The minister told me that he had outlying lots in Boston; that when the city stretches out to them—which it is fast doing—George will be worth hundreds of thousands of dollars. Just think of that, now," said Mrs. Flemming, with a quick snap of her fine black eyes.

"I am glad to hear that, mother, for his own sake," said Eva, quietly; "for he will more easily forget his disappointment up here when he takes hold on the cares and glitter of riches. I do not care for money myself—at least as the price of what I should consider dishonor—for I do not love George Merill, and if I married him for his money, I should be ashamed to look him in the face."

"To be sure you would," said Hope, speaking for the first time, "and I should be ashamed for you."

"George promised to take me over the seas to see the fine pictures of the old masters," said Reuben, with a sigh; "but I guess that's all up now;" Even Reuben reproached her; but she laughed and said:

"Perhaps not. I think there is something between you and the old pictures that will sooner or later bring you together, Ruby."

"Don't put such stuff into his head, Eva," said her mother, curtly.

"Is it stuff, mother? I only meant to comfort him!" she answered, with a sad smile, while her eyes flashed with unshed tears; the strain was getting too much for her.

"Yes, I call it downright stuff. Reuben must learn to be useful, and not expect to go about the world mooning and daubing, and doing nothing but read." Reuben sighed, picked up his book and sought refuge on the heights of the ideal, and soon forgot the family discussion going on around him. His mother always let such a *douche* down on him that he was glad to escape, shivering with the shock and chill of it. "And I think, Eva, since we have come to talk of it," continued Mrs. Flemming, after quenching Reuben, "that you have done a *very* foolish thing to reject George Merrill."

"I am sorry, mother," she said, gravely; "but I do not wish to marry—least of all will I marry George Merrill."

"Many a one just as positive as you are have changed their mind," said Mrs. Flemming. "There's Prudence Rogers; why, she and Sam hated each other after they got acquainted, for more than a year; then, after all, got married; and there was not a happier couple about, was there, father?"

"And I read once of an audacious man that beat and cuffed and kicked a high-born lady who had refused his suit; and she, either to wipe out the insult, or because she was afraid that the next time he would kill her, married him. But if George has the spirit of William of Normandy, he'll find no Matilda of Flanders in me, mother," exclaimed Eva, whose spirit was up so high that she could not wait to hear the history of Sam Rogers' happy marriage.

"Well, perhaps you'll *repent*, Eva; repentance and changing one's mind are perhaps different things," said Mrs. Flemming, with a provoking smile.

"I shall never repent of this, mother, rest assured of it. I ask nothing better than to stay here with you and my father in the dear old place where I was born, as long as I live," said Eva, more quietly.

"And here you are welcome, my child, as long as you live," said the Elder. "Your mother and I ought to rejoice if we can keep you; for the old place will seem too empty and silent when you all go away to new homes."

"Well, well, don't fret over what I said, Eva. I am outspoken. I *am* disappointed; there's no use denying it. I should be glad to think I'd have you with me all my life; but I don't want you to be an old maid, like that forlorn, dried-up old aunt of Huldah Sneathen's," said Mrs. Flemming, whose mother-heart, always true and good in its instincts, was at last touched. Pride and ambition for her beautiful child had held sway long enough—it was pulsing to the right music now; and Eva went over, and drawing up a low cushion, sat at her feet, and leaning upon her knees, lifted her eyes appealingly to her face and said, "Then you are not angry with me, darling?"

"Well—no—I'm not angry," she replied, while she laid down her knitting and smoothed the soft, golden brown hair away from Eva's pure forehead. "I can't say that I'm angry, but *disappointed*. I had counted so on seeing you a great lady down to Boston——"

"Wife! wife!" exclaimed the Elder.

"Why! mother!" said Hope.

"It's no use," said Mrs. Flemming. "I mean

just what I say. I counted on seeing her a fine
lady in Boston, riding in her own carriage and
dressed in rich silks, laces and jewels, and showing
that the New Hampshire hills are no way behind
the flats of Massachusetts in the way of handsome
women. Now if that's a sin, it is out, and I'm
done with it; so let the subject be dropped."

Eva buried her burning face in her hands. She
felt humiliated to think that her own mother had
been having such sordid thoughts about her. The
Elder did not speak for several minutes, but kept
walking up and down, while the knitting needles
clicked with vim. At last the Elder said slowly, in
his kindly, even tones, "My daughter, you did
right. You have my approval."

"Thank you, father," she replied very quietly.

"Now let us be as we were before," said Hope,
snuffing the candle. "I declare I feel as if we had
been in a Scotch mist."

And they tried "being as they were before;" but
the shadow had flitted over them, and each one
had an indescribable and indefinite prevision that
the harmony of their life was broken. But Mrs.
Flemming began to talk of farm matters and the
coming spring work, a subject always full of interest to her, and asked, "What are you going to do
with that corner lot, father? It's a perfect quag-
mire."

"Drain it, and put down Swedish turnips, I think."

"It's a great waste of soil, I think. They're nasty things."

"I like the sharp taste of them, rather," he replied; "they are splendid winter feeding for stock, and will make your butter look like gold, mother."

"Yes, I guess they will. I hope you'll put down a good lot of mercer potatoes on that slope; they'll come early there, and fetch a high price. I should not wonder if you get four or five dollars a barrel."

"Yes, they'll bring about that, if I can get them into the market early enough. But if we have a late, soggy spring, how then?"

"It'll be a poor chance for early potatoes, and hard on people who have nothing but their crops to depend on. Have you seen the Deacon lately, father?"

"No. I shall have to see him in a day or two, about that lumber business. Our partnership expires in a month or so; and if he should take it into his head to make a change, it will be a great disappointment as well as loss to me."

"Land-sakes! such a thought never entered my head," exclaimed Mrs. Flemming. "Why! what are you thinking about? The idea of Deacon Sneathen throwing you over for anybody else, and just now, too, when you are clearing something on your outlay!"

"It does seem like sheer nonsense, even to think of such a thing," put in Nicholas, who had been amusing himself tickling the cat's ear with a straw. "The Deacon was only talking about it last night, and seemed very anxious to know if you'd like to keep on for another term, father."

"Was he?" remarked the Elder, folding his hands behind him, while he still walked up and down. "I hope he will continue in the same mind. The business is a profitable one."

CHAPTER X.

MRS. FLEMMING HAS A GREAT SHOCK.

THE snow was beginning to melt on the southern slopes of the hills, and in sheltered nooks the star-wort shot its dark waxen leaves up among the soft green mosses, while now and then, on sunny mild days, the low musical warble of the bluebird —like stray notes from heaven—floated out and melted on the air. It was cold enough yet, with too much frost in the ground for ploughing, and too much frost in the air for the regular out-door farm work to begin ; but there was no lack of work for all that. The men were busy getting their

farming implements in order, burning brush, hauling manure, and mending fences. The Elder was
busy fencing in a piece of poor land, which per-
sisted in growing nothing but wire grass, to turn
his sheep into as soon as spring opened, and on
rainy days in manufacturing the framework of a
hay-tedder, having bought the metal teeth from a
travelling agent of the inventor the preceding au-
tumn. Hay-tedders were novelties then, and all
novelties were looked upon then, as now, by old
practical farmers, as ruinous innovations; but the
Elder had lost a whole field of hay last season for
want of hands to get it in in time, and having seen
a hay-tedder at work somewhere down the country, was so convinced of its utility that he determined to defy prejudice, and use one upon his
farm. He had great mechanical genius, and being
very much interested in his experiment, had succeeded in making, from the diagram furnished by
the agent, a tedder which would have borne favorable comparison with those made in Boston.
Nicholas had gone back to the pine forest, and
Reuben was happy at last in the prospect of
making himself useful: he was to paint the
window frames and doors of the old homestead, a
plan about which Mrs. Flemming had serious misgivings, for she was "morally sure," she declared,
"that before they knew where they were, Reuben

would have faces staring out at them from the panels, and the house would look like a circus; he couldn't help it, poor boy; he was possessed, she was afraid; poor, dear Ruby! and she couldn't think, for the life of her, what ever would become of him." But the Elder laughed and told her not to fret, that he would see that there were no faces painted upon the panels. The girls were also busy preparing Hope's wedding outfit, for she was to be married in May to John Wilde, which, together with their regular domestic duties, left them no idle time ; while Mrs. Flemming helped everybody, governed her household and administered its affairs with reference to the comfort and well-being of all, and had, every day, two hours left for her carpet weaving. One letter had come to Eva from George Merill, which she gave unopened to her father, declining altogether to read it, who put it away into a private drawer of his desk, with a natural regret that Eva had set her face so resolutely against her own interests ; but he made no remark one way or the other on the subject, nor did any of the rest of them.

One day Huldah Sneathen and her aunt, Miss Deborah Wyatt, came to spend the day with the Flemmings. The girls huddled together over the fine and beautifully made *lingerie* of Hope's *trousseau*, and talked, and chattered, and cut patterns

and sewed on ruffles, and embroidered, until one
would have thought they must exhaust themselves,
but the subject and the work were too interesting
by far for that, and their nimble tongues and fingers, instead of showing signs of weariness, grew
more voluble and busy every moment. Mrs. Flemming and Miss Deborah were entertaining each
other in their peculiar way, Mrs. Flemming inwardly fretting over the two hours she was obliged
to lose at the loom; but nothing loth, and with a
pardonable motherly pride, to talk over Hope's
good prospects, to all of which Miss Deborah listened with an expression on her countenance which
said plainly: "I hope you won't be disappointed;" which meant—when literally translated—"I
shouldn't be sorry if you were." She was an an-
gular, uncomfortable-looking person, and had a
way of cocking up her nose and chin to take
square aim with her eyes whenever she addressed
any one, which was embarrassing to some, and almost terrifying to such as had weak nerves. She
had never been handsome, and the wine of her life
had long ago turned to vinegar. She wore her
thin dry hair drawn up to a knot on the top of her
head, and rolled into two little flat rings on each
side of her narrow forehead, where they were held
in place by side combs. Her eyes were sunken
but sharp, and her voice thin and wiry, but, as

old Sarah Gill said, "went through and through
your head, like a gimlet." Her neck was long,
wrinkled, and decorated with two rows of large
gold beads, Miss Debby's fortune, invested in that
shape for safe keeping and not for ornament, she
having a dread of banks, and as little love for the
vanities of the world, as her attire of plain dark
woolen stuff, without braid, cord, or button to trim
it, testified. She had kept house for her brother,
Deacon Sneathen, ever since his wife died, and if
Huldah hadn't got a start in life under the tender,
cheerful care of her mother, she would have been
blighted and quenched by Miss Debby, who was a
firm believer in total depravity and that world-re-
nowned precept of Solomon's : "Spare the rod and
spoil the child," which proves that Solomon with
all his wisdom sometimes gave utterance to impracticable theories. So, according to Miss Debby,
there was no cure for total depravity in a child except the rod, until they reached the age of reason
and obtained the "saving evidence" of conversion ;
and she and Huldah had a spirited time of it,
which resulted in Huldah's setting everything that
her aunt advocated at utter defiance, and heartily
hating everything that she liked. So Huldah loved
to dance, to sing songs to read "Sir Charles
Grandison," and "Evelina," the only two novels
she had ever seen, which she found one day in a

barrel of old papers in the garret where she had
been sent for punishment, and with which she was
so charmed, that she repeated her offence next day
and the day after, that she might be sent up there,
where she could revel to her heart's content in the
new, wonderful world she had discovered. She
loved to wear ribbons, laces and jewelry; and she
had some rare old treasures of both among the
things her mother had left; she liked ruffles and
bright colors, and artificial flowers, and "purple and
fine linen," and now that she was grown, would
never read the Bible at her aunt's bidding; or at
all, unless she felt like it; indeed, I'm afraid that
Miss Debby had got Huldah to think of God pretty
much as she used to think, when she was a child,
of the ogre that lived in the clouds upon the top of
Jack's bean stalk. She shuddered when, sometimes
alone in her mountain-side rambles and sometimes
at midnight when the wintry storms were howling
outside her windows, the thought of God, the stern
and terrible Judge, the merciless executioner of
justice and wrath, who might at any moment reach
out His iron hand from the heavens and thrust her
into the living and eternal flames of woe; the God
her aunt had taught her to believe in, came like a
dark, fearful shadow into her heart, making her
tremble and shrink even in the bright sunshine, and
hide her head in her pillows in the darkness. So

it is not strange that Huldah grew up, under such
influences, into a sort of amiable, light-hearted
pagan, flying from all voluntary thoughts of this
religion of horrors, and, like an epicurean priestess
trying to cover the skeleton with flowers. Only in
one thing had she profited by her aunt's guardian-
ship ; she knew all the mysteries of domestic econ-
omy in all its branches, and was noted through the
neighborhood as the " nattiest, smartest" young girl
in it. She liked house-keeping ; and having good
taste and ambition, she beautified the old brown
house under the elms, and excelled in whatever she
undertook.

Miss Debby had already snubbed Mrs. Flemming
—it was her way—and taken the girls to task for
frivolity, when the Elder came in from his fence-
building, his face all aglow with ruddy health, and
gave cordial greeting to his guests, whom he was
glad to see as neighbors, and because their coming
seemed like a friendly indication of what he might
expect about a renewal of the partnership, concerning which he had, somehow, without any tangible
reason however, had strange misgivings. After he
got fairly seated, and they were all waiting for dinner, Miss Debby stuck up her chin, and taking sure
aim at him with her eyes, said sharply :

" Wal, now, Elder, I hear you're making one of
them tedder things."

"Yes; I have it nearly finished. It is a good thing for harvesting hay."

"It's a great shame, to my thinking. It's taking the bread from the poor. I don't hold with any such machinery!" she snorted out, elevating her chin still higher.

"Labor's hard to get sometimes; meanwhile the hay gets spoiled. The tedder works so fast that you can go over your field three or four times if it is necessary, and if there's a good hot sun, get heavy grass cured enough to go in the same day."

"I don't believe a word of it. I don't like new-fangled things. They're unlucky. I saw one of them things at work in Captain Jones' field last summer, and it looked like a grasshopper kicking out its legs. It seems fooling with Providence, and will make our lads as lazy as Virginny nigger drivers."

"The world moves on, Miss Debby, in spite of prejudice, and I'm afraid you'll see more tedders than mine at work this harvest," he said with a quiet smile.

"And I hear you're hauling pond muck to put on your fields! Land sakes, Elder Flemming! I think you must be getting a screw looser in the head in your old days! Who ever heard the like!" she said.

"It's one of the best fertilizers in the world," he replied, good-humoredly.

"You got that out of books, I suppose! Book farming's ruined more men than a few."

"I'm a pretty old farmer," said the Elder, poking up the fire, with just a shadow of annoyance in his countenance, "but I don't think pond mud will ruin me, if I do get the notion from the 'FARMER.' You'd better try some on that slip of ground west of your orchard, where nothing will grow but rag-weed."

Miss Debby sniffed and was silent. That sterile lot was the eye-sore of her life; and the Elder could not have found a more certain means to end their dispute than the mention of it, if he had taxed his ingenuity for an hour. Then she turned sharply around toward the girls and said, "Eva, how could you flirt so with George Merill? I'd like to see Huldah treat anybody so."

Eva's face crimsoned, but she made no answer. "I say, it was shameful of you, Eva, and he so rich and handsome. Land sakes! have you lost your tongue!"

"I have never flirted with any one, Miss Debby. Hope, give me that sleeve, and tell me how it shall be trimmed," said Eva quietly.

"Wal! and so techy about it, too. There must be something in it. I wish Huldah had such a chance."

"I wish she hadn't, then," answered Huldah saucily. "I wonder you didn't set your cap for him, Aunt Deb." The old lady bridled, and got red in the end of her nose; but the subject was quenched. Then, defeated on one point, she flew to another, and said, turning toward the Elder:

"Next Sabbath's Saycrament day, ain't it, Elder?

"Yes."

"That jest 'minds me, now I come to think about it: What become of you the last three months at the table of the Lord's Supper? I looked 'round and didn't see you nor hear your voice, either singing, nor yet praying. The Deacon says you was up to the Pines."

"Yes," he replied, "I was at the Pines."

"Wal, I s'pose you'll be along Sabbath. It seems sort of strange not to have you there in your place." Fortunately, at this moment Reuben and his mother came into the room together, and the cat running to meet Reuben, whose especial pet she was, he trod upon her tail without seeing her and was so startled at her outcry and the tangle she got into under his feet that he lost his balance and pitched forward with full force, falling across Miss Debby's lap, just as he, with a beaming smile, had stretched out his arm to shake hands with her, almost upsetting her and the chair together; she instinctively grasping at something to save herself

from falling, seized Reuben's long golden hair, and
the next instant would have boxed his ears soundly,
when Huldah grasped hold of her wrists, and with
much laughter told Reuben to escape, which he did
forthwith, glad of the opportunity to get somewhere
to laugh his fill. It was an absurd scene; even the
Elder's grave eyes had a merry twinkle in them,
and Mrs. Flemming was so choked with laughter
that she could scarcely find breath enough to
say: "I declare! I do wonder what will ever become of Ruby?" while Eva and Huldah and Hope,
bent over their sewing almost in convulsions. Miss
Debby gained her equilibrium, but not her temper,
and went away directly after dinner, to the great
relief of the Flemmings, to whose amiable and
happy tempers she was under all circumstances and
at all times a moral nettle.

That evening Mrs. Flemming, after a long and
thoughtful silence, said: "Father, it does seem
strange to me that you have not been to meeting
the last three Sabbaths of the Lord's Supper. I
hope nothing will take you off next Sabbath."
She had been secretly troubled for weeks about
this, but had forborne speaking, under the impression that her husband's absence from his usual
conspicuous place on these solemn occasions was
of absolute necessity; but Miss Debby's remarks,
so full of ill-concealed malice, determined her to re-

lieve her mind by speaking out. The Elder did not answer her at once; he only moved uneasily in his chair, lowered his heavy eyebrows, and tapped slowly with his fingers on the page of the old Bible which he had been poring over. At last he said in a slow, deliberate voice: "There's no business to take me off. *But I shall not be there.*" Mrs. Flemming dropped her work and looked at him in speechless surprise, and in her face there was a flickering look of terror, an appealing, silent demand for the meaning of his words. It had been laying heavy at her heart for three months, but she had kept silent, hoping that when the next "Sacrament Sabbath" rolled round, her husband, of whom she was justly proud as the impersonation of all that was true and good in man, would be there at his post the burning and shining light, the golden candlestick of the sanctuary; and now to hear this! He would not be there!

"Did I understand you, father? Did you say that you would not be present at the Table of the Lord?" asked Mrs. Flemming in a low, excited voice.

"You did not misunderstand me, mother," he replied, speaking slowly: "I shall not go."

"And why? Oh husband! husband! what does it mean?" she exclaimed. "It can't be that you are a backslider after all these years of christian, godly life? You of all men!"

"I may be that in a sense," he answered, "but I will not be a hypocrite."

"Hypocrite! Why, father, *what* do you mean? Eva, Hope, Reuben! go away; I want to talk to father," she exclaimed, almost beside herself.

"Stay where you all are, children. I have no secrets from you, least of all in such matters as this," said the Elder, lifting his head and looking out of the great truthful eyes from one to the other of them, as they, full of wonder at the strange scene, looked with almost frightened faces towards him. ' I have something to say to you, wife and children, —a something which has troubled me for years, and made a miserable man of me whenever I have partaken of the bread and wine of the Sacrament. I would have kept my secret still buried in my own breast—for I know of no help for me—but, as you see yourselves, circumstances compel me, as it were, to reveal it, at least to you, my wife and children, for fear you may judge me as having been guilty of hidden sin, and be scandalized in me."

"O Wolfert! Wolfert Flemming! what awful temptation has got possession of you?" exclaimed Mrs. Flemming, from whose face every vestige of color had fled, and whose eyes were dilated and fairly gleaming with excitement.

"I don't know," he said, sadly; "I don't fully know, myself. I feel blind, like Sampson, and may.

be am pulling the temple roof down to my own destruction. But I can bear it no longer! I was not
born to be a hypocrite—I'd rather die than be a
hypocrite."

"Father," said Eva, going round to him and
standing by his side, while she laid her arm tenderly about him and drew his grand, handsome
head to her breast : " Tell us what difficulty you
are struggling with? We may not know how to
help you, but we do know that whatever the
cause is, it is an honest one, and we can respect
and sympathize, and try to soothe——. Oh, father!
you who are so truthful and good, *why* should you
be so troubled ? It must be something of great
weight to move you from your foundations like
this."

"Sandy foundations, child !" he said, folding her
hand for a moment in his own. "But I will un-
bosom myself, then ; think as you may of me, you
will never despise me for hypocrisy."

" Dear father!" whispered Eva, leaning her cheek
against his gray head. Mrs. Flemming could not
speak. She put her hand to her throat once or
twice, and a quick, deep-drawn breath, like a sob,
escaped her lips ; and folding her hands together
in her lap, she turned to listen to what her husband
might have to say.

CHAPTER XI.

LIGHT OUT OF DARKNESS.

SHE sat listening to hear what he might say, with a dull dazed feeling in her head, as if she had received a heavy blow upon it, wondering all the while if that strong energetic will and intelligent mind, to which she had been wont to look as to something higher and better than other men's, were drifting into the eccentricities of coming madness, so strange and terrible a thing it was to her to hear from her husband's lips words which meant something little short of apostasy. Then, all the consequences of such a fall swept like a torrent through her brain; she saw his place empty in the sanctuary, his "candlestick taken away;" she saw him shunned by old neighbors and friends, and instead of being looked up to by all as a model of every manly and christianly excellence, she saw him treated with contempt, pitied with cold sneers by some, avoided as a leper by others; and as the possibilities of worldly misfortunes, dearth of prosperity, and the ruin of her children's prospects mingled gloomily together in her thoughts, she felt a tightness grasping her throat, like the clutch of old Massasquoi's bony fingers, almost suffocating her. But she did not utter a word; and with her slim little hands clasped tightly together, resting upon her knees, and her handsome black eyes flickering with the fever of her heart, she waited, wondering if it was in the scope of human ingenuity to show good reasons for such backsliding. She had not to wait long; for the Elder, after glancing with grave but tender looks on the dear faces, all bent with anxious interest upon him, said :

"It is a bad cause which can show no good reason to support it; and while I do not seek to defend myself, which would argue that I doubt the justice of my conclusions, I am willing to explain to you, my wife and children, the cause of my refusal to partake any more of the Sacrament of the Lord's Supper as administered among ourselves. I am not a learned man, and have but little knowledge of other religions outside the sect in which I was bred; but from a constant study of the Scriptures, doubts and troubles have arisen in my mind, forcing me to the inevitable conclusion that my religious opinions are full of error and deceit——" Mrs. Flemming gasped for breath, and a spot of crimson flamed out on either cheek, while an inward tremor ran like an electric chord through the hearts of the rest; but no one spoke, and the Elder went on : "I will not now go into the history of my doubts; some other time will do; but I will explain, as I said before, why it is utterly impossible—unless I could stoop to a base hypocrisy—for me to unite in a rite which strikes me as an audacious human invention entirely opposed to the plain and literal meaning of its divine Founder. To make myself better understood, I wish you to listen attentively, not losing a word, while I read to you the sixth chapter of St. John's Gospel.*

Then the Elder, in his clear even tones, read, slowly and impressively, the chapter from beginning to end; Eva still standing with her arm resting upon his shoulder, and her eyes fixed upon the page of the old Bible, with its quaint illustrations, from which her father read. When the last word dropped from his lips he again looked around him, and scanned with deep pity in his heart the countenances of those near and dear ones, to whose hearts he well knew he was bringing grief and disquiet. But as we said before, the Flemmings were people who let nothing obstruct the working out of a principle which to their mind was clearly right: and although the Elder felt the first throes of the sacrifice at hand, he went bravely on. "The first thing," he said, " to be noticed in this chapter, is the account of the great miracle, the most wonderful perhaps that the Saviour had yet wrought;

---

* What follows was the genuine experience of an intelligent Protestant mind, who—at the time—had never heard of the doctrine of the Real Presence, and we render it in all its simplicity.

a miracle which was a manifestation not only of a divine power, but of a divine priesthood, and at the same time a figure and a fact: the figure and preliminary preparation for a great mystery which he was about to announce to them, and a fact by which the physical hunger of five thousand men, besides women and children, was satisfied with material bread, which, blessed by the Lord, was multiplied by His power in the hands of His apostles, who distributed it to the multitude. But the carnal-minded Jews recognized only the fact: their hunger had been appeased in a wonderful manner, and in the first flush of their gratitude they declared Him to be a great prophet, and would have taken Him by force and made Him a king, had He not fled from them, concealing Himself from their sight; but they discerned neither the divinity of His power or the symbolic meaning of the miraculous feast, and cared for no other manifestations from Him than such material ones as would benefit themselves. 'He is a wonder-worker,' they thought, 'and can found a rich and powerful kingdom, of which we shall be the princes.' Full of such thoughts, they determined to follow Him the next day, hoping to witness greater miracles."

"In the next point there is a hidden and holy meaning to me, which seems separate from the great mystery of the mystic feast announced by the

Lord, and yet linked indissolubly with it in the order of faith. I mean the appearance of the Saviour walking on the stormy waves of the midnight sea. His disciples had sought for Him ; and not finding him, probably thought He had passed over to Capharnaum, and ' took ship' to go thither ; when a storm arose, and coming out of the darkness of the night, walking upon the rough waves of the sea, they beheld a form advancing towards their ship, and they were terrified, thinking that it was a spirit, until He spoke : ' Be not afraid. It is I.' In this miracle he revealed Himself in a real and spiritual presence, disguised by the miraculous character of the occasion, which was utterly at variance with every natural law ; and they did not know Him, until He said : ' It is I '—when, consoled and full of joy, they took Him into the ship ; a lesson, it seems to one, of faith to His own disciples, some of whom, we shall presently see, after all, turned back and walked with Him no more.

" The third point to be considered is His discourse on the bread of life, in which He declares Himself to be the Son of God, and enforces the necessity of ' believing in Him,' as a condition to inherit eternal life- -meaning clearly, from what follows, a belief in His doctrines, especially in the great and mysterious one of the partaking of His body and blood.*

" The next day, the multitude who had been fed —full of human curiosity and ambitious designs— sought for Jesus ; but not finding him, ' they took shipping' and came across the sea of Tiberias to Capharnaum, where they found Him teaching in the synagogue. They said to Him : Rabbi, when camest Thou hither ?

" Then Jesus rebuked them saying : Amen, ámen, I say unto you, you seek Me, not because you have seen miracles, but because you did eat of the loaves, and were filled. *Labor not for the meat which perisheth, but for that which endureth unto eternal life which the Son of man. will give you.* For Him hath God the Father sealed.

" What shall we do, that we may work the works of God ? they said to Him.

" This is the work of God, that you believe in Him whom He hath sent : Jesus answered them.

" What sign dost Thou show us that we may see, and may believe Thee ? they said therefore to Him. What dost Thou work ? Our fathers did eat manna in the desert ; as it is written : He gave them bread from heaven to eat.

" Amen, amen I say to you : Moses gave you not bread from heaven ; BUT MY FATHER GIVETH YOU THE TRUE BREAD FROM HEAVEN ; Jesus said unto them.

" Lord ! give us always this bread ! they besought Him.

" I AM THE BREAD OF LIFE : he that cometh to Me shall not hunger ; and he that *believeth in Me*, shall never thirst : Jesus said to them. But I said to you, that you also have seen Me, and do not believe. All that the Father giveth Me shall come

* The reader must keep in mind that these impressions are the unaided results of an uninstructed Protestant experience, and the writer is only transferring them from a regularly-kept journal to her pages.

to Me ; and him that cometh to Me I will not cast out : *Because I came down from heaven,* not to do my own will, but the will of Him that sent Me.   Now this is the will of the Father who sent Me, that of all he hath given Me, I shall lose nothing, but should raise it up again at the last day.   And this is the will of my Father that sent Me ; that every one that seeth the Son and believeth in Him,* may have everlasting life, and I will raise him up on the last day."

"Then the Jews"—still discerning nothing beyond their carnal ideas—murmured at Him, not because He had said He was the Son of the Father, but because He said : I am the living bread which came down from Heaven.   "And they said : Is not this Jesus the son of Joseph, whose father and mother we know ?   How then saith he, I came down from heaven.

"Murmur not among yourselves," Jesus answered and said unto them : "No man can come to Me, except the Father, who hath sent Me, draw him :† and I will raise him up at the last day.   It is written in the prophets : And they shall all be taught of God.   Every one that hath heard of the Father, and hath learned cometh to Me.   Not that any man hath seen the Father, but he who is of God, he hath seen the Father.   Amen, amen I say unto you : *he that believeth in Me, hath eternal life.*"

"Now," said the Elder, looking out of his grave gentle eyes with unspeakable love upon them all, as they sat reverently listening, "we hear how solemnly and emphatically He declares, over and again, His divinity, in calling Himself ' the Son of the Father,' who ' had seen the face of the Father,' who ' had been sent to do the will of the Father,' and so on ; and how He insists on their believing in Him as a primary and absolute condition to their inheriting eternal life.   Do *we* believe Him to be the Son of the Father, or do we not ?"

* Receiving Him in the Blessed Sacrament.

† Not by compulsion, nor by laying the free-will under any necessity, but by the strong sweet motions of heavenly grace.

"We believe that! How can any one, who believes the Bible at all, doubt that?" said Mrs. Flemming quickly. "And believing that He is the Son of God, and our Redeemer who died for our salvation, is enough. It is all that is required of us. God is not pleased with subtleties."

"No; God is not pleased with subtleties," said the Elder in his calm, quiet way. "And it seems to me, from what follows, that something more than a personal and historical belief in Him is necessary. This belief must embrace the acceptance of His doctrines. The devils themselves—as we are told in holy writ—believe and tremble, but their belief is without profit; therefore He must have had a deeper meaning in exhorting them *to believe in Him* than is now apparent. There are no half-way doings with God. We must believe entirely not only in His existence, but in His law revealed to us by Jesus Christ His Son.

" Up to this point of our Saviour's discourse all seems easy, because it sounds symbolic or figurative, and can be adapted in a mystical sense to our spiritual comprehension; but I believe with all the power of my soul that He was teaching a *substantial* truth, hence I am no longer satisfied with either type or shadow, and will seek for the substance, which is Himself under the form of bread. He *speaks of three sorts of bread.* The first is that with

which he He fed the five thousand on the mountain
—a miraculous bread, miraculously multiplied, and
figurative of a greater mystery; but He calls it
'meat which perisheth'; the second is *manna*,
which the Jews called 'bread from heaven,' but
which Jesus declares with the solemnity of an oath
was not: 'Amen, amen I say unto you: Moses
gave them not bread from Heaven. . . . . I am the
bread of life.' Here now we have the third kind of
bread, and He tells us what it is: 'Your fathers
did eat manna in the desert, and are dead. This
is the bread which cometh down from heaven: that
if any man eat of it he may not die. *I am the
living bread which came down from heaven.* If
any man eat of this bread, he shall live forever:
and the bread which I will give, is My flesh for the
life of the world.'

" When the Jews heard these sayings, they strove
amongst themselves, thinking He meant His flesh
in a carnal sense, and said to one another : ' How
can this man give us His flesh to eat ?' Here was
the time and opportunity for Jesus to have explained His meaning if He spoke a parable, or
meant His words to be understood in a figurative
sense; for He knew that He was speaking through
them to all time, and it would have been the work
of a devil and not of God to leave them in error on
so vital a question. He saw how eagerly they

awaited His answer, and how the minds of His own disciples were troubled by His words; but, so far from doing this, He declared in plainer terms if possible, ratified by the solemnity of an oath, the same mystery: ' Amen, amen I say unto you: except you eat the flesh of the Son of man, and drink His blood, you shall not have life in you.' Who was the Son of man? Himself. Who was He? Jesus Christ. Who was Jesus Christ? The Son of God. We believe this. Then must we also believe Him when He tells us how we are to believe in Him, when He declares squarely and without a shadow of prevarication or hidden meaning, in simple, straightforward, but awful words: ' He that eateth My flesh and drinketh My blood hath everlasting life: and I will raise him up in the last day. For My flesh is meat indeed; and My blood is drink indeed. He that eateth My flesh, and drinketh My blood, abideth in Me, and I in him. As the living Father hath sent Me, and I live by the Father: so he that eateth Me, the same also shall live by Me. This is the bread which came down from heaven. Not as your fathers did eat manna, and are dead. He that eateth this bread shall live forever.' Not only the Jews who thronged the synagogue that day to hear His words scoffed and cavilled at His doctrines, but some of His own disciples, who had witnessed the multiplication of the loaves, and afterwards on the midnight sea saw Him walking upon the stormy waters ; who, terrified because they thought it was a spirit, were consoled by His voice whispering : ' It is I : be not afraid,' and took Him into their ship with joy : doubted Him now, and turning back walked with Him no more. But He did not recall them. They ' had seen Him and *did not* believe ;' they had been taught of God, but profited nothing. We believe in Him as the Eternal Truth, the true Son of God, the Redeemer who assumed flesh that He might die in the flesh for us, then we must believe Him when He tells us that to inherit eternal life we must eat of this bread which is His flesh. To abide in Him and Him in us we eat His flesh and drink His blood ; and," continued the Elder, "I believe His words, and because I believe them I can no longer make a mockery of them by partaking of symbols. There must be somewhere among God's people a solution of my difficulty. The truth cannot perish. I know nothing beyond Congregational opinions ; and they do not hold it. I do not know where, or how, to seek this life-giving bread. My ship is tossed on waters of stormy doubts and fears, and in the darkness and uncertainty of my soul I see Him afar off ; He is yet but a spirit to me and I tremble, for I know not who holds the divine and life-giving legacy He has bequeathed me, the great and awful trust, the miraculous feast of the body and blood of Jesus Christ which to inherit eternal life I must eat. This, my wife and children, is what has troubled my spiritual life for some years past. I have sought to stifle it as a temptation and false doctrine, but it has pursued me until my thoughts are so full of it that I could as easily doubt my very existence as the belief that it is necessary to my salvation to eat of this heavenly bread."

" Oh, husband ! your delusion passes all belief. It is a temptation ; never doubt that. There, there —read that !" exclaimed Mrs. Flemming standing beside him, and pointing to a verse which she read in a triumphant voice : " ' It is the spirit that quickeneth : the flesh profiteth nothing. The words I have spoken to you are the spirit and the life.' "

" Yes, mother ; dead flesh separated from the spirit, in the gross manner they supposed they were to eat His flesh, would indeed ' profit nothing. That is what He meant. In proposing the feast of His body and blood, don't you see that it bestows spirit, grace, and life, inasmuch as in partaking of it He abides in us and we in Him, marking us for His own, worthy by it of inheriting eternal life ? Paul says that whosoever shall eat of this bread and drink of this cup unworthily shall be guilty of the body and blood of the Lord, and ' he that eateth and drinketh unworthily, eateth and drinketh judgment to himself, not discerning the body of the Lord.'* "

" Wolfert Flemming! you are wresting the word of God to your own ruin! I fear that you are possessed of a devil, if you are not crazy," exclaimed Mrs. Flemming, laying her hand on his broad forehead and looking into his calm gray eyes, which regarded her troubled countenance with a look of ineffable love and pity. "Oh, what delusions to come to such a soul! Husband, send for Father Ray."

" Father Ray cannot help me, mother. He tried, but gave me no comfort or light. Only God Himself can aid me. I look for Him to stretch His hand out of the darkness to lead me, for He knows how earnestly I seek Him; and though He slay me, yet will I trust Him. I can be a hypocrite no longer. The scriptures themselves have led me into deep waters; perhaps I may sink, but I hope not. I hope not. Like Tobias, I know not the way, nor whence to find a faithful guide; but I ' believe' for all that, and I know that God will not suffer me to perish through ignorance. But I must break off from the old lines, they are too narrow for the needs of my soul."

" But, father, consider!" cried Mrs. Flemming, her voice tremulous with excitement and distress.

* I. Corinthians, xi.

"Consider how you are looked up to by old and young as one strong in the faith, and what a hurt it will be to souls to see you falling away from pure and simple Gospel doctrines, to run after visionary ideas. Consider, too, the discredit it will be to you, you who come of such old true-blooded Puritan stock; think of the hurt it will be to your business, and the disgrace it will bring upon your family—Oh, dear me! I never heard of such a dreadful thing in my life. And the girls—I'm sure their prospects will be ruined if you go off and backslide in this way."

"Little wife," said the elder, kindly and gravely, "I must not labor for the meat that perisheth, but for the bread of eternal life. I will abide in the promise of Him who commands me to believe in Him. I am groping for the truth, which must be somewhere on God's earth; and if I find it by His grace, I shall be ready not only to suffer, but rejoice, if need be to die for it."

"Oh, dear me!" bewailed Mrs. Flemming, "what will that righteous man, Father Ray, say? What will the Deacon do? What will John Wilde think? I never had such a shock in my life. Why, Elder Flemming!" she cried, growing irate: "You must surely be bewitched."

"No, mother, I am not bewitched. Don't distress yourself so—it pains me," he said quietly.

"I'm glad it does; it's a good sign, Elder Flemming, to have something pain your conscience; it shows that you are not quite 'given over.' I've felt *something* coming for weeks and weeks. I didn't know what, but it made a cold spot on my heart all the time, that wouldn't let me forget even for a minute that it was there. Ever since that idolatrous Irish papist was here, I have felt so. I wish it had been in the good old times for him, with his crosses and superstitions." Which meant that Patrick McCue would not have got off with flying colors, but would probably have got a "rise in the world," as they say out in Nebraska when a man is hung. "Only see, now, how God has punished us for sheltering an idolater."

"Mother, do you remember the words : 'I was a stranger and ye took Me in. I was hungry and ye fed Me,'" said the Elder.

"No, I don't forget them; but there were no wandering Irish papists going about in those days, destroying the peace of christian families." Then Mrs. Flemming, out of breath, and half beside herself with grief and anger, went back to her chair and tried to resume her work.

Hope and Eva had not spoken; the whole scene surprised and distressed them; they were not prepared for any such thing, and the sudden breaking down of accustomed lines, or the uprooting of lifetime traditions, is always painful; but on the whole they sympathized and almost believed with their—father, it all seemed so straightforward and indisputable; but Reuben for once forgot his book, and regarded with something akin to a speechless terror what appeared to him very like a great moral earthquake of apostacy. Elder Flemming got up, and walked up and down the room; his soft, firm footfall, and the creaking of a plank here and there of the old floor as he stepped upon it, and the sparkling of the fire caused by the falling apart of a great blazing log, were the only sounds, except the low shrill whistle of the wind around the northwest angle of the house, that were heard. They were all full of busy thought, and it seemed to them that a curtain had been suddenly rent away before them, revealing a chaos into which they were being driven. At last the Elder paused in his monotonous march, and taking his accustomed seat, said: "We will have family worship;" then he turned over the leaves of the old Bible, and in his calm even voice, full of the spirit of the Psalm* he read, fell soothingly upon the mortal unrest around him; after which, from the fulness of his own soul, upon his bended knees, he poured out his cry for help. Afterwards Hope and Eva bade him and their mother a tender good night and went away. Mrs.

* Psalm lxvi. "Deus misereatur."

Flemming lit Reuben's candle, and sent him off to his room with a charge "not to read in bed," then she took up her own candlestick, and went round inspecting the fastenings of doors and windows, and looked to see if the old *beaufet*, with its sparkling treasures, was safely locked ; and finding that the Elder did not move she fidgeted around, jingling her key-basket a litte while longer, and then said · "Rake up the fire carefully if you are not coming, but don't stay up too late, father; you need sleep."

But he did not feel like sleeping, and after she went away he took the light and went to his "work-room" and sat down to think, but his mind was so tempest-tost that he could not bring his thoughts to anything like order, and he determined to go to work on the accounts of "Sneathen and Flemming " and prepare the new terms of partnership, the old one expiring ten days hence ; he would go over it all, and see what he could do to find out what virtue there was in algebra for a troubled mind. So thinking, he went to his desk, and in turning over and assorting his accounts he picked up Patrick McCue's keepsake, which he had entirely forgotten, and in a vague absentminded way he opened it, and his eye lit upon these words : "First, supposing it possible that Jesus Christ had deceived the Jews at Capharnaum, and even His disciples, and His very apostles, in the solemn asseverations which He, six times over, repeated His real and corporal presence in the sacrament when He promised to institute it; can any one believe that He would continue the deception on His dear apostles in the very act of instituting it? and when He was on the point of leaving them? in short, when He was bequeathing to them the legacy of His love?* . . . ." The strong man's soul trembled as he read! What was this, and whence, so aptly fitting his needs? Could it be that help was at hand, and from such a source? Was it this book, which weeks ago he had thrown aside with contempt as defiled with false doctrine, which was to enlighten him? He did not stop to parley with the past, but read on, and on, until he came to the end of the subject, then he turned hungrily to the first page of the book and began anew; he must see it all, and find if other questions of his soul could be answered by it; and forgetting time and rest, he stood at his desk leaning upon his elbows, devouring its contents, so full and satisfying to his mind, until with a sudden upflirting of light, the candle, burnt down to the socket, gave one flash of light and expired, leaving him in darkness. Exterior darkness only, for the lamp of his soul was alight, its shadows were fleeing before the divine illumina-

* " Millner's End of Controversy," page 229.

tion; he had found a guide at last who led him with a strong, strange power into the ways of truth, and his very blood pulsed with a new and perfectjoy. But he could not stop. He must learn more ; so he kindled his fire and lit the swinging lamp over his work-bench, and drawing his great leather-backed chair to it, he sat down and resumed the book.

Mrs. Flemming had passed a restless, feverish night. Now and then she dozed from utter weariness, then starting up, wondering what was the matter with her, and put out her hand to her husband's pillow, to see if he had come to bed; but finding it empty, turned away with a sigh half of anger half of alarm at his absence; and tried to sleep, but when hour after hour passed on, and the sky showed streaks of light through the clear window pane, she sprang up terrified, and hurrying on her clothes, trembling in every limb, ran down to the old sitting-room where she had left him—her heart stirred with the first anger she had ever felt towards him—but he was not there. Full of wild apprehensions and scarcely able to walk, she was so agitated by she knew not what, she dragged herself along until she came to the "work-room," and with a sick fear at her heart of not finding him there, she softly opened the door, and there, his head leaning back on his chair, he was sound asleep, with a look of such

peace and joy and a smile of such perfect restful-
ness on his countenance that Mrs. Flemming stopped half way, wondering if it could be the red and
golden light from the morning sun that brightened
up her husband's grand massive face with such
strange soft brightness. He stirred at the moment;
and the book falling from his hand to the floor,
awoke him.*

———

CHAPTER XII.

THE NEW DAY.

Mrs. Flemming felt thankful, so thankful that she
could have ran and thrown her arms about her husband and told him how gl d she was, after all her
imaginary terrors to find him there safe and un-
harmed; but then she got a little angry at having
been made so uneasy without rhyme or reason, and
thought if in addition to his new opinions—which

---

* This narrative was commenced two years ago. Elder Flemming's conversion, from reading " Milner's End of Controversy,"
occurred more than forty years ago ; and another individual, of
whom we knew, had her doubts entirely silenced by a copy of
the same work which she got from an ignorant Irish woman,
who kept a little Catholic library in Baltimore, twenty-five years
ago. The writer makes this explanation, lest some might think
we are making use of "Gropings after the Truth," by Dr. Hunt-
ington.

threatened trouble enough—he was going to adopt
new habits, and upset their regular godly way of
living, she would try to nip it in the bud, so she
said with some asperity of tone :

"This is a way for a Christian man to spend the
night, sleeping in a chair in a cold room without
even your old cloak to cover you! I couldn't sleep
even in my bed, for wondering what had become
of you ; but that is a small matter."

"Why, mother, I believe I have spent the night
here!" said the Elder, a little bewildered at first.
"And I have been asleep too. What a night you
must have had ; forgive me ; I did not expect to
spend the night here. I came here to think awhile,
then I began to overhaul my accounts, and found
this book in my desk, which I opened, and got so
interested in it that I forgot how the time was passing. I really don't know when I fell asleep." Then
he got up and stretched his great limbs, and looked
out at the glorious sky flushed with crimson and
veiled with transparent fleeces of cloud, with here
and there a dash of gold gleaming through, and
streaks of blue, like great veins pulsing with light,
showing dark, and beautiful, between the splendors that tinted every salient point with edges
that shone like the jewelled diadems of kings. He
drew a long, full breath, an inspiration of deep
happiness ; it was in his heart to cry out with

Davia: "The heavens declare the glory of the Lord'"—so typical was the new-born day of the light that had risen upon his darkness; but he repressed his emotions—his wife standing there, looking so coldly and reproachfully at him, would not understand him; so he only said: "The new day is very beautiful, mother. I never saw so fair a morning."

"Yes," she said, shortly; "it's a good day. I'm glad you found among your books one that could interest you so much. I hope the sound doctrine of it will bring things right. Better put out that sputtering lamp overhead. You'll find your clean things on the chair—I suppose you haven't forgot it's the day to change—when you feel like going to your room to slick up for the day."

"Thank you, little wife," he said as she turned away with an injured air and left the room. "Clothe my soul, O Lord, in fresh garments this day," he whispered as the door closed. A great peace filled the man's soul, through the medium of which all things looked more fair; he felt as if a film had fallen from his eyes, as if a new day had indeed risen upon his life; as if—having been so long buffetted and tossed by contrary winds of doctrine— he had suddenly found safe port for his soul; for as he had turned page after page of that book so providentially thrown into his hands just in his

greatest need, and found question after question
answered, doubt after doubt removed, and very
contradiction that had troubled and tormented him
solved and harmonized; he indeed forgot how the
night was passing; he only knew that he had discovered that there was truly and verily a divine
Faith upon earth, established by Jesus Christ, its
great Founder, and perpetuated through all time
by His power. His natural reason had long ago
assured him that God cannot be the author of different religions; for, being the Eternal Truth, He
cannot reveal contradictory doctrines; and being
at the same time the Eternal Wisdom and the God
of Peace, He cannot establish a kingdom divided
against itself.* The result of this reasoning was,
that consequently to be worthy of its divine origin
the Church of Christ must be itself ONE: one in
doctrine, one in worship, and one in government.
This mark of unity in the true Church, so clear
from natural reason, was made still more clear to
his mind from certain passages, which over and over
again had arrested his attention as fraught with
deep and connected meaning, while perusing the
pages of his old Lutheran Bible; as, for instance,
when the Saviour, speaking of Himself in the character of the good Shepherd, says: "I have other
sheep (the Gentiles), which are not of this fold:

* Milner.

them also must I bring, and they shall hear My voice and there shall be ONE FOLD and ONE Shepherd.* To the same effect addressing His heavenly Father, He says : " I pray for all that shall believe in Me, that THEY MAY BE ONE, as thou Father art in Me, and I in Thee."† In like manner St. Paul, inculcating the unity of the Church, writes: We being many, are ONE BODY IN CHRIST, and every one members one of another.‡ Again, he declares : There is one Body, and one Spirit; as you are called in one hope of your calling : One Lord, One Faith, One Baptism.‖

The settled convictions of Wolfert Flemming's mind, from a study of the Bible alone, had long ago tended to the firm belief that Christ founded a visible Church upon earth, and in this Church there must necessarily be a unity of faith, doctrine, and government; but he was without chart or guide ; his aspirations were earnest, but he had no clue and was entirely hedged about by narrow sectarianism and all the human inventions called religions, that he was perfectly ignorant *where* and *what* this Church, which was so full of all that could satisfy the immortal cravings of his soul for truth and consolation, was to be found, until this night, when it was revealed to him as we have described. Oh,

* John x, 16. † John xvii, 20, 21. ‡ Rom. xii, 5. ‖ Ephesians iv, 4. 5.

God! how his soul expanded; how greedily it drank
in the knowledge of the Truth; how gladly his eyes
brightened in the light risen out of darkness; how
his weary heart rejoiced to behold a straight and
narrow way beyond the tangled wilderness! He
had been drifting alone upon midnight seas, without helm or compass, when lo! the morning dawned,
and he found himself near the boundaries of the
glorious land he sought! Oh, what peace it was
to know with a certainty, which it did not once
enter his mind to doubt, that there was indeed a
Divine Faith upon earth; a Church—holy, apostolic,
and universal; a sheepfold having One Shepherd; a
Creed acknowledging and confessing one Lord, one
Faith, one Baptism; a Body of which Christ is the
head; a great, holy, divine truth, containing and
covering all truth; a Church endowed with all the
Godlike powers which had been exercised by its
Divine Founder upon earth; upon whose altars He
abides through all time, offering Himself from the
" rising of the sun unto the going down of the same,
a perpetual sacrifice to the Father;" the food and
the guest of His children; the " bread of life "
which is a guerdon of everlasting salvation to all
who eat worthily of it!

It was all plain to the man's clear and logical
mind, and as he finished the book he exclaimed:
" If this is being a Roman Catholic, then, my God,

I am one—heart and soul. There is nothing left
for me but this, or infidelity. If the Catholic religion be not the true one, then all religion is a lie.
But it is true. I feel it in the depths of my soul,
stirring it to new life; my reason responds to it;
my heart thrills responsive to it. My mind submits to it with gladness and freedom. It is clear
and indubitable. I am a Catholic. I believe all,
because I believe in Jesus Christ. I accept all.
O God! Thou hast enlightened me while I dwelt
in the shadow of death ; Thou has led me thus far ;
I see the way, I believe, but yet I am afar off from
actual communion with the One Fold ; lead me still
nearer, until I and my household enter in." Have
you not sometime read of certain philosophers who,
observant of effects, spent a lifetime of patient investigation, and tireless study, and ruinous experiment, to ascertain their natural cause, and finally
when almost worn out by disappointment, poverty,
sleepless nights, and the stolid indifference of the
world to the great principles of science, have suddenly and in the most unexpected manner solved
the mysterious problem, and understood at once,
as by inspiration, *how* it was to be applied to the
grand march of the world's progress ; you have
read of their exceeding and exultant joy, of the
sense of triumph and delight which almost killed
or crazed them? But this was nothing, aye, less

than nought, to the profound peace and content
which flowed in and pervaded the whole being of
the man who sat there in his little workshop reading through the long dark hours of night, finding,
as he read, the solution of his soul's great problem.
Just before the day dawned he turned over the last
page of the book; but, not satisfied, he again
opened it, and was reading and re-reading certain
portions, when—throwing back his head to think
of the dragon's teeth that Luther had sown, and
the sharp conflicts he had with the heresies born
of his own apostacy—he fell asleep.

When Elder Flemming came into the quaint old
family room, brightened by the cheerful noisy fire
and glorified by the splendor of sunshine streaming
through the windows, he found his slippers and
dressing-gown by the fire, just where his wife had
been in the habit of placing them for the last thirty
years; there was his table, with the old Bible open
upon it; there stood his chair waiting for him; the
breakfast table in its spotless linen and neat
polished china suggested thoughts of the dear faces
soon to gather around it; there was nothing
changed except himself, and he felt at that moment
a certain assurance that this change would involve
such sacrifices as would perhaps turn all this
domestic peace into gloom, and disperse forever
the earthly happiness of his household. He could

not tell. The crucifixion came after the palms and
hosannas. But he was prepared for every crucial
test, seeing that the kingdom of God is not of this
world, and he that enters in must be prepared for
sacrifice and conflict. It is only when a soul enters
into the true Church that real sacrifice is made.
To go from one denomination or from one communion to another scarcely excites remark, and certainly involves no radical change of opinion, no
revolution in faith ; it is looked upon by Protestants
as a simple exercise of freedom of conscience ; but
when a man comes out from among them to become a Catholic, the act has a deep significance ;
it means persecution, warfare, and sacrifice ; his
whole being, intellectual and spiritual, sloughs off
its old life, its old association of ideas, its errors
and all arrogance of will, and submits with simple
submission to the divinely established authority of
the Church. Neither fame, worldly considerations,
family ties, riches, honors, or human respect in any
form can compromise the integrity of this faith : if
they stand in the way they must be sacrificed ; or
he must, like the young man spoken of in the Gospel, turn back and go sorrowful away. To become
a Catholic a man must be prepared to sacrifice not
only material goods, but also to hear himself called
" visionary"—a " seeker after novelties"—" crazy"
—"a hypocrite,"— and be accused of every unworthy

motive ; all of which goes to prove more conclu-
sively that the kingdom of this world, with its
human inventions of creeds and religions, is separate and distinct from the kingdom of Christ upon
earth, which is the Catholic Church.

But we have forgotten Wolfert Flemming standing there in the cheerful glow and warmth of his
fireside, full of peace and high earnest resolve,
counting the cost as nothing when compared with the
certainty of eternal gain ; for this thing was for him
a question of eternal import, before which all earthly considerations faded into utter insignificance.
Presently the girls came in with their pleasant
smiles and good morning kiss, and, shortly after,
Mrs. Flemming and Reuben ; she in her high-
backed, beaded chair—he close beside her, seated
upon a lower one. Mrs. Flemming said nothing ;
but her soul had been sorely exercised. " Suppose,"
she had asked herself at least twenty times, " he
should give up family prayer ? Perhaps he will.
But I will go in, and seem to feel no difference.
Come, Ruby," she had said aloud ; "come, it is time
for family worship. Don't keep father waiting."
Her mind was soon placed at ease by seeing her husband go towards his table and seat himself as usual ;
and everything seemed so natural that she wondered
if she had been dreaming ; she almost imagined she
had, and her heart melted within her as she listened

to the unction with which her husband read the
sacred word, and prayed as if he were in the very
presence of God. "No doubt," she thought, "it
was the book he read last night;" and she thanked
God, without knowing for what, that he had sat up
all night to read it, never doubting but that it was
a doctrinal work of their own belief which had set
all his doubts and difficulties at rest. She moved
about briskly and cheerily, sure that her husband's
temptations had passed away : and it was pleasant
to them all to see the little mother whom they so
dearly loved and reverenced, standing with such
a blithe happy smile upon her countenance at the
head of the breakfast table, as they gathered around,
waiting for their father to offer thanks; when to
their amazement he raised his right hand and signed
himself with the sign of the cross in the name of
the adorable Trinity, after which he asked the blessing. Mrs Flemming started and turned very white
It was the very thing that the Irish pedler had
done at this very table.

"Father!" she said sharply, "what do you mean
by doing that?"

"I mean, mother, that as the cross is the stand-
ard of Christ, and the sign of our belief in Him, to
use it in this way to help me at all times to bear
in mind His death and passion," replied the Elder,
his grave, quiet tones unruffled and kind.

"But that is popery. It is like being a papist—"

"I am a papist, my wife: in other words, I am a Roman Catholic."

"Lord have mercy on me!" wailed Mrs. Flemming; and she would have fallen from her chair if Hope had not sprung forward and caught her in her arms. She had fainted—the second time in her healthy, happy life. The first time was when the dying Indian squaw, Massasquoi, throttled her; and now when something ten thousand times more terrible to her had come upon her, risen as it were out of her very hearth to strike her down. Her husband was not a backslider, as she had feared he was a papist, her dread and abhorrence, the antithesis of all that was good and pure, religiously and morally. The Elder lifted the limp little form very tenderly in his strong arms and laid her upon the sofa, chafing her hands, while Hope opened a window and Eva ran to get hartshorn. It was a long faint, but presently she revived and was bewildered for a little while, then she fixed her eyes on her husband's face with a look full of pity, entreaty and reproach, and burst into sobs and tears. It was something new in this peaceful household, such a scene as this; nothing like it had ever happened among them before, and it almost frightened them to see their mother, always so full of strong, cheerful life, so unselfish in her ceaseless efforts for

their comfort and happiness, stricken down in such
a way.

"Mother," said Flemming, smoothing her cheek
tenderly with his broad hand, "don't get fretted
and miserable until we have a little reasonable talk
together over this matter. When you come to
know what good cause I have to change, you will
no longer blame me or be unhappy about it."

"I would rather have seen you dead! I would
rather have seen you dead!" she cried.

"Mother, we won't talk over this now," he said
gently, for he knew how deeply she was struck.
" Come and get a cup of hot coffee, and don't get
miserable over a thing that fills me with unspeakable joy. At least be patient, and understand distinctly that I am prepared to sacrifice everything
on the face of the earth—yea, life itself—rather
than go back a hair's breadth from the saving faith
I have found."

There was nothing to be said after this; Mrs.
Flemming knew her husband too well to argue
with him when he asserted himself in this master-
ful, positive way; and, not fond of scenes, she
gathered up her energies and returned to the
breakfast table. There was but little talk, every
one being full of his own thoughts; the Elder finished his breakfast, again signed himself reverently
with the sign of the Cross, gave thanks, and left

the room to go about his daily tasks on the farm,
and Mrs. Flemming and the girls to theirs in the
household.   They were all very quiet: a sort of
awe filled the hearts of Wolfort Flemming's daughters, as of an unseen presence; but, swift-footed
and practical, they did not stop to brood over it
all: there was not an idle bone in their bodies, and
it was one of the principles of their life to put duty
before everything; so their domestic affairs received the same scrupulous attention, and things were
arranged in their accustomed order. The only difference was the silence.   There was no cheery conversation, no blithe snatches of song, no loving little romp with each other, flitting here and there
like sunbeams through the house.   Their father a
Catholic!   It was incomprehensible to their minds.
They could not have been more amazed if they
had seen the topmost peak of Chocorua spread out
a pair of black, spined wings, and fly out of sight.
How did it happen?   And "how did it happen?"
they asked each other again, when seated together
over their sewing.

"It was the pedler," said Mrs. Flemming.   "I
knew and felt all along that something dreadful
would follow having him here.   He contaminated
a christian household with his rank idolatries, and
now see what had come of it."

"Father is not a man to plunge recklessly into

absurdities," said Hope; "even if he should, he is not the one to stand by them just for the sake of making a point."

"I used to think so," sighed Mrs. Flemming.

"If father has changed his religion, depend upon it he has good reasons for doing so," said Eva: "and I hope that he will explain it all to us, for it must be a better way than we know of or he never would have taken such a step."

"Hush, Eva, this moment. How can you, who have never been converted or baptized, know of such things," said Mrs. Flemming.

"No, it is true, mother, I don't know much about religion; I only know that father is a good and just man, who has served God without guile ever since I can remember; and my highest aspiration, whenever I have thought of being religious, was to be like him," replied Eva.

"If all that he said last night be part of the change, *I* believe with him so far," said Hope.

"And I," quietly added Eva. I don't see how we can doubt a word of that, seeing that Christ Himself said it all. I believe it as He said and meant it.

"How many pounds of butter did you churn, Eva?" inquired Mrs. Flemming.

"Ten, mother," she answered looking up quickly at her mother's flushed, unquiet countenance, for the sudden and irrelevant question had almost taken her breath away.

"Did you give the buttermilk to the pigs?"

"Yes. Did you wish me to do so, mother?"

"Of course." Then they fell to talking about other domestic matters ; and at dinner time the Elder, before and after meat, made the sign of the Cross upon himself when he returned thanks, and Mrs. Flemming was thoroughly miserable. "After all these years of peace, happiness, and family harmony, to be visited with such a trial!" And it is only those who know anything at all of the puritan sentiment forty years ago in New England— not yet extinct—against the Catholic religion, who can understand the magnitude of Mrs. Flemming's trial. To have declared one's self an open disbe- iever, would not have been half as scandalous, or banned a man more completely than for him to proclaim himself a Catholic in those days. It was not in reality the Catholic religion which these people, who served God earnestly according to their lights, were so bitterly prejudiced against; but a huge, idolatrous, devilish system, which their founders, teachers, and writers, represented to them as such, to suit their own purposes, taking good care that they should not be undeceived. The Catholic religion, as it is, was as sealed a mystery to them as the Sphinx.

CHAPTER XIII.

MRS. FLEMMING AT BAY.

MRS. FLEMMING was really sincere in her belief in the doctrines she professed. There was just enough spirituality in them to lift them above the common, and they were just narrow enough to come within the scope of human reason; all above that being a dead letter, about which she gave herself no con- cern whatever. "Why should it?" she thought; "for that which had served the ends of salvation for her pilgrims forefathers was not only good enough, but the best for her." Besides it was a comfortable religion, which gave one great liberty of action in the sharp commerce of life, provided all things were done in a decorous and sanctimonious way; and was not too exacting in its demands for God : for while they claimed certain portions of the Bible for their rule of faith, and certain congrega- tional doctrines for their dogmas, a close observance of the Sabbath and its ordinances was their actual Shibboleth. This was a most convenient arrange- ment for all human purposes, as it left them six days to toil and prosper in, unfettered by any higher law than the law of the land; and all that troubled their conscience growing out of their daily life was healed by the unction of this day of expiation.

Such as it was—and it was the best and only one she knew of—Mrs. Fleming clung to the meagre outlines of what she called her faith; it was good enough for her, it had been good enough for the ancestral Flemmings and the ancestral Babsons, all of whom had been righteous men and women, faithful to their calling, stern in their opposition to everything that even savored of Popery, and fore-handed with the world. She and her husband had been happy together all these years; they had prospered, and held a high place, not only among their own brethren, but were looked up to by all with respect and something nearly akin to affection; indeed, as the distressed little woman had said only a short time back, "There was truly nothing left for them to wish for; their 'basket and store' was full and overflowing with blessings in every shape." But now this dreadful thing had happened; her husband was an apostate; he had done worse than apostatize; he had turned Papist; and she felt that they were all ruined and to be brought to disgrace and poverty. Then, leaving loom and everything else to take care of themselves, she shut herself up in her room, and prayed and wept as she had never prayed and wept before, that her husband might be saved alive out of the fiery temptation which threatened him, body and soul, with utter ruin.

That night they were all in their usual places in

the quaint fire-lighted old sitting-room ; there was
an attempt at conversation ; and the girls, trying to
be cheerful, talked now to their father, now to their
mother, but seeing that it was no use, began rallying Reuben about a picture of Miss Debby Wyatt,
which he had painted on an old biscuit board, much
caricatured, but faithfully like her ; but Reuben was
in one of the dreamiest of his dreamy moods ; he
just shook back the golden mane that hung about
his beautiful face, answered " Yes," and " No," then
turned his eyes back to the visions he was behold-
ing amidst the glowing coals, the Sinai where, veiled
by smoke and flame, his fancy had many high
revealings. At last Mrs. Flemming said :

" I should think you'd be sleepy, father, after
sitting up all night."

" I expect I shall be pretty soon, mother. You
know I am a great sleepy-head," he answered
pleasantly.

" What book was it that interested you so much
as to keep your eyes open all night ?"

" It is called ' Milner's End of Controversy.' "

" I never heard of it before."

" Nor I, until very lately. I should like, mother,
to read portions of it to you if you will listen."

" Yes, you can read what you like. There's no
book belonging to this house, thank God, that can't

be read to a Christian family. Is there anything about Luther and Romanism in it?"

"Much, mother. But there is something I want to read, which is a sequel to what we were talking over last night." Mrs. Flemming, still thinking it was one of the old volumes from their own book-shelves, full of pure doctrine, settled herself to listen while the Elder, sprang his mine—hoping almost against hope that she would hear something that would upset completely the destructive spiritual novelties he had adopted.

"In the sixth chapter of John, which I read last night, we saw how Jesus Christ instructed His apostles by His express and repeated declarations concerning the nature of the sacrament which He promised them, thereby preparing their minds for the sublime simplicity of His words in instituting it—words which sealed His meaning in the most solemn manner. 'For whilst they were at supper, Jesus took *bread* and blessed it, and broke it, and gave it to his disciples and said: Take ye and eat; THIS IS MY BODY. And taking the cup, He said: Drink ye all of this; FOR THIS IS MY BLOOD OF THE NEW TESTAMENT, WHICH SHALL BE SHED FOR MANY UNTO THE REMISSION OF SINS.'"*

"Yes," said Mrs. Flemming, "we always hear those words, and solemn words they are, when we

*Matthew, xxvi, 26, 27, 28.

go to the table of the Lord; but they mean nothing except that we are to partake of the bread and wine in *memory* of His sufferings and death."

"HE does not say that, or mean it," replied the Elder in his calm, deep voice. "The apostle declares that when He took it into His hands it was *bread*, but when He gave it to them He said: THIS IS MY BODY. He did not say it was bread, or tell them to eat it in commemoration of Him, or intimate that it was a symbol of His passion and death. He said, as He gave them that which *had been bread:* THIS IS MY BODY. Then, taking the cup, He gave thanks and gave it to them, saying: 'Drink ye all of this, FOR THIS IS MY BLOOD of the new testament, which shall be shed for many unto the remission of sins.' How can we disbelieve this clear and explicit declaration of the Son of God, without accusing Him not only of prevarication but of imposture? thereby bringing Him to naught. It was a solemn moment; it was a time fraught with the consummation of the ransom He was to pay for the salvation of the world, and He was giving into their hands for all time the legacy of His body and blood, which was to be unto all who partook worthily an assurance of everlasting life. Can we—believing in Him as the Eternal Truth—imagine for one instant that on this solemn occasion, and under the stupendous circumstances, He would have given them mere bread, and declared that it was His Body; and mere wine, declaring it to be His Blood?"

"I couldn't believe such a doctrine to save my life," said Mrs. Flemming excitedly, "nor do I see how any enlightened person can."

"I can't help believing it. It is all there in the Bible," said Hope.

"To disbelieve it, it seems to me, would be to lose all faith in our Saviour," said Eva. "It seems unreasonable to doubt His own actual words, however hard they may be to our understanding. And yet, father," she said, suddenly turning to him, "is it harder to believe this than to believe that the Son of God assumed the flesh and nature of man for our salvation, as He did?"

"No. Of the great mystery of His Incarnation there was no human witness; all that we know we receive from the lips of the Virgin Mary His Mother; but here in this great sacramental institution we have His own words, repeated without variation, adding to, or taking from, by each of the evangelists, who wrote—as a note here tells me—their gospels in different places and at different times. No Christian doubts the account given by Mary of the Incarnation, yet how many doubt the words of her Son, whom they profess to believe is the Eternal Truth! Strange inconsistency of man!"

" Did you say there was something about Luthei in that book?" asked Mrs. Flemming fidgeting. "This discussion is disagreeable, and I should like —if you don't object—to hear something that I can understand."

"Here is something, mother, about Luther, but I don't know how you'll relish it. ' Martin Luther,* in one of his epistles on the subject in question, says : ' I cannot tell you how desirous I was, and how much I have labored in my own mind to overthrow this doctrine of the Real Presence, because,' says he (and let us note his motive,) ' I clearly saw how much I should thereby injure Popery ; but I found myself caught, without any way of escaping: for the text of the gospel is too plain for this purpose.' Hence he contined, till his death, to condemn those Protestants who denied the corporal presence, employing for this purpose sometimes the shafts of his coarse ridicule, and sometimes the thunder of his vehement declamation and anathemas.' "†

" We are not Lutherans," said Mrs. Flemming sharply.

" No, not exactly ; but you know that Luther is the rallying cry of the Protestant world. They regard him as the apostle of the Reformation, the

* Epist. ad Argenten., tom. 4, fol. 502, ed. Wittemburg.

† Milner's End of Controversy, p. 232.

root of their tree, the founder of their sects. Listen to this,'' said the Elder, turning back the pages
of the book : "'No sooner had Luther set up the
tribunal of his private judgment on the sense of
the Scriptures, in opposition to the authority of
the Church, ancient and modern, than his disciples,
proceeding on his principle, undertook to prove
from plain texts of the Bible that his own doctrine
was erroneous, and that the Reformation itself
wanted reforming. Carlostad,* Zuinglius,† Œco-
lompadius, Muncer,‡ and a hundred more of his
followers wrote and preached against him and
against each other, with the utmost virulence, still
each of them professing to ground his doctrine and
conduct on the written word of God alone. In
vain did Luther claim a superiority over them ; in
vain did he denounce hell-fire against them, saying :
'I can defend you against the Pope—but when the

---

* Luther's first disciple of distinction. He was Archdeacon
of Wittemburg. Declared against Luther, 1521.

† Zuinglius began the Reformation in Switzerland some time
after Luther began it in Germany, but taught such doctrine that
the latter called him a pagan, and said he despaired of his salvation.

‡ A disciple of Luther, and founder of the Anabaptists, who,
in quality of the *just*, maintained that the property of the wicked
belonged to them, quoting the second beatitude : "Blessed are
the meek for they shall possess the land." Muncer wrote to
several of the German princes to give up their lands to him,
and at the head of forty thousand of his followers marched to
enforce the demand.

devil shall urge against you (the heads of these changes) at your death, these passages of Scripture, and when Christ, your Judge, shall say, *they ran and I did not send them,* how shall you withstand Him? He will plunge you headlong into hell.'* In vain did he threaten to return back to the Catholic religion : 'If you continue,' he says, ' in these measures of your common deliberations, I will recant whatever I have written or said, and leave you. Mind what I say.'† All in vain : for 'he had put the Bible into each man's hand to explain it for himself.' This his followers continued to do in open defiance of him, as we see in his curious challenge to Carlostad to write a book against the Real Presence, when one wishes the other to *break his neck,* and the other retorts : ' *May I see thee broken on the wheel ;'* ‡ till their mutual contradictions and discords become so numerous and scandalous as to overwhelm the thinking part of them with grief and confusion.' "§

" That seems to be a curious sort of book. Elder Flemming, tell me where you got it?" said Mrs. Flemming, with indignation too big for words.

" This book," he answered, speaking slowly, " which has been ' as a lamp to my feet,' as a guide

---

* Oper., tom. vii, fol. 274.
† Oper., tom. vii, fol. 276, ed. Wittemb.
‡ Variat., b. ii, n. 12.
§ Milner's End of Controversy, p. 36.

showing me the way, and making the crooked paths straight, was left upon my desk by the Irish pedler, McCue, the morning he went away. I threw it into the desk, determined to send it back to him, little dreaming what a treasure it was, or that in it I should find comfort and enlightenment, until last night in turning over my papers I came across it and opened it. The very first words I read arrested my attention, and I sat up all night reading it; and the result of this reading is that from that hour I am a Catholic—a Roman Catholic."

Again Mrs. Flemming felt that tightening around her throat; she could only gasp: "I knew it. I knew that Irish Papist was at the bottom of it. Wolfert Flemming, I know that you are a hard-headed man, and that once you have made up your mind to a thing there's no power on earth can change you; I've no hope to do so, but I tell you you've broken my heart and ruined your family; mark my words—you have."

"Neither, I hope, little wife. All I ask of you is to give this matter a cool, intelligent investigation, earnestly praying the while to be enlightened."

"Enlightened!" repeated Mrs. Flemming with sarcastic emphasis.

"As it regards all else concerning earthly prosperity and the like, I have counted the cost and made up my mind—made it up fully. It would be small profit to me to gain the whole world if I lose my own soul," said Wolfert Flemming emphatically.

"But why need you lose your soul ?" she asked ; you have always been a good man, serving God."

"According to the light I had, mother, I tried to serve God ; but I have felt for years past that there was something wanting. I was not satisfied ; and now that I have discovered a true, soul-satisfying faith, one which every faculty of my mind responds to as divine and necessary for my salvation, I shall —nay, I do embrace it, counting all things nought for it. It is the way for me, and if I should try to climb up by any other I should be like a thief and a robber, and be cast down."

"I, dear father," said Eva, "should be glad to know something of a religion which seems so vital and sublime that all things are counted but nothing for the sake of it. May I read that book ?"

"And I too, father," said Hope. "All that I have heard sounds like truth."

"To save time," replied the Elder, while his eyes brightened with a tender light as he looked at the two fair earnest faces of his daughters turned with confiding love towards him, "I will read it aloud every night to you. Then we can talk it over as we read."

"That will be much better," replied Hope.

" Although I don't expect to become a Catholic, I should like to hear what Catholics do really believe."

" I suppose," said Mrs. Flemming, " you won't forget that you are to see Deacon Sneathen on Monday about that business."

" No, indeed. I shall have everything ready, mother, and it will all be fixed by Monday night; then, sometime during the week, I shall have to go up to the Pines. Reuben, did the Deacon say he'd come here, or am I to go there?"

" He didn't say, father," answered Reuben. " He only said he'd see you."

" I haven't seen John Wilde either, for a week; where is he, Hope?" asked Mrs. Flemming.

" He went to Boston, mother, to buy furniture and carpets, and won't be back for a week or two," answered Hope, blushing.

" I should like to know what *he'll* think of all this!" said Mrs. Flemming to herself. " Popery, of all things in the world, to come into this household! I do believe it will kill me."

Hope and Reuben went to meeting with their mother on the following Sabbath. Eva remained at home to read and converse with her father on the all-important subject which engrossed his thoughts, and which now also claimed her deepest attention. Mrs. Flemming carried a heavy heart with her into the old Congregational meeting-house that day. She already felt some of the grief arising from a " divided house." How could she face the congregation, knowing all that she did? knowing too that the most of them—her neighbors and friends—would miss her husband from his accustomed place, and begin to wonder at his absence, and ask her all sorts of questions before she got home; questions which she could not fully evade or set aside. She almost wished that the Indian woman had choked her to death, to have been spared this unspeakable trial.

Father Ray missed the Elder as soon as he arose in the pulpit and cast his eyes over the congregation. Deacon Sneathen glanced round, then up and down, hoping to see his old friend somewhere; Miss Debby deliberately mounted her large tortoise-shell spectacles upon her nose, and took a long stare through them at his empty seat, then cocked her chin a degree higher than usual, and fixed her eyes with a supercilious expression on Mrs. Flemming. I am sorry to say that Reuben, who noticed her impertinence, was very much tempted to make a face at her; but he resolutely turned away so that he could not see her; while Hope, who had also observed her offensive manner, fixed her calm, grey eyes for a moment steadfastly on her, then lifted them to the old minister who in tremulous tones was giving out the hymn.

Father Ray had a sermon prepared for the day and occasion; but when he discovered that Wolfert Flemming—whom he loved as David loved Jonathan—was again absent, his heart misgave him; he felt sure that the man had at length yielded to the doubts which had so long beset him, and delivered in the place of it a startling discourse on the perils of backsliding and apostasy, which he wound up by describing with quaint eloquence the wretched plight of those disciples who after having been the friends and companions of Jesus,—who had listened to His words, and perhaps daily touched His hand and held sweet converse with Him,—turned away at last and left Him, because all that He said did not exactly suit their ideas and comprehension, and walked with Him no more. "They thought," said the old man, "that he meant that He was going to give them His own body and blood to eat; when, if they had been patient and staid where they were, if they had been more humble and faithful, they would have found out their mistake, and understood that their Lord spoke in a figurative sense; but no! in the pride and conceit of their hearts they turned their backs upon Him, and it is only reasonable to suppose that they were given over to perdition; for, brethren, we all know that the condition of a backslider is ten thousand times worse than his first state of sin."

The old man's utterances were full of blended ire and pathos, and Mrs. Flemming felt every word like a blow as she sat there listening to her husband's condemnation; with all a woman's keen sensitive perceptions she understood the whole drift of his meaning. But, when the time came, she went up with the rest to receive the bread and wine of what her sect call the Sacrament of the Lord's Supper; and when she took the bread, and heard the words THIS IS MY BODY, a thrill, an awe, such as she had never felt before, passed swiftly like an electric shock through her heart; and when the minister presented the cup, saying, " Drink ye all of this, for this is my blood of the New Testament which shall be shed for many unto the remission of sins," her impulse was to thrust it from her and run from the place; for suppose, after all, her husband was right? But then she remembered that it was really nothing but common bread and wine, simply set apart for this occasion; all that was left over, after the rite, being generally given to the sexton's wife to make toast out of, and season lier puddings with. Then, trying to think that it symbolized and commemorated the death of the Saviour, she drank a few drops, and the cup was passed on.

After the congregation was dismissed, and they were all standing outside waiting for their chaises and wagonettes to be brought round, everybody came up with inquiries about the Elder. "Was he ill?"—"Did he have to go to the Pines again?"— "Where was he?"—"Why was he not at meeting?"—"It was the fourth Sacrament day that he was absent; what could it mean? they thought.

Mrs. Flemming stood her ground bravely, saying as little as she could, consistent with the truth, yet enough to give them to understand some of the facts of the case. "No; Elder Flemming was not ill," she said to one; "he is in excellent health." "He is not at the Pines," she answered another; "he is at home." "He did not come to meeting," she said to a third, "because he preferred staying at home;" but to the last query, made by Deacon Sneathen, she replied stiffly: "He is not here, because he has changed his opinion on some doctrinal points which he thinks erroneous, and I guess he'll break off altogether from the old lines." Her voice quavered, and she had nearly broke down, but the brave, loving little soul was determined that—no matter what *she* might feel at liberty to say *to* her husband—they should all find themselves mistaken if they expected her to stand still while they pulled him to pieces in her presence. So she acted on the defensive. Deacon Sneathen grew purple in the face, and was seized with vertigo, which sent him staggering against the horse-block; Miss Debby cocked up her chin in the most aggressive manner,

and cleared her throat in such a tumultuous way
that several persons ran towards her, thinking she
was strangling; meanwhile Mrs. Flemming and
Hope stepped into the chaise, and Reuben drove
briskly off. Before they were out of sight, every
man, woman, and child there knew that Elder Flemming was a backslider. If Mrs. Flemming had told
them that he had turned Papist, I am at a loss to
imagine to what heights their excitement would have
risen.

CHAPTER XIV.

SACRIFICE.

I WAS sitting one summer evening in a pavilion
built upon a bluff overhanging the sea, watching
the long lines of surf, as the strong swift billows of
the Atlantic swept shoreward over the bars, and
listening with mingled awe and delight to their
reverberating thunders as they burst in creamy
whiteness upon the shingly beach, roaring and raving with impotent fury at the failure of their as-
sault on the dry land, as driven by the invisible
and inexorable power which let them " come so far
and no farther," they rushed backwards like a
routed army, their only spoils the scattered drift-

wood and sea-weed deposited along the shore by the last flood tide. As the tumultuous sounds subsided into low and more distant mutterings, there rose above me the wild sweet song of a bird which was brooding on its nest under some carved wood-work on the apex of the roof. It sang, or seemed to sing, in ecstasy of peace, gazing out the while at the rose-tinted clouds, the turbulent ocean and the rocking ships; and the sounds fell upon my heart like balm; but presently the booming and bursting of the surf below drowned the flute-like symphonies, and I feared that I should hear them no more; but when the defeated billows were again dragged back moaning and sobbing, I distinguished through the din a faint sweet trill: then as they receded still farther, leaving a short interval of quiet, the wild wondrous music floated out again in rich fulness, and I knew that it had not been hushed, but that the bird had been singing on as heedless of the thunders of the sea as of the stillness of the land.

The little bird singing there on the edge of the noisy turbulent ocean was like the peace that had made its abode in the soul of Wolfert Flemming. Disturbing elements clamored around him, and there were moments when his own nature beat like great waves against his soul, and his out-look in the future seemed so dim and stormy that although the sweet singer, brooding in its depths, never ceased murmuring blissful hymns of peace, he should not hear them, but when the discords of life and nature ceased, they thrilled through every avenue of his being, consoling him with the sublime consciousness that his faith was at last and indeed anchored on the eternal Rock of Ages. And in this deep peace, he learned to "possess his soul in patience," knowing that however tempestuously the waves might beat against him, however angrily they might threaten him, they could come just so far and no farther; and his great trusting heart looked up, and was glad.

After the trial which his wife's distress of mind on account of his change of faith caused him—and it was not a light one—he thought that nothing could pain or disturb him to the same degree, but he was mistaken. Old Father Ray came down to see him, losing no time. He came on Monday morning, and with a countenance in which severity struggled with an expression of sorrow which he could not conceal, he entered the house, returning the welcome greeting he received by cold, curt salutations.

"I have come to see your father," he said to Hope, "and I wish to see him alone."

"I will go and fetch my father directly. He is out somewhere on the farm," replied Hope, folding up her work. And she went out, leaving him alone with her mother.

"And you, Martha Flemming, how is it with you in these times of faithlessness?" he asked in quavering tones.

"There is no change in me. I am satisfied with pure gospel doctrine," she answered stiffly; then a flood of thoughts came surging through her mind, and with a low cry of anguish, she sobbed: "Oh, Father Ray! Father Ray! it will kill me. My husband has turned papist!"

The old man was startled and nearly frightened by such an unexpected outburst of emotion, and if she had said, "My husband has turned infidel," he could not have felt a more deathlike sickness at his heart; but it was impossible to sit silent in the face of such a sorrow as this, and making an effort to collect his scattered wits, he began to utter some consolatory words, when Wolfert Flemming's footsteps sounded along the passage, and she hastily left the room before he entered it.

No one was present at this interview. Mr. Flemming led his guest away to his little work-room, and they shut themselves in. There for three hours they talked together. Now and then the old minister's voice arose in loud expostulatory tones; then he pleaded and denounced alternately, and as **he grew** more excited its thin treble sounded like a shriek, and sometimes sunk into hoarse trembling whispers, for throughout the interview every moment convinced him of the utter futility of arguing the case with this man who—grave, calm and assured—had scripture, reason, history, and, above all, faith, with which to rebut and crush out all that he could say ; this man whose sense of religion was so pure, whose moral nature was so grand, whose conscience was so upright, and whose very earnestness impressed even him—angry as he was —with the perfect sincerity of his belief in the strange and incomprehensible doctrines he had adopted ; doctrines which to his darkened and narrow mind were " damnable idolatries." Baffled and wounded—for as we have said elsewhere, old Father Ray loved Wolfert Flemming as a father loves his first born—and full of bitterness, he gave up the contest and left him ; remembering the doom of Ephraim, who was joined to his idols, he " let him alone," and shaking the dust of his house from his feet he went out, refusing Flemming's offered hand, and mounting his horse rode slowly away, feeling as if a gulf had suddenly opened and swallowed the last earthly happiness of his life, destroying the one mortal tie that above all others he had held most dear for time and eternity.

"That's what's come of it all," said Mrs. Flemming bitterly, as she and Eva and Hope stood at

the window looking after the old minister. She
saw him refuse her husband's hand, and almost
imagined that the words she saw him uttering, but
could not distinguish, were curses, for there was no
blessing in the look he cast back to the house, no
relenting in his hard pinched features, which they
saw as he wheeled his horse around to ride homewards. She watched her husband as he stood
motionless and almost breathless on the spot where
the old man had parted from him, then turned to
come into the house, and she saw that his features
were pale and set, that his lips were compressed,
and that his eyes, over which his heavy brows hung
lowering, had a steely gleam in them she had never
seen there before : then she knew that he had had
a fierce struggle in his inner life and that his
powers of endurance had been taxed to their utmost.
He poured out a flagon full of cool water which
had just come from the spring, and drank it every
drop ; then stood a few moments, his elbow leaning against the window frame, looking out through
the budding vines, at the distant mountain ridges
edged with sunshine and the deep calm blue of the
heavens beyond ; and the passion waves subsided
within him, and he heard the sweet whispers of
faith and peace. He did not refer to his stormy
interview with Father Ray ; indeed he did not
speak at all, until, as he was leaving the room, he

stopped for an instant beside Mrs. Flemming's chair, and laying his hand tenderly upon her head, said : " Mother, I am going down with the men to harrow in the oats; if Deacon Sneathen comes, send for me."

" Very well," she replied coldly, even while her heart was full of wifely pity for him, dashed with anger that she could not help. " Deacon Sneathen, indeed !" she added, as he left the room; " mark my words, girls, Deacon Sneathen won't come ; see if he does !"

" I hope he will," answered Hope. " I don't see why he shouldn't. My father's change of religion can't affect the business in which they've been engaged in so many years. I think it will be a most unreasonable thing in the Deacon to break off his connection with father, because—" Hope hesitated a moment, and then added bravely, " he has become a Catholic."

" Where is Reuben !" asked Mrs. Flemming, sharply, to change the conversation, for every reference to her husband's change of faith was like a stab. " Where can that boy be ?"

" I don't know, mother," replied Eva, " I have not seen Ruby since breakfast time. I hope he is not going to have a sick turn ; I thought he looked very white this morning."

" So he did ; I noticed it too. Do go, Hope, and

find out if any of them have seen him," said Mrs. Flemming anxiously, " I can't tell what makes Ruby so ailing all the time." Then Mrs. Flemming went up to the weaving room and sat down to think—not of Reuben and his feeble, useless life, which generally caused her much anxious concern—but of the heavy trial which had fallen upon her, which she almost imagined to be a judgment from heaven to punish her for having been too proud of her husband, and for having loved him too entirely.

But Reuben could not be found ; no one had seen him since early in the morning, and each one of the family began to feel seriously uneasy about him. Dinner time came and passed, and still he did rot come. Mr. Flemming and his men came in at sunset, but there were no tidings of Reuben ; and urged by his mother, who was half distracted by her anxious fears, they were making preparations to go in search of him, when he glided in like a ghost out of the twilight, and sunk down on the old oak settle by the fire, pale, speechless, and exhausted. They set to sponging his face with vinegar, rubbing his hands, and feeding him with elderberry wine, which revived him, then they began to question him all together in such a chorus of sounds and confusion of words, that he burst out laughing, although he was still too weak to answer them.

"You're all right now, Ruby," said Eva, kissing his forehead.

But where in the world have you been, Reuben? Do tell! To give me such a fright!" said Mrs. Flemming, sitting down and folding her hands on her lap while she looked at him, puzzled beyond expression by idiosyncrasies which made the boy's life a perpetual mystery to her. "You should not have done so!"

"I didn't intend to, mammy, indeed I didn't," he answered, disarming her anger at once by the tender, sweet appellative which he always used as a shield and defence, whenever he wanted to propitiate her, or when she was displeased with him. "I went straggling around, digging and poking among the thorn bushes, and turning over big rocks searching for something I wanted, until I got so far from home that I thought I should never be able to get back."

"What in the land's name were you hunting up, child? I never did see the like of you in my life!" exclaimed Mrs. Flemming.

"Gold, I guess," said Hope, laughing.

"No," said the boy, gravely, "I was searching for soft stone."

"Now do tell! Why!" exclaimed Mrs. Flemming, quite exasperated at what she considered his extreme foolishness. "I do think, Reuben, of all

your vagaries, this one beats. Soft stone! But
listen now to what I have to say. I will have no
more such shiftless doings, and sinful waste of
time. You can't work; you're really not strong
enough; and you shall help me in the dairy, and
learn how to spin. Indeed you shall. I will positively put a stop to this aimless sort of a life. Soft
stone, indeed!"

"But there *is* soft stone; mother, I have read
about it, and how to find it, and I shall keep on
looking for it, too," answered Reuben, a little crestfallen, and a little doggedly.

"I guess you learnt that out of the book the Irish
pedler gave *you*. It would be just like the rest.
Soft stone! When you find it, let me know; maybe it will do to stuff the pillows with." Reuben
was silent. He knew that he might as well be, and
he was very tired; so he leaned back, closing his
eyes, and seemed to doze, she watching him all the
while. Then she lifted up his long tapering hand,
as fair and white as a woman's, and laying it across
her own, sat looking thoughtfully at it, and like one
speaking in her sleep, said: "It is exactly like the
hand in the old portrait of my great grandmother,
Lady Pendarvis;" then she smoothed it, and folded
it against her heart with an indescribable yearning
for this gifted, half helpless, and best beloved one
of her children. Reuben was not asleep, and he

raised himself up and put his arms about her, and leaning his head upon her shoulder, said : " I'd like to find it, little mammy. I want it for something great."

" Have you eaten anything to-day, Ruby?" she asked, while she smoothed back the golden tangles from his face. "No! Get up, and let me hurry them with supper." And forgetting her great sorrow for the time, the busy little woman began to bustle around, and presently left the room.

" Did you hear what mother said about the old portrait?" said Hope. " This is the first time I ever heard the proud-looking old lady's name. Mother never mentioned it, and I thought she was one of the dead and gone Mrs. Babsons."

" So did I. Lady Pendarvis! That sounds quite grand!" said Eva, laughing.

" It is just like mother's old 'Mayflower' pride never to have spoken of it. Maybe she thought it might make us vain or proud to know that we have noble English blood in our veins," said Hope.

" All the blood of all the nobility on earth could not make a nobler man than my father," answered Eva. " I'm prouder of him than of old Lady Pendarvis, even if she were of the blood royal."

" So am I," said Hope. Then they fell to talking of the old portrait, and Hope remembered to have heard her father tell some one, years before, that the original had been a zealous persecutor of the English Puritans and had disinherited her only child for marrying one; and that the picture had not been kept out of reverence for her memory, but because it was painted by Hans Holbein, and considered to be a master piece of art, besides which the picture itself was remarkably beautiful. "And" —whispered Eva, looking towards Reuben, who was now really asleep—"Ruby is the living image of her. Well! mother has good reason for being a little spiteful. It seems a little like retribution that Lady Pendarvis' portrait should have been hanging against the walls of a Puritan house all these years. I wonder it has not walked out of its frame; and her very name not known to her descendants."

"Suppose now, Eva, just suppose that she was a Catholic?" suggested Hope.

"Why! how strange it would be! I should like to ask mother, but dare not. Poor little mother, she is so troubled!" replied Eva.

Deacon Sneathen did not come to see about the partnership. It was too late for him to come now, and Wolfret Flemming's face wore an expression of anxiety and gravity; he felt, somehow, that difficulties from unexpected quarters were beginning to gather around him. Mrs. Flemming tried to think that something had happened to prevent the Deacon's keeping his engagement; but she had her suspicions, and bitter ones they were; however, she made no remark; and although the girls had a vague feeling of uneasiness on the subject, they did not refer to it in any way, but exerted themselves to be cheerful, efforts which their mother could not refrain from uniting in when she saw the look of care on her husband's countenance and knew what it boded.

That night Wolfert Flemming began to read aloud "Milner's End of Controversy" to his family. Hope and Eva, with their sewing, brought their chairs closer to him, and listened with the deepest interest. Mrs. Flemming hurried Reuben off to his room to bathe his feet and go to bed, he being feverish after his day's tramp, and she did not return until prayer-time.

CHAPTER XV.

LETTERS.

IT did not take long for such news to spread, and if Wolfert Flemming's old friends and neighbors had heard that he had been transformed into a fiery dragon, they would not have been more wonderstruck and dismayed than they were when they learned that he had become a Papist. Papist is not a pleasant word, being a term of reproach always used by our separated brethren when they wish to be particularly and emphatically bitter against Catholics; but it was a word they understood as meaning all that they had been educated to dread and despise in religion; nor could they have comprehended the word Catholic, as applied to the spiritual *bete-noir* which they called Popery, to have saved their lives; hence these good people thought that their Elder had given himself up body and soul to certain destruction. There had never been such an excitement in that quiet romantic region since the old Indian scalping times, and the old Puritan witch-burning and ear-cropping days! Some believed the report; and some grieved and astonished, refused to credit it. Some mean little souls, who had always secretly envied the man his good fame, which set him by tacit consent above them, were glad, and inwardly rejoiced; others were sorry because they feared such an example would scandalize the weak and set them to running after novelties; others deplored it, because they had sincerely loved and reverenced his strong, guileless character, and could not bear the idea of severing their intercourse with him, a thing which, under the circumstances, they would feel bound to do; while to many the event afforded a new and highly spiced subject for gossip. But

the limits of my narrative restrain me from describing the excitement. All who knew anything
at all about the sentiment of the New England of
that day against the Catholic religion, can imagine
it more vividly than any words could paint it. I
must confine myself to the effect it had upon those
who were immediately connected with the Flemmings.

Deacon Sneathen was one of the first to hear the
tidings. He was at the old minister's house when
he got home that day from his stormy interviev
with Wolfert Flemming : had stopped on his way
down to the Old Homestead, to keep his engagement about the partnership, to ask Father Ray
some confidential questions in relation to the erratic
state of mind the Elder seemed to be in about religious matters, and heard more than he had
counted on ; for the minister, still smarting under
the hurt of what had passed on that occasion,
told him all about it in pretty strong language
But the Deacon, never remarkably quick, got so
bewildered and confused that he could not follow
him, or clearly comprehend what he was talking
about ; until by dint of questioning him at every
few words the facts of the case began to dawn upon
his dull understanding, when the most fanatical
wrath and enmity against his old friend took possession of him. There's a saying that "it takes a

surgical operation to get an idea in the head of certain people," and Deacon Sneathen was one of that unfortunate class, with this difference : when the idea did get into his head, it took full possession of him, to the exclusion of every other, and became the motive power of his being. He understood it all now. His old friend and former partner in business, the man whose son his only daughter expected to marry, the man whom he had always looked up to, and likened in his own mind to one of the apostles, had gone and turned Papist! Here was a pivot to turn on, and he forthwith began to spin. The first thing he did, when there was nothing more to be said between Father Ray and himself on the subject, was to go home instead of keeping on down to the Flemmings' ; his next was to go straight up into his room after he got there, and, after locking himself in, sit down to the heavy task of inditing and writing a letter. "Joe Gargery's" efforts were nothing to his. He felt as if he would burst, and couldn't get a word right. He was confused by two personalities. Elder Flemming the Puritan, and Elder Flemming the Papist! Elder Flemming the burning and shining light of their congregation, and Flemming given over to Antichrist! Elder Flemming his friend and partner, and the Flemming that he intended to throw over at all risks! The nearness of all their previous relations made the task more difficult; and the more he thought it over, the worse he floundered. He spoilt nearly two dozen sheets of paper. He broke out in a cold perspiration, and felt as if bees were humming in his ears, and jerked about n his chair until the buttons of his suspenders flew off. Then he got up and opened a little cupboard in the wall, took down a dusty-looking bottle, and poured out a tumbler full of clear, amber-colored, oily liquid, which he drank, with his eyes rolled up to the ceiling as if he were praying; then hastily restoring the things to their receptacle, he locked them up, put the key into his waistcoat pocket, washed his mouth, and with his courage renewed "like an eagle's," he sat down and wrote the following:

ELM COTTAGE, March 28th.

W. FLEMMING: Sir, Sence I herd that you have forsook the true Gospil religin in which you wor bred and born, and hev jined the ranks of Antichrist, I dont feel willing to renoo the pardnership. If you will give up poppery and be what you was before in the house of the Lord, I am willing to let the bisness goon as it wor, which you must let me know. But if not I will take into pardnership a Bosting man with a big capitol, that will put up Steam Sawmills at the Pines, and has a gift in prayer, for which latter the Lord will prosper the bisness.

Your obedient servant to command,

SHADRACH SNEATHEN.

This was the ridiculous missive which was to carry consternation into the camp of the Flemmings, and its results were as effective as if it had been written in the most stately English, interlarded with legal clauses in Latin. Broken glass and bits of rusty iron can do as mortal execution as minnie balls, if fired with true aim ; so the Deacon's bad sample of orthography, etymology, syntax, and prosody, did not fall a hair-breadth short of his intentions when it reached its destination. But I will not anticipate. When Deacon Sneathen at last finished his letter, without a single blot, or a word scratched out, he read it over and felt very proud of it, and would like to have read it out in meeting ; but as that was impracticable, and his vanity was hungering and thirsting to display his epistolary talent to some one, he unlocked his door, and went down stairs into the kitchen where his sister and Huldah were making doughnuts, pies. and other comforting things for the stomach, and after telling them the news he unfolded the letter. Miss Debby, her arms covered with flour and her hands stuck up with soft dough which hung down from her fingers like fringe, dropped breathless in- to a chair, her chin in the air and her whole being thrilled with a delightful excitement, exclaiming : " Du tell neow !" It was all that she could say. For once in her life she was bereft of volubility of speech. Huldah was standing with a spoonfull of stewed pumpkin in her hand, just ready to drop into the light shell of flaky paste she had prepared for it, when the news burst like a petard among the Penates of the hearth ; and so she stood motionless with surprise and grief, the color mounting in crimson flushes to her face, and her handsome eyes flashing fire, while the Deacon read his letter.

" You ought to be ashamed of yourself, father, to write such a letter as that to Elder Flemming!" she exclaimed, when with a flourish of his hand he finished reading it.

" Wal, neow!" he said, looking amazed, " how dare you speak so to me?"

" Because I am ashamed of you !" she repeated, rapping the large spoon upon the table until the stewed pumpkin flew round in every direction. " To go and write a letter like that, to such a man as Elder Flemming, and throw him over because he's gone and done what he has a right to do if he wants to. Popery can't be so bad a thing, if he's taken it up ; and whatever it is, I think it must be better than your religion, which will let you go and do such a thing to a good man, and your old friend too."

" I'll box your ears, you sarcy jade," responded the Deacon, quite purple in the face.

" No you won't !" she answered, fearless of consequences, in her zeal for the friends so dearly loved and so unjustly injured. " I'd like to know what the battle of Lexington and Bunker Hill, and all the other battles that you all make such spread-eagles over, training days and Independence Day, were tought for, if it wa'n't for liberty of conscience, and to keep people from being hung and quartered, if they happen not to be Puritans? What right have you got to meddle with Elder Flemming, even if he was to turn Pagan or Jew, so long as he don't cheat you, which you know he has never done?"

"Huldy, hold your tongue. I'll have no Papist in my business, nor in my family either; do you hear that?" he exclaimed, loosening his neckcloth.

"Yes, father, I hear you," she replied, defiantly. "I hear you; but that does not change my opinion in the least. And if you don't take care, you *will* have one in your family more than you count on."

"Huldy Sneathen!" said Miss Debby, holding up her dough-fringed hands, "I wonder the bears don't rush down from the mountings and devour you! To talk so to your father, who is doing nothing but a righteous act."

"If the bears ever eat me, aunty, it will be when they come after you and get scared at the looks of you. Bears don't like skin and bone," said Huldah, with a saucy, angry laugh.

"Wal, neow! I'd like to know!" gasped Miss Debby, white with rage.

"Father," said Huldah, laying down the spoon, and speaking more gently and gravely, "*don't* send that letter to Elder Flemming. I am sorry I spoke saucily to you, if that will do any good; but don't send it."

"Don't meddle with what don't concern you, Huldy," answered the Deacon, refolding the letter. "It's to go."

"Huldy Sneathen, you're a sassy piece of goods; and I reckon if it wasn't for Nick Flemming you wouldn't be so dretfully cut up," at last broke out Miss Debby.

"It will make no difference between me and Nick, whatever happens; depend upon that. I'd marry Nick Flemming if he was the Pope himself," she exclaimed, her handsome eyes flashing with anger. "And I tell you again, father, you ought to be ashamed of yourself to do such a thing as you are going to do." Then she turned her back on them, her heart throbbing passionately and tears blinding her as she pretended to busy herself over her pies.

Miss Debby whispered something to the Deacon as he went towards the door, and he stopped to consider for a moment, then said: "I say, Huldy, don't be going down to Flemming's any more. I won't allow it."

The girl turned round and looked at her father, her face pale now, and a look in it as if she did not quite comprehend him.

"What did you say, father?"

"I say you are not to go to Flemming's any more," he repeated.

"Father!" she replied, looking straight into his eyes, while her thin nostrils expanded, and the color came back in hues of brightest carnation to her cheeks and lips. "Your command is both unreasonable and cruel, and I won't obey it. I shall go to see the Flemmings as long as they will let me come."

"I do admire to see such impidence! I'd lock you up, and keep you on bread and water," exclaimed Miss Debby, in an ecstasy of anger.

"Try it—any of you," answered Huldah, turning her back once more. The Deacon, almost suffocated with excitement, went out without another word, to send his letter away by a messenger on horseback, that it might the sooner reach its destination; and Miss Debby began a severe lecture, which Huldah put a stop to by telling her if she did not hold her tongue she would turn her out of the kitchen and lock the door; and as Miss Debby knew that her niece had not only the spirit but strength to put her threat into execution, she sniffed, took a good long stare at the girl, standing there with such a determined look as if only waiting for the slightest provocation to do as she said, gave her chin an extra elevation, cleared her throat vociferously, and said:

"It is wasting breath to talk to you, Huldy Sneathen;" then held her peace.

Huldah did not behave at all like a model young lady in defying her father, and threatening her aunt as she did; but her nature had been engaged, ever since she could remember, in a life-long conflict with an injudicious training, which instead of crushing had developed the spontaneity of her impulsive character; and if she had not propriety on her side in this instance, she had justice. Particularly improper—if she had only known it—was her allusion to the Pope; but she only meant to let them know, in the strongest terms she could put it, that she would marry Nicholas Flemming if he were ten thousand times Catholic.

The next day the Deacon received the following reply to his letter:

April 10th.

SHADRACH SNEATHEN,

SIR : Your letter informing me of your decision in relation to the partnership hitherto existing between us is received. The accounts of Sneathen & Flemming are all balanced and can be closed at once. My son Nicholas has my authority to settle up my share of the concern. Respectfully yours,

WOLFERT FLEMMING.

"He's jined to his idols," muttered the Deacon, who felt much crestfallen as he read and re-read the brief note; "and he's too proud even to thank me for the offer I made him. In fact, he don't notice it any way. Wal! I've done my duty."

Flemming's religion was too far above all sordidness to be dragged into the mire by such an offer as Deacon Sneathen had made him; he did not give it a second thought in connection with the business, the loss of which, it is true, would bring upon him a crowd of cares and anxieties and pecuniary troubles, which he scarcely dared to think of; much less did he listen to the faintest whisper of temptation to compromise his faith for worldly gain—his faith, for which he was prepared, if needs be, to sacrifice all. Then he wrote another letter, this one to Patrick McCue, in which he told him of the great change wrought in his religious sentiments by the book he had left him, thanked him with eloquent sincerity for the gift which had been productive of such great results to him, and asked him to select other Catholic books, doctrinal and devotional, and torward the package to him by the stage. He enclosed fifteen dollars, and though he did not know that it would ever reach him, he did not even know that the pedler was in Boston, he thought it something worth the risk; and asking the blessing of Almighty God on his intention, he rode over to Wier's Landing, the nearest post-office, where he mailed his letter. Then he wrote to Nicholas, informing him of the events and changes that had so recently occurred, and directed him to wind up their

business at the Pines as speedily as possible and
return home.

It was a day of surprises to Nicholas Flemming,
who had never received more than one or two letters in his life, to get three in one day; one from
his father, which alone would have given him enough
to think over for six months to come; one from
Deacon Sneathen, telling him that he withdrew his
consent to his marriage with his daughter, "Huldy,"
and ordered him not to visit her any more. The
grotesque pigeon-English of the Deacon would have
made Nick Flemming laugh if it had not been for the
terrible things it meant, being nothing less than the
destruction of his best earthly hopes and the
wrecking of a career just begun. The third letter
was from Huldah, written in a storm of anger and
affection, which really did make him laugh and cry
together.

"You know, Nick," she wrote, "that it is no use
to mind father or Aunt Deb. either. I don't.
I never did. I know exactly what *she's* after, for
she's been nagging me about it ever since Eva
threw George Merrill over; but it won't do,
although she has succeeded in talking father over
to her plans. Not all the George Merrills in the
world, if every one of them wore a crown, and had
Alladeen's lamp to boot, could induce me to change

my mind. I don't care a snap; and if you don't want to be off, I am

"Affectionately and faithfully yours,

"HULDAH."

Nicholas Flemming had never in all his life experienced such an excitement. "Here," thought he, "is trouble in a heap. My father, of all men in the world, to go and turn Catholic; the business broken up, and I ordered not to see Hulda, whom I have loved ever since she was a little girl! A pretty kettle of fish for a man to jump into. I wonder if I am awake? Yes, I am wide awake. That pinch convinces me that I am not dreaming. I suppose there's trouble enough at home among them all; and there's my poor little mother! I wonder how *she* takes it? She hasn't much love for Papists, I know that. My father is right to do what he pleases with his own soul—but, by George! it's mighty inconvenient! I know that he must have had weighty and good reasons for what he has done! * * * Whew!" Then Nicholas Flemming doubled up one fist, and holding the Deacon's letter in the palm of his other hand he pounded it, then tore it into small bits and scattered them on the cold gusty air. Then he went into his hut, stirred up the coals on his hearth, filled his pipe, and sat down to smoke and think it all over.

CHAPTER XVI.

TRIALS COME NOT SINGLY.

WHEN a Protestant disassociates himself from the sect with which he has been in communion, to join some other Protestant sect holding different doctrines, it is only necessary for him to present a " certificate of good membership " from his former pastor to be received. This certificate he obtains without difficulty, and however loth his pastor and brethren may be to lose him, they attach no odium to the act, which they look upon as a simple exercise of liberty of conscience, and which they consider one of the most sacred prerogatives of a free-born American citizen. He suffers neither in reputation or estate, and enjoys, with unctuous meekness, the coddling of his new co-religionists.

But the case is different when a man becomes a convert to the Catholic faith. That means sacrifice. It means humiliation. It means contempt. It means false accusations. It means the standing aloof of friends and neighbors. It means the Cross. It means, even now, everywhere in this broad free land of ours—where " liberty of conscience " is the political boast of the demagogue, and the favorite sounding phrase of the pulpit—anathema. For when a man becomes a Catholic he enters not only into an entirely new spiritual life, but must be prepared for the painful rending of many ties which made the old one pleasant. He begins a warfare of grace against nature. It is a religion which accepts no compromise, because it is divine; a faith which must reign supreme in the soul, and over the will, intellect, and of its children : which being in sweet subjection to it, become elevated and holy.

This contrast is full of a deep and significant meaning, which can be explained in no other way than that the kingdom of Christ upon earth, which is the Holy Catholic Church, being not of this world, all the thousand contradictory sects whose doctrines are human inventions—and, consequently of the world—are engaged in perpetual conflict against her ; and while they claim Christ as their Head, reject the doctrine He has revealed, tear to pieces His divine word to substantiate their fallacies, and trample Him under the feet of poor finite human reason, and a more than half-pagan philosophy!

Why is it that when a man eminent for learning and talents becomes a Catholic it is immediately said by his former co-religionists that " He always wanted balance ;" " He was a very eccentric person ;" " In fact, his friends always thought him *just not* crazy, and some of them dreaded that he was entirely so." Then with a smile of derision, they

"Hope with his visionary ideas that he may stop short of actual atheism." Of other converts of less repute they declare them "Always to have been hypocrites; and their going over to Rome was for wider license to sin, for which they could get ablution beforehand;" or that "Their ignorance had been imposed upon, and their senses led astray by religious pomps and ceremonies;" of the poor and obscure, who seek, as in a city of refuge, the heavenly consolations of a true faith, they say: "Poor ignorant souls! we are well rid of them, and Popery is welcome to all such weeds. Let them support those whom they have perverted;" then they are stripped of employment and turned adrift to join that great army which is one of the distinctive marks of the true Church, the innumerable army of the suffering poor, of whom our Lord said: "The poor ye will always have with you."

There is no surer test of the truth of the Catholic religion than this undying, ceaseless persecution, and the spirit of sacrifice which it involves in its warfare with the faithful soul, enabling it in the end to exclaim: "I have fought the good fight"; then to go covered with the glorious scars of the conflict to receive its eternal reward.

Many err through the accident of their birth and surroundings; some err, sincerely believing they "do God a service" when they persecute His peo-

ple ; and others through ignorance; but alas! for
those who, more enlightened, close their eyes and
see not, and their ears and hear not; who stifle in
their souls the whispers of grace and truth, and
strike blindly against a divine faith which not even
the "gates of hell" can move! Alas for such!—
were it not better that they had never been born?

Wolfert Flemming felt that he was getting into
deep waters; but a peace passing all human understanding now filled his inner life and gave him courage.
The out-look was not cheering. There was a
mortgage on part of his property, which he had
expected to clear and have a handsome profit over
from the lumber business; but, as I have related,
he was cut quite off from that by Dacon Sneathen's
fanaticism. He could see no mode of relief except
by selling, which it went sorely against his heart
even to think of; for he had invested all his ready
money the year before in building the large addition to his house, in erecting a new stone barn and
other outhouses, and in enriching and fencing in
his lands. It is true that he had a year before him
in which to look round and manage for the best,
but his way was so hemmed in just now, that if he
could manage to pay interest and get the mortgage
extended it was as much as he dared hope to accom-
plish. In addition to this serious cause for anxiety,
there was his wife growing thin; the light had

faded out of her eyes, the cheerful ring was gone from her voice, and she was miserably unhappy. And the boy, Reuben, the idol of the household, grew more dreamy every day ; sometimes wan and drooping, at other times glowing and brilliant with feverish excitement, he was an enigma which none of them could comprehend. The doctor had been sent for, and his scrutiny into the case resulted in the sage opinion that " he must be let alone. He was too fragile for bleeding and physicking, and must be as much as possible in the open air. He could not decide whether the case was one of inertia, or, what was worse, softening of the brain." So Ruby had his liberty, which above all things he desired just now ; and he really was selfish enough to feel glad that they were all uneasy enough about him to follow the doctor's sensible advice. Had it been otherwise some of his fine plans would have come to grief. For Ruby had a secret which he guarded with jealous care ; and when his keen-eyed, anxious little mother found out that the boy was making a mystery of something, it added to her unhappiness, and she wondered with a dull ache at her heart if he was going daft? She had never got over the talk about the " soft stone," and nothing could have convinced her that it was not a feature of mental hallucination in him to imagine such a thing.

Then Nick had run down for a day and night from the Pines to get some instructions from his father relative to a final settlement of his affairs, and he told them about the letter he had got from Deacon Sneathen ; the poor fellow bore it bravely enough, for he had Huldah's faithful, cheering letter as an offset to it ; but his father and mother knew that this sudden turn in the affairs of his young and happy life was no light burden for him to bear, and they comforted him as best they could, " speaking words of endearment, where words of consolation availed not."*   Altogether the situation of the family at the Old Homestead was grave.   But Wolfert Flemming had counted the cost ; and come weal or woe, the peace of his soul was undisturbed, his faith unshaken.   The readings from Milner's " End of Controversy" went on regularly every evening—Mrs. Flemming now habitually absenting herself.   Her quaint high-backed chair looked forlorn and empty ; they not only missed her presence, but deplored the cause ; even the great tortoise-shell cat, which was wont to sleep curled up at her feet, seemed to understand that something was amiss, and finally one night mounted quietly into the chair, where she sat sadly blinking at the fire until her mistress came in to prayers, then springing lightly to the floor she met her half-way, rubbed

Longfellow.

her sides against her and lay down in her old place
at her feet, where she dozed contentedly. This
grotesque little episode occurred every night, and
no one disturbed Griselda, who, like her famous
namesake, behaved with the greatest propriety.
Meanwhile Eva and Hope became more and more
interested, and more sincerely convinced by the
arguments they heard that the Catholic faith was
the one, only true, and holy apostolic faith, upon
earth. Convinced of the divine origin and truth of
the Church, a belief in its dogmas necessarily followed, although their faith in some of these was
not altogether clear; for instance, the doctrine of
Purgatory, so unlike anything they had ever heard
of or conceived, was a drawback; also Tradition
and Invocation of Saints were subjects which they
discussed night after night with their father, who
in his grave patient way turned first to the Bible
and then to Miiner, linking the proofs together by
his own strong natural reason and the inspirations
of grace, until they felt at last that however strongly
their human reason might be opposed to such doctrines they could not see how they could believe
otherwise, and experienced for the first time in their
lives that grace is supernatural, and above all worldly
reason and philosophy; that the high mysteries of
God are not to be solved by mortal minds, or
dragged into the mire of human understanding, but

were to be reverenced and adored. Then it occurred
to them that the mystery of the Trinity, which they
had always believed, without the shadow of a doubt,
was a greater and more inaccessible one than any of
these new dogmas they had been hearing about, and
which they desired to accept; yet they had never
thought it necessary to seek to fathom its meaning,
or even troubled themselves for a single moment
about it; they simply believed it, and if need be
would have suffered death rather than deny their
faith in it. They had many talks together over
their sewing in the daytime, when their mother
was not present, on the subject of the previous
night's reading; grave, quiet conversations, indi-
cating not only an appreciation of new and strange
information, which in itself affords a certain pleasure to intelligent minds, but the dawn and awak-
ing of a spiritual life which already inspired them
to place their will in subjection to the supreme will
and service of God. And Eva daily meditated on
the picture that the pedler gave her. She had
learnt much about that Virgin Mother who stood
weeping at the Cross. Her Bible told her in its
prophecies and in its gospels who SHE was; and
Milner told her how and why the Church venerated
her and sought her intercession—and the thought
of MARY became more deeply precious to her; it
was her companion in solitude; it was the purest

and tenderest motive of her soul, the model by
which she was interiorly striving to fashion her
own life. She was the sinless Mother of Jesus;
through Him she was also hers; she was the new
Eve who had brought healing and salvation to her
progeny, instead of malediction and eternal woe as
did the first Eve. She suffered in her soul all that
her Son suffered in His body, that the ruin wrought
by our first mother might be healed; and—thought
the girl—lest her Son's passion should become,
through our own perverseness, fruitless for us, she
intercedes without ceasing for us, for whom she
suffered a supreme martyrdom. Then Eva began
to understand that the little statue in old Missis-
quoi's room was not an ideal "Peace" or "Charity,"
but an image of the holy Mother and her Divine
Babe; and in a little while the table was covered
with an embroidered drapery; it was drawn out
from the side of the wall and set in the middle of
the room, with the ivy-covered window for a back-
ground, and before the statue she daily placed a
vase of wild flowers. Into this retreat Eva used to
steal at twilight, sometimes at sunrise, and in fact
whenever an opportunity presented itself, to offer
her pure devotions, to read and meditate on all the
wonderful and sublime truths which were gradually
illuminating her spirit, and ask with timid yearning
love the intercession of the Mother of Jesus. After

a little time the family got to know where Eva was
to be found when she was missing, for she now
often took her sewing with her, and sat there full
of content and peace, thinking and thinking of her
sweet Virgin Mother until all earthly things were
lost sight of. One day her mother surprised her
there. Mrs. Flemming stood on the threshold and
saw it all: the image, the flowers, the embroidered
draperies; and, above all, Eva sitting there on a
low chair, her hands lightly clasped over her knee,
and her face uplifted, gazing with a rapt far-away
look in her eyes upon the fair likeness of MARY.

"Eva," she said, in a hoarse, harsh voice, "What
is this? Has it really come to image-worship
under this roof? Are you all mad or possessed?"

Eva started and looked round. "Not worship-
ping the image, mother," she answered quickly, as
she rose and stood, making a little gesture with
her hand towards the statue. "It represents the
Mother of Jesus; and I was thinking of her holy
life and exalted virtues, and wishing that I might
even in a feeble and imperfect way, imitate them."

"She was no better than any other converted
woman. I don't deny that she was converted," *
said Mrs. Flemming; "but you ought to be
ashamed of yourself to practice such idolatry as to
be paying her honors which are due only to God,

* This was said to me by an intelligent Protestant lady a few
weeks ago.

you who have been sitting under the teachings of the gospel so many years."

"Mother!" asked Eva, in her grave, sweet way, so much like her father's, "is it idolatry for me to love you, to think of you, to desire to resemble you, and to ask the aid of your prayers? Is it giving to a creature the worship which is due to God to do this?"

"It is a different thing entirely. It makes me sick, such false reasoning," she replied, nervously.

"Dear mother, if it is not idolatry for me to love you and try to imitate your virtues, it is not idolatry for me to love the Mother of Jesus who was sinless and holy, and try to model my poor life on hers," said Eva, while a soft glow crimsoned her cheeks, and her brave truthful eyes beamed with an unearthly brightness.

"It is all foolishness!" exclaimed Mrs. Flemming. "I wish to hear no more of it; it would take a miracle to change my opinions about all these new-fangled superstitious doings and doctrines." Then she went away, ready to cry out in her desolation and anger; she went into her own room and threw herself upon the floor, weeping in the bitterness of her soul and wondering no longer that the Jews, in their time of affliction, used to put ashes upon their heads and wrap themselves in sackcloth; some such thing would have been a great relief to her, but she was a Christian, to whom all Jewish rites, as well as all religious pomps and ceremonies, were abominations; so she could only try to pray. But latterly the heavens had become as brass over her head, and whenever she had sought consolation in prayer she could only weep those hot bitter tears, to which, until the perversion of her family, she had been a stranger.

"Eva," said her father, that evening, "your mother tells me that you spend much of your time in old Massisquoi's room. Be careful, for I think the ceiling is unsound. There has been a leak in the roof this long time which should have been mended."

"Is the ceiling cracked, father? I did not notice!" replied Eva.

"Yes, cracked entirely across; but it is not very perceptible; however, I will see to it. I am glad the room is used. A shut-up, never-used place like that in a house, is not canny!" he said, with one of his old pleasant smiles.

Then came a day when Wolfert Flemming was summoned before his Church to answer for his contumacy and backsliding.* His family wished him to spare himself the humiliation; and although he would not have sought it, still less was he going to avoid the opportunity that it gave him to con-

* This scene occurred as described.

fess the Faith openly; so he signified his intention of appearing before them on the following Sunday afternoon.

Never was the old meeting-house so crowded. People came from far and near to hear what he would have to say to extenuate his course of conduct. They were full of vague expectation and curiosity, many of them hoping that at the last moment he would recant the errors into which he had fallen and ask to be restored to the membership he had forfeited in his Church; and when he arose and stood before them in all his dignity, his grave noble countenance and frank honest eyes confronting them calmly and fearlessly, the silence became almost breathless. Then he began in clear level tones to set forth his "reasons for the faith that was in him," which carried to the mind of each one present the conviction that the man was speaking the "words of truth and soberness." He went over the whole ground of his religious experience, describing in simple and graphic language how his doubts were first awakened by observing the contradictory doctrines of the various sects composing the Protestant world; how he became still more disquieted by studying the scriptures in search of a solution of his difficulties, which so far from silencing his doubts, plunged him into still greater; he spared them nothing of the mental ex ercises he had passed through, and from the Bible and Milner's End of Controversy, in clear, lucid and simple terms, told them how at last his soul had found rest, as "under the shadow of a great rock in a weary land." His heart kindled still more as he talked to them; the truth inspired him with strange eloquence, and, without a word that could pain or offend the bitterest Puritan there, he set before them with logical force the pre-eminent claims of the holy Catholic Church to a divine origin and incorrupt Faith. He explained in simple style her dogmas, and spoke of her sacraments and consolations with a zeal, a fluency and pathos which amazed all who listened to him.

Many were filled with wonder at the strange doctrines he discoursed about; some heard him in anger, some were almost persuaded to go and do likewise; some of the women wept, and all listened to him with rapt attention. Old Father Ray sat through it all with his head bowed and his face covered with his hands, never once trusting himself to look towards him. Deacon Sneathen, his face purple, as with threatened apoplexy, from the beginning to the end of it gazed intently into his hat, which was stuck between his knees, as if it were the well in which truth abode. Miss Debby "sat in the seat of the scorner," her chin stuck up to its highest possible angle, and upon her hard face a more grim and unpleasant expression than usual. Mrs Flemming, who, with the spirit of Puritan and Spartan combined, had determined with wifely and womanly devotion to be present, to stand if need be by her husband's side, and show them all that whoever forsook him she would abide with him, could not forbear thinking, as she listened to arguments which she had never heard before, that there was much plausibility in them, and received impressions which she did not until a later day acknowledge. Nicholas—who was also there—thought his father had made his case good and defended it ably; while Eva and Hope held up their heads proudly, gazing at him with fond affection, believing as he believed, and rejoicing in every word that fell from his lips. Reuben, who had shown no interest one way or the other in the spiritual disturbance in the family, had slipped off directly after dinner for one of his solitary rambles, and could not be found when the chaise started from home; consequently he was not there. Huldah was sitting near her aunt, and nodded and smiled to the Flemmings in the face of the congregation, who fluttered with indignant surprise at such an infraction of Puritan decorum, to say nothing of the disapprobation they felt at her noticing people who were actually under the ban of public opinion. But Huldah did not observe the sensation she caused, and would not have cared a snap for it if she had.

It was high noon when Wolfert Flemming began to speak; when he finished, the last golden beams of the setting sun shone through the old hemlocks around the windows. Then Father Ray got up, and, in tones whose tremulousness he in vain attempted to control, read to the congregation the formula which severed Wolfert Flemming from all religious communion with them; a most senseless thing, as he had sometime before voluntarily withdrawn himself. But the humiliation which gave him an opportunity to confess and defend the faith, sunk into the smallest insignificance by the side of its results.

When the people all left the meeting-house, some few came up out of very shame and shook hands with Wolfert Flemming, then hurried off as if fearful of contagion—but the others stood aloof, neither speaking or shaking hands, or by even a nod recognizing him, except Huldah Sneathen, who left her father and aunt and marched up before them all, and with a heightened color in her cheeks and a brighter sparkle in her handsome eyes held out her hand to her old friend, who, touched by the act under the circumstances, pressed it in his broad palm and said: "God bless you child." Then she stood chatting with Hope,

Eva and Nicholas, throwing defiant glances to the right and left about her, until Miss Debby, unable to bear it another instant, came up, and grasping her by the arm exclaimed: "Huldy Sneathen, I admire to see you! Ain't you ashamed of yourself! Come 'long, and don't keep your father waiting!"

"I'm coming to spend the afternoon with you and Eva to-morrow, Hope," said Huldah, in her old familiar tones. "Good-by all." Then she turned to Miss Debby, and in hearing of every one said: "I declare! I thought the bears had me! You ought to be ashamed to give me such a scare, Debórah!"

To be called Debórah, with the accent upon the o as was the fashion in those days, always stirred up the wrath of this severe maiden; but on this occasion the allusion to the bears and the Debórah together were overpowering, and rendered her quite speechless.

CHAPTER XVII.

JOHN WILDE.

John Wilde was at last ready to leave Boston and turn his face homeward. He had been away nearly four weeks, including his journey thither, and it would be almost five before he got back;

for he had a hundred miles to travel with his two heavily loaded wagons, over roads which in some places for a stretch of miles were worse than the famed corduroy roads of the South, and in others amounted to nothing better than old Indian trails, up hill and down, through marshes and over disintegrated rocks which seemed to have been dropped at random from the clouds, or were the debris—as some gravely assert—of glaciers long since melted. But John Wilde gave himself no trouble about the difficulties of the route except to get over them the best way he could, nor puzzled his brain about the natural phenomena that originated them ; he was far too happy and too full of bright anticipations of the future to let himself be disturbed by such trifles ; and, as far as he could see, there was not a shadow to darken the aureole that crowned it. He was not a man given to building castles in Spain ; but he often found himself, as the sturdy team crept slowly along dragging the great creaking wagons loaded with his household goods, thinking of how his home would look when Hope Flemming —soon to be his wife—brightened and consecrated it with her presence. He wondered how she would like his purchases, and in which rooms she would place this or that piece of furniture, certain that however she arranged them they would bear the impress of her good taste. He knew how good, without pretence, she was; how pure and true, without dissimulation; how thoroughly domestic and womanly in her habits; how thrifty in all her ways; and he longed for the hour when he could look on her grave beautiful face again, and watch the brightening of her eyes and the soft blushes mantling her cheeks as he discussed their future plans and talked over his purchases together. Sometimes a lurch of the wagon aroused him from his pleasant dreams; sometimes a sudden halt of the tired horses interrupted them; sometimes they melted into the music of the bells upon the horses; sometimes they were rudely broken upon by the unexpected bursting of a mountain storm, which threatened, while it lasted, to sweep him and his dreams and household treasures away together. And he felt truly and happily thankful to find, after the flurry was over, that everything was safe; for he was very proud of his purchases, knowing that Hope would like them—he knew her tastes so well. The real mahogany sofa and work-stand; the gilded cane-seat chairs; the large round centre-table, standing on carved claws tipped with brass, upon which she would arrange the choice books he had bought her; the handsome cherrywood furniture for the bedrooms; the green carpet covered with roses; the crimson carpet covered with garlands of oak leaves; the blue carpet covered with

white daisies ; the beautiful pieces of furniture ;
chintz—real French ; tne neat gold-banded china ;
the new bright kitchenware ; and, above all, a gilt
oval-framed mirror for the best room ! How could
Hope fail to admire them, and give credit to his
good taste ? It was a rare thing in those days for
a young bride, up there in the hill country to go to
housekeeping in such nice style, but then Hope, he
thought, was without her equal, and must have
suitable surroundings. John Wilde spent nearly
eight hundred dollars in Boston, but if it had been
five thousand he would have thought it scarcely
worthy of one so fair, so good and beautiful. Then
he went on dreaming of the time when her home
should be the stateliest and most elegant in all
New Hampshire ; and, when, about middle life,
when his hair would be touched with white, and
fair sons and daughters gathered about him and
their beautiful mother, he would go to Congress,
and finally take his seat in the National Senate !
Then he thought of Hope presiding over the refined
and cultivated society of the metropolis—for there
really was in those days a refined and cultivated
society there—and gracing with sweet dignity the
high position he had won for her—when the wagon
wheels slipped into a gully, and brought John Wilde
down from his seat upon the flanks of his horses,
dispersing his day dreams, and giving him no end

of actual trouble in getting things to rights once more. So we see that the man had ambition too ; but it was for her. It is astonishing what capacity there is in the mind of these quiet practical people, who apparently don't know the difference between a rose and a thistle, for castle building ! and how happy they are in the beautiful structures sprung into existence by virtue of rubbing the lamp they carry about, hidden in their bosom ! I don't say that this sort of people originate their fair imaginations in idle day-dreaming. Far from it. They must have, as John Wilde had, a real substantial foundation, and fair outlooks to build upon ; then nothing seems impossible to their fancy, nothing too high or noble for their aspirations.

John Wilde was a happy man the day he caught sight of the old gables and high chimney-tops of home. He whistled the old tunes that he and Hope had learned together in singing class ; he looked over his broad rich acres of farm and woodland, beautified by cascade and mountain slope, and his eyes brightened at the thought of endowing her with these and all other of his worldly goods ; if he had been master of a world he would have thought it worth nothing unshared by her !

Mrs. Wilde heard the wagon bells far off, winding around the moutain and crossing the little valley nestling between the hills, and she knew that John was nearing home; that he was coming straight under a cloud to meet a trial such as he had never dreamed of; and she had not the heart to go out to welcome him, for she knew that what she had to tell him would shake his brave, honest heart to its depths. He feared that she was sick, when he did not see her standing as usual on the vine-clad porch, waving her handkerchief to him, as she always did when he came home from a journey; but his uneasiness merged into something like anger, when he got in and found her quietly moving around, setting the tea-table! He knew that she must have heard the bells, and wondered why she did not meet him as she had always done ever since he was a boy; then he noticed a restraint and reticence in her manner, which altogether made his welcome-home the coldest he had ever experienced. It was like the first heavy rain-drop of a coming storm, before the blue sky and sunshine are obscured; and it fell with a sudden chill into the warm, loving nature of the man. But he had enough to do outside; so, instead of staying there sulking, he left Mrs. Wilde still pottering about the table, her heart so full that she was ready on the slightest provocation to burst out crying, and went to assist the men in unloading his treasures from the wagons, for, mark you, these were things to be handled with the greatest care, that *she*

might receive them without "scratch or scaur.
After stowing them away carefully—as you may
believe—in the new part of the house, where he
and Hope were to live, which was full of the clean
pure smell of whitewash and fresh paint, and
where not a speck of dirt or litter was to be seen ;
he locked the door and went back to the sitting-
room, the old sitting-room with its low blue ceiling
and black-walnut chair-boarding, which he remembered from his earliest boyhood, and which he had
made over with all the old portion of the house to
his mother, that she might still be mistress there ;
and where, as she said, " she would not be turned
out of the old tracks she had been walking in for
nearly forty years;" adding : " It is better, John,
for young married folks to live alone, and get used
to one another without anybody meddling. I had a
hard time with my mother-in-law and other step-
kin, who came nigh breaking up my happiness and
heart together; and I determined then never to
live with you and your wife, if I could help it; and
I won't, for human nature is human nature, just as
certain as twice one makes two ; and we mightn't
understand each other ; then, where would *you* be ?"

Mrs. Wilde was sitting at the head of the table,
ready to pour out his coffee, when he came in.

"I am glad to have you home again, John," said
Mrs. Wilde, who had a pale, scared look in her face.

"Are you sick, mother?" he asked, looking fix-edly at her.

"No, indeed. What put that into your head? I am never sick."

"Well, I don't know. It seems like there's something the matter. You never met me like this before. Surely, surely, mother, the thought of my wife is not getting disagreeable to you. I have heard of such jealousies!"

"Make your mind easy on that score, John. Should Hope Flemming ever be your wife, there'll be no jealousies between us, depend upon that."

"Should Hope Flemming ever be my wife! What nonsense! when we are to be married in two weeks! I'd like to know what you mean, mother? There seems to be something of a mystery," he said, feeling scared as he went on. "Is Hope well? Is there anything the matter at Elder Flemmings'?"

"Finish your supper, John, and we'll have a talk," said Mrs. Wilde, stirring her tea, and look-ing down into her cup. She would have burst out crying if she had met his eyes.

"Are they all well down there?" he asked, sternly.

"Perfectly well," she answered; "but eat your supper, my boy; there, try a muffin, and eat some of that custard pie. Do, John, try and eat your supper."

"Try and eat!" It is the way with some people to think that eating is a panacea for all troubles, and that others who are stricken by griefs and trials, which almost crush them, can be materially relieved by "a nice hot cup of tea," a "delicious broiled chicken," or "some of the nicest preserves, now, you ever tasted;" and urge their pleasant remedies persistently upon them, until, driven to desperation, they gulp down the hot tea, choke themselves with muffins or broiled chicken, as the case may be, and swallow the preserves, altogether careless whether they are honey or gall, just to rid themselves of well-meant importunities and thereby add the horrors of indigestion to the sum of their sorrows.

But John Wilde was made of sterner stuff; so he pushed his plate and cup back, saying he had finished his supper; then reverently returning thanks for blessings which it was not the fault of Providence that he had rejected, he got up and told his mother that he was going to saddle his horse and ride down to Elder Flemming's to see what all this was about."

Then she bade him stay; and, taking his hand tenderly in hers, she led him to the sofa and told him all that had happened at the Old Homestead while he was away. Elder Flemming—no longer Elder—had become a regular out and out Papist,

and had been turned out of meeting; and Eva and
Hope—yes, Hope too—professed openly the same
idolatrous creed! All of them, except Mrs. Flemming; who was much pitied by every one, but who
kept very stiff and silent about her troubles; and
Reuben—he stuck by his mother. But Nicholas,
he had told Father Ray right out that "the fact of
such a good man as his father becoming a Catholic
convinced *him* that the Catholic faith had something in it that was at least worth inquiry; and he
intended reading and examining into it from beginning to end; and if it come up to his ideas of
what religion should be, he would go with them at
the risk of everything. It was the first religion he
had heard of," he said, "that cost a man anything,
and that a man was ready to lose all for; therefore
he thought it must be something more than singing and praying and preaching once a week."
"He said all that, John, to Father Ray, and Father
Ray is so cut up by it all that he looks ten years
older. You know he thought the sun rose and set
in the Flemmings. Then Deacon Sneathen
wouldn't renew the partnership with Elder Flemming, and they say has broken off the match between Nicholas and Huldy!"

Here was a batch of trouble; for John Wilde
was a conscientious Puritan, serving God according to his lights, and believing himself to be walk-

ing in the laws of the gospel, and it was apparent
to him at once that unless Hope could be reclaimed
from these Popish errors there was much unhappiness in store for them. How could he marry a
Papist! It seemed better to him to marry a
pagan, who might in the end become converted!
But a Papist! a brood of papistical children!—a
house divided against itself! It was a great blow
to the young man. His mother said all this to
him too, repeating his own unuttered thoughts,
and told him that Father Ray and his friends had
expressed the same opinions. He was in great
distress, but he had not seen Hope herself. It was
too late to go down to the lake now, but he would
go early after breakfast the next morning. It had
all come upon him like an earthquake, tumbling
down the fair fabric of his life about his ears with
a crash. It was almost more than the man could
bear. His mother heard him walking his floor all
night; and when, towards daylight, not being able
to bear these signs of his distress any longer, she
went in to him to try and comfort him, he laid
his tired, aching head upon her shoulder, and,
completely unmanned, sobbed like a whipped
child.

"Don't cry, John," said Mrs. Wilde, almost
blinded by her own tears; "may be Hope won't,
after all. You go and have a good, long talk over

it with her, and I guess she'll give it up when she finds there's danger of losing you."

"Not if she thinks it right, mother. You don't know Hope Flemming. She's like her father. She'd burn at the stake sooner than give up a principle she thought right," he answered.

"The Flemmings are all alike, that's a fact," said Mrs. Wilde. "If they once take up a thing, and believe it to be the right thing, you might as well attempt to move the Sandwich Mountains into Lake Winnipiseogee as to expect to change them. But, John, trust in the Lord! His arm is strong; have faith in Him and He will not fail you in your hour of need. I don't want to believe that, after all, it will come to pass that you and Hope Flemming will not be man and wife! I tell you, John, I've shed many a bitter tear since all this trouble came about; and when I heard the wagon bells tinkling 'way off there on the mountain, and knew you were coming, I felt like running away to hide myself, I dreaded so much having to tell you sorrowful news. It's hard on me too, for I've been counting so surely on ending my days here with you and Hope, and the children God might see fit to send you. But lay down awhile, honey! It won't ease your mind, but it'll rest your body. It must be near daybreak, for all it's so black out; and don't forget, John, that the very darkest hour of the night is that just before dawn." And the good woman drew his head to her bosom as she stood beside him, he sitting on the bedside, and pressed her wet cheek down among his tangled brown curls, with a prayer in her inmost soul that God in His mercy would pity her child and avert from him this great trial of his life; which meant, from their stand-point, a desire that Hope Flemming would cast aside the errors in which she was entangled, otherwise it was clear to both of them that the marriage must be broken off.

But the human heart is prone to seek even in the depths of misery for the sweet solace of hope; and John Wilde, like a drowning man grasping at floating seaweed, at last began to lay hold of the possibility that things were not quite as bad as they had just appeared. He began to take into consideration the spirit of exaggeration which always prevails in small communities, to which their own neighborhood formed no exception; and to make allowance for the bitter feelings among his sect against Romanism; also for the stale fact that as gossip travels its dimensions as surely increase in substance and bulk, as a snowball does that is rolled in the snow. Anything better than giving up Hope. He couldn't stand that. It is strange that it never once occurred to him that Hope of her own free will might reject him because he did not believe as

she did ; that she, on her part, might not be willing
to compromise her happiness—as well as he—
knowing how widely their beliefs differed.

The next morning early he drove down to the
Old Homestead, taking with him some little presents
he had brought for Hope's acceptance.

The Flemmings were all glad to see him, and the
welcome they gave him differed in no wise from
the cordial welcome of other days ; there was no
change outwardly that he could see, and yet there
was an indefinable something, originating possibly
in his having heard all that he had and in the unpleasant position it had placed him in, which made
him feel as if a transparent but impenetrable mist
had risen between him and them. Then, little by
little, he began to notice things which to a casual
observer would not have been in the least apparent.
He saw that Hope's cheek had lost some of its
roundness and bloom : and that her eyes, as they
met his now and then in the old frank way, wore u
grave and somewhat sad expression ; and he listened in vain for the low sweet laughter which
always sounded to him like the warbling of a bird.
Mrs. Flemming's face wore a look of care, which he
noticed more particurly when she was not speaking ; she had lost flesh and color, and there was a
heavy troubled look in her large black eyes once so
full of life and spirit ! But she was very glad to

see John Wilde, and in her heart hailed him as an ally who would give her help in these religious difficulties, which, like the waves of a rising flood, were sweeping her near and dear ones away from her to certain destruction. Wolfert Flemming and Eva were more cheerful than he had ever seen them; and it was a strange sort of cheerfulness, so full was it of serenity, and so far above all levity, yet so genial and kind, that when they asked him about his journey to Boston and back, and he became interested in describing the wonders of the city and some of the perils of the road, he almost forgot his troubles; for the conversation became general, and it seemed like the old times again. But presently the family one after another went away to their various occupations, leaving him alone with Hope, and he realized his position with such a sick feeling at his heart that it almost blinded him. He placed the presents he had brought her—a pearl brooch and a plain heavy gold ring—in her hands. She opened the morocco case and looked at them, as if admiring them, then laid it quietly on the workstand beside her without saying a word.

"I thought perhaps you would like them, Hope!" he said, mortified at her indifference.

"They are beautiful," she answered, "and I thank you for thinking of me." Then they were both silent; she stitching away on a linen wrist band for her father—he watching her, full of a great love and sorrow.

"I have heard strange news since I came home!" he said at last, unable to bear the strain of uncertainty any longer.

"I suppose so. You mean my father's conversion to the Catholic Church?" she answered.

"Aye, and of all others of your household, yourself included, Hope," he said.

"It is true. I am also a Catholic for life and death, John," she replied, in firm low tones.

"How in God's name did it all happen? Tell me, Hope! It is the most remarkable thing I ever heard of—and, to me, the most painful," he exclaimed.

And Hope told him how it had all come to pass, giving him reasons, as she went on, for the faith that was in her. Nor did she falter, at a loss for words, or arguments, or proofs; simply and truly, almost eloquently, she made her reasons for becoming a Catholic clear to his mind, but not to his faith. Then he discussed the whole matter with her; he argued and pleaded, and appealed to her by the love which had grown up between them, and by the regard she ought to feel for his happiness, to abandon the errors and idolatries into which she had been led, and return to the religion taught by the gospel; almost his wife as she was, he had a right, for the sake of their future, to ask this of her. But so far from yielding in the slightest degree to anything he said, she told him plainly, while her eyes kindled, and her cheeks, a little while ago so pale, glowed: "That no earthly consideration or motive could change her conviction of the truth of the Catholic religion; and that so far from relapsing into the darkness and errors which she had just abandoned, she would not rest satisfied until her union with the Catholic Church was consummated by a reception of its Sacraments. "For this," she added, "I am ready to give up all things, even you, John, unless God by His grace converts you to this holy and true faith."

"I have no thought of changing, Hope. God forbid. I am satisfied with what the gospel and the Westminster Catechism teach. Least of all could I become a Papist. I could not believe all the nonsensical idolatrous things that Papists believe, to save my life," he said in low husky tones.

"The Catholic faith is not nonsensical or idolatrous, as you would find if you would take the trouble to inform yourself. Promise me, at least, to read a book which I will lend you. Or come down of evenings and let us read it together," she said pityingly.

"I will do that, Hope," said the poor fellow, "but I couldn't believe anything more than I do, or in any other way, if I was to try from now until doomsday."

"Try, John; try for your soul's sake—and for the sake of our happiness," she said, in a low voice. "You know how impossible it will be for us to marry, entertaining religious beliefs so widely differing. The case seems, no doubt, peculiarly trying; but this newly-found faith is so essential to my salvation, and so suited to all the demands of my reason and soul, that I repeat there is no earthly motive or power that could induce me to relinquish it. Knowing this, the best that I can do is to implore you to examine this holy faith, which you will find based and founded and built up on the Bible, and adopt its creed if you can. In that case we can be happy together; otherwise we must become as strangers to each other."

"It is a hard, bitter case," said John Wilde, bringing his clenched hand heavily down on his knee; "and it seems to me that you take it coolly, Hope, and think no more of wrecking my happiness than you would to sweep away a cobweb."

"I cannot tell you," she said, her voice tremulous with emotion. "I cannot tell you all the extent of this trial to me, or give you an idea of its bitterness. Remember, John, that if you have to lose something, I also sacrifice somewhat that was dear to me; but not to gain the whole world would

I consent to lose my soul, or even place it in peril."

"Hope," he said at last, raising his head from his hand, "you have never earnestly sought conversion; if you had, you had never fallen into this delusion and error. Lay aside these novelties, at least for a season, and pray to be truly converted!"

"I do not and never have believed in that sudden, instantaneous, extatic change of soul and nature which you call conversion, and which has always seemed such an unutterable state that I could never think of otherwise than as a delusion," she replied. "It seems to me that conversion is a deliberate response of the will to the grace of God, placing itself under subjection to His will to work out the soul's salvation. Religion is a warfare, not a duel. It is a science which we must learn with simplicity and humility, from its very rudiments, grace assisting our will. First the seed, then the plant, then the flower—after all, the fruit. The result is not the effect of a sudden transformation, but gradual progression, 'and if there are examples of men regenerated by a single experience, they are so rare as only to prove the general rule of patient progression.' I feel that having found the right path, which is essential, that I can only advance a step at a time, stumbling and often falling back at that, that I must be engaged in an incessant warfare with my own nature as I go; that I must labor and work out my salvation and be influenced and governed in every motive and act of my life by the thought of the end for which, through the merits of Jesus Christ, I strive. This is what the Catholic religion and my own reason teaches me about conversion."

"Could you not do all that in the religion you have abandoned?" he asked.

"No, John. To be a Christian I must feel sure that I am running not against, but according to the divine law. I must be satisfied that the Church to which I belong has a divine origin and faith, and is not divided against herself; but is one, holy, true and immutable—having one Lord, one Faith, and one Baptism. Everything must be clear to my faith and to my reason. All this I have found in the Catholic religion. What its other consolations are, I do not know experimentally, not having had the happiness to receive the Sacraments."

"Hope, I see that you are irretrievably joined to your errors. My God! it is a bitter trial to me; after all these years of looking forward to the time when you would be my wife to find everything broken up like a sudden shipwreck!" he exclaimed.

"Don't you see, John," she said, laying her hand upon his arm, "that if I were even willing to peril my faith and happiness by marrying you—

which I am not—how impossible it would be for you, holding the opinions that you do, to marry a Catholic?"

"It is true, Hope. I could not marry a Catholic. And here we are, just on the eve of our marriage, with a gulf as wide and as deep as death suddenly sprung between us. It is more than I can stand!"

"The grace of God bridges over deeper and wider gulfs than this," she said in low tones, while her eyes filled with tears that she could not keep back.

John Wilde got up and walked to and fro the room. The man's anguish was very deep, the woman's equally so, the difference being that hers was consecrated by a sublime spirit of sacrifice for the love of God, while his was the result of error and prejudice, the offshoot of old sectarian hate blended with a fear of the judgments of men.

"I can't go away like this, Hope," he said at last. "I will at least come and read that book with you, and see what shadow of excuse you have for your unaccountable change. I can do no more."

"I have nothing else to offer, John. A religious change except from the very highest and best of motives, is like a house built upon the sands, or like a flower that springeth up in a night to wither at noontide. I have too great faith in your integrity of mind to believe that even for my sake you would profess a creed which you could not sincerely believe."

"No, not for your dear sake, Hope. But some arrangement, some little yielding on both sides, may be possible!" he said standing before her.

"Not on mine," she said quickly, while a sudden paleness which overspread her face, succeeded by a crimson flushing, showed how the crucial tests were hurting her nature. "I can yield nothing, not to the smallest iota of my faith, either of dogma, precept, doctrine, or practice. Do not hope for that."

"I hope for nothing now," he said wearily, as he lingered near her. Then pointing to the brooch and ring which lay upon her work-stand glistening in the sunshine, he added : "Keep these at least, for my sake ;" and wringing her hand, almost crushing it in the grasp of his, he went away, but came back a moment after to tell her that he would come again the following evening to read with her.

CHAPTER XVIII.

PATRICK M'CUE AND HIS LETTERS.

THE foreign mail was in—an event of not very freqent occurrence forty years ago, as some will remember—and the Boston post-office was besieged by an expectant crowd which extended from the delivery-window clear out to the sidewalk, all jostling and shouldering each other in their eagerness to get nearer and be the first to receive the letters they hoped for. There were faces there full of expectation—there were faces full of anxiety : some full of dread—others beaming with hope ; the occasion formed a crisis in the moral life of many of them, out of which their real natures looked without conventional mask or veil, and it was a study to watch the eager countenances of them, every emotion suddenly intensified, every eye more wistful as the delivery-window was thrown open and the business of the day commenced. There were men who had sent ships loaded with priceless cargoes to sea, months and months ago, who had had no tidings from them—ships which had probably gone down in some of the terrific storms which had swept the world's waters that winter of tempest and wreck— and now they stood waiting, hoping against hope, for tidings which would either add to their prosperity or cripple their fortunes for years to come. There were others who had sent rich ventures to newly opened foreign ports, who knew that their ships had been spoken at sea, and knew that they were homeward bound with stores of " golden fleece ;" but weeks stretching into months had passed since they were due, and no word had come up from the "deep" concerning them. They also hoped to hear news of their argosies; for if they had foun-dered and sunk it meant nothing more or less than utter ruin to them. There were others waiting— whose near and dear ones were travelling abroad, bearing with them in search of health the fading, perishing darling of the household—who now stood with lips firmly compressed, and bated breath, until the crowd thinned out a little, and almost thankful for the delay before they called for the letter so fraught with joy or dole to them ; for the last one that came told of increased pallor and fee-bleness, of quickened breath, and cheeks that were growing thinner and whiter every day. There were hard-faced, keen-eyed stock and money-brokers, eager for news from the Bourse and London Ex-change ; here were merchant-princes who had branches of their business in Paris, in London, in Bremen, in Canton, and the Brazils, jostling against editors impatient for their foreign budget; there were women whose eyes were bright with the hope of hearing good news from distant relatives, friends, husbands, brothers. Mixed up with them all were the poor emigrants mostly from Ireland and Ger-many, men and women almost dead with home-sickness and hungering for letters from over the sea as they had never hungered for food.

But in this motley crowd there was only one with

whom we have to do; a tall, round-shouldered man with grizzly red hair and beard, who was plainly dressed in gray frieze and held a square basket upon his arm filled with packages, a basket which provoked many a sharp and muttered oath from those with whose ribs its corners came in contact. But the man could not help it; he was jammed in the very thick of the crowd, and although he was better than half a head taller than any there, it gave him no advantage whatever, unless looking like a lighthouse amidst that surging sea of faces could be called one. But he was a good-humored genius, and now and then his jokes, full of pungency, and flavored with a generous brogue, created roars of laughter around him. At last, by dint of watching his opportunity and edging his way an inch at a time, he got to the window, and asked the tired, perspiring clerk if there was a letter for him.

" Name?" growled the clerk.

" Misthress Noona McCue, my own mother, God bless her, at Clanmoosie, County Meath, Ireland," answered the man.

"Is the letter *for* your mother?"

" No, faith! the letter I'm expecting is from the dear ould soul; and I shall be sorely disappinted not to get it!" replied the man, taking off his hat to mop his face.

"And what in the d——, what's your name, man?" shouted the exasperated clerk.

"Patrick McCue's my name, and I'm not ashamed to own it!"

"Well then, here's a letter for you, Patrick McCue; and next time you come to inquire for a letter, tell a fellow who it is to, not who it is from!" said the clerk, handing him a letter, but not the one he expected, as he afterwards found out. He could not get out, for the stream of people coming in was steadily increasing; so, literally wedging himself back in an angle of the wall, and thrusting his basket down between his feet, he, all impatient to hear from the "old mother at home," tore open the letter and run his eye over the strange hand-writing, then read its contents. Wonder and joy struggled together in his homely countenance as he read; then "Glory be to God and the Blessed Virgin" burst from his lips, and snatching up his basket, which he hoisted to the top of his head that he might get through the crowd more quickly, while he held his letter like some sacred trophy to his breast, he forced his way towards the door.

"Hilloa there!" shouted the clerk; "here's another letter for Patrick McCue. From Ireland."

"That's from the mother of me—God bless her. Take good care of it, your honor, I'll be round for it this evening!" he shouted back. "Converted!!

By this and by that! it's aiqual to the conversion of St. Paul: may he be promoted in glory. Up there, away amongst the icebergs and snow, with no more idea of the holy Catholic Faith than cannibals, to be converted, and be after writin' to me to get them Catholic books! It bates Bannagher!

And they hatin' the sight of the cross too, and calling me names, and talking to me as if I had just come up through the earth from the middle of Chiny and had never heard of Christianity in my life. Faith, and it'll do me good to send them books." Patrick McCue was thinking aloud; and everybody around him heard what he said, and thought him crazy, for his words sounded incoherent and without sense to them, and they moved as well as they could out of his way, by which means he soon reached the door.

Of course you remember our old acquaintance, the pedler? It was really he, and the letter which so excited him was the one written to him some weeks before by Wolfert Flemming. The news it contained almost overpowered him; it seemed nothing short of miraculous. He had heard nothing of the Flemmings since he left their house months ago, and although he had never ceased praying for their conversion, the recollection of their hospitality and kindness was always embittered by the thought of their deeply-rooted hos-

tility to his Holy Faith, and their undisguised contempt for the Cross and the Pope. And now to
get a letter from the grave, stern Puritan himself,
telling him that "he was converted to the Catholic
Faith, and there was good hope for thinking his
entire household would before long follow his example." "Why," said Patrick McCue afterwards,
"it gave me a chill; and you might have knocked
me down with a feather, the surprise of it made
me so wake." But Patrick happily did not fall
over, but managed to keep his feet and hold on to
his basket beside, until he finally got clear of the
post-office building and found himself standing in
the street. Here he rested for a moment to draw in
a few breaths of the cold wholesome air, then hurried away and did not stop until he came to a
church, the door of which being open, he marched
reverently up the empty aisle towards the rich altar,
and prostrating himself before the Blessed Sacrament, offered with simple and fervent devotion his
thanks to Almighty God for the conversion of his
benefactors. Then rising he crossed over to a lat-
eral altar, the altar of the Blessed Virgin, where
he again knelt, and like a child thanking its mother
for some unexpected happinesss, poured out his
gratitude to her who had obtained the great boon
of Faith for those for whom he had been so long
praying. When he left the church there were

great drops glistening on his grizzly beard which looked strangely like tears!

"Thanks be to God!" said Patrick McCue, standing at the church door, still holding his hat in his hand and looking undecidedly up and down the street; "it is the wondherfullest thing, out an' out, I ever came across, and I'm most at my wits' end." Then he fell to thinking, and presently exclaimed, with a radiant countenance: "Now I've got it, surely! I'll go sthraight with my dilemma to the Bishop—may he be promoted forever—and get the favor of him to put down a list of the right kind of books, rale convincin', tunderin' books, that'll knock the last bits of heresy that's left in thim to smithereens." And full of a zeal and joy which no language on earth can describe, for it belonged to the realms of the soul, Patrick McCue, still lugging his basket and holding the unfolded letter to his breast, went to the Bishop's house.

It was not a "palace," not even a "mansion;" it could scarcely be dignified with the title of "residence;" it was simply a plain old two-story brick house, not far from the cathedral, whose door-bell the poor and humble were not afraid to pull, whose threshold the sorrowful and poverty-stricken ones of his flock could cross without dread of pampered servants or worldly grandeurs, or the fear of a rebuff from the prelate, who was indeed their good

Shepherd and faithful friend. The door of the dingy little library, which was filled with ancient and modern lore on abstruse questions in theology and philosophy, and many a treatise worth its weight in gold even according to worldly valuation, rich in volumes collected here and there from the old monasteries of Europe and Asia, some written in languages almost forgotten, besides some rare relics of early Christian literature—that door ever opened with Christianly welcome, admitted the lowly as well as the great, the sinner as well as the saint; and to each one the good Bishop listened patiently and sympathizingly; and however great the needs of those who came to him for counsel, however hopeless those who came hither for aid, none ever turned from his presence without consolation.

"Who is it, Dan?" he would say, looking up perhaps from his polyglot Bible, or perhaps from some of the deep sentences of Thomas Aquinas. "Who is it?"

"And it's only a poor beggar-woman and a boy, Bishop; hadn't I bether tell her how busy ye are?" returned Dan.

"Tell her to come in, poor soul; then fetch some coals in, and if I ring my bell bring in some bread and meat," replied the Bishop, always amused at Dan's tricks to secure him an hour's quiet and at the same time save the household expenses.

"Faith! I don't know how your Grace'll ever get through them hieroglyphics if everybody—Tom, Dick and Harry—'s to come upon you whinever they like to," Dan would mutter. "But it's no use. I'll take her and her brats in; she'll make about the twentieth since the Bishop's Mass; all comin', comin', to impose upon the soft heart of him, and keepin' him stript of money, and wearing old clothes not fit for a scarecrow. An' I'll get the bread and mate ready, for that bell's sure to ring."

This was the Bishop's way, and this was also the way of his old *major-domo*, Dan.

Patrick McCue rang the door-bell and was admitted without delay to the Bishop's presence, his face beaming with delight as he knelt to get his blessing and kiss the consecrated ring upon the good prelate's finger.

"I am glad to see you, my man; but won't you sit down?" said the Bishop.

"Thanks to your lordship," answered Patrick McCue; "an' if you'll kindly allow me to stand I think I can get through what I've come about better nor if I was sitting."

"Very good, my friend; but I think if you'll notice what a short neck I have, and consider that it will be apt to give me a crick in it if I sit here looking up at you—why, man, you must be descended from the Kerry giants—you will take that

chair beside you, just for the comfort of your poor
Bishop," said the Bishop.

"Faith, your Grace, if it would comfort ye I'd
go and sit upon the top of the cathedral," replied
Patrick, dropping into the chair, confused and em-
barrassed, and blushing all over his face and head.

The good Bishop laughed; he had gained his
point; then he said: "Now—your name?"

"McCue, your Grace!"

"Now, McCue, I am glad to see you, and you
have made me very comfortable by sitting down
when you are bid; tell me what I can do for you?"

Then Patrick McCue handed Wolfert Flemming's
letter to the Bishop, and with many digressions to
the right and to the left told him about the Flemmings and all that had happened up there in the
winter. The Bishop listened patiently, picking out
the kernel of the nut Patrick was so awkwardly
cracking, until he fully understood the pith of the
matter; and, deeply interested, he—as soon as
McCue finished his narrative—opened the letter
and read it from beginning to end. Then he said:

"This is good news, excellent news, McCue.
What do you wish me to do?"

"Why, don't you see, your Grace, that being an
ignoramus, with nothing to boast of except my
Faith and my country, I thought you'd know better
about the books—" stammered Patrick.

" I see now. You wish me to make a list of the proper books for you ?"

" Just so, your Grace ; I mightn't hit upon the right ones if I set about it myself."

" You made a very good hit in leaving ' Milner's End of Controversy' with your Puritan friends. But I will of course write a list for you. You did right to come to me ; it was a wise thought, my child. God has honored you greatly in allowing you as it were to become the instrument of the salvation of these souls. Give Him thanks. I will not forget them, or you, in offering the Holy Sacrifice." And the Bishop dipped his pen into his inkstand and wrote rapidly the titles of several books, and handed the list to Patrick McCue, who had sat watching him, and wishing that he might throw himself down and kiss the floor that the good man's feet rested on, his great, tender Irish heart was so full and overflowing with those filial sentiments of reverence and affection towards his spiritual superior so well understood among Catholics.

" Is there anything else I can do for you, my child ?"

Yes. There was something on Patrick's mind yet, and waxing a little bold under the gracious and simple kindness of the Bishop's manner, he determined to find out, if he could, what had been a mystery and puzzle to him ever since he had heard it; and he began: "There is, if your Grace will be so good—. But I'm thankful to see your lordship in such health; may it continue."

"Thank you, Patrick; but you know that 'the race is not always to the swift,' nor the highest health to the fat," said the Bishop, laughing. "Now I'll tell you a secret. I have not seen my own feet for five years, but for all that I have my aches and pains like the rest of the world."

"It must be a great incumbrance to your Grace, so much flesh; and this"—said the cunning Patrick —"brings to my remimbrance something I'd be glad to be insensed* about, if your reverence won't take the asking of it for impidince."

"Not at all, not at all, Patrick," replied the Bishop, whose genial nature delighted in a little innocent recreation. "Ask whatever you please."

"Well, thin," said McCue, assuming a most confidential attitude, while he screwed his courage up to the highest point, "I've thought many a time, your Grace, seein' how fleshy you are, how in the name of the world ye ever got up that long laddher, some time ago, to the loft where the two men were dyin' with ship fever?"

The Bishop burst out laughing. He remembered it all: his fright as he clambered up the

* Made sensible of.

steep creaking ladder, wondering after he got up how he should get down; and he remembered the two souls saved by his ministrations, whose pressing needs had made all perils to his own life or limb sink into insignificance. "Upon my word, Patrick," he said, "I would tell you if I could; but it has always been a mystery to me how I did get up there, and a greater one how I got down—the ladder creaked and swayed with my weight in such a way!"

"And it is a wondher, your grace, that it didn't smash up with the weight of ye," answered McCue, naively. "But that was nothing, your reverence, to the way you got down into the ould granite quarry to hear the confession of the man who kilt himself and broke every bone in the skin of him? I'd be thankful to know the way you reached him!"

"Oh! well, well, my man! there were some of your brave countrymen there, who with the assistance of Almighty God helped me to do His work. It was a tough job though, getting down to the poor mangled fellow, who died in my arms just after receiving the Holy Viaticum; and I was a little out of breath when I got back 'out of the depths' of the quarry," said the Bishop.

"And no wondher—God reward your lordship for your charity. It's a meracle altogether, cou-

siderin' the weight of you, how you got out of it
alive. And, faith, I shouldn't be surprised if your
grace could walk on the tight-rope itself if some
poor soul at the other end of it should call for
your assistance !"

"God forbid such a thing happening!" said the
good Bishop, diverted beyond measure at the genuine simplicity of the man. "I should have to try,
you know, at all risks, Patrick."

"The Lord save us! and deliver your reverence
from all such divilthry as that. But I must be
goin'," said Patrick gravely, as he took his hat
from under the chair, uncoiled his long legs and
picked up his basket, standing before the good
Bishop, who said: "I should like to learn something more of these converts, McCue; whenever
you hear from them, come and let me know; and
don't forget hereafter to call me what all my good
children in Boston do, 'Father Ben.' I like that
above all. God bless you, my child." And the
Bishop gave him his blessing as he knelt before
him, then he went his ways feeling happier and
more elated than he had ever been in his whole
life.

Without going home to rest, Patrick McCue
trudged on a mile farther with his heavy basket to
the then only Catholic bookstore in Boston, and,
presenting the list written by the Bishop, was

fortunate in getting all of the books he had recom-
mended. Among them was a "Catechism of the
Council of Trent," "Cochin on the Mass," a Catholic prayer-book, an "Imitation of Christ," and
several others. To these Patrick McCue added of
his own selection, "The Papist Represented and
Misrepresented;" and "The travels of an Irish
Gentleman in Search of a Religion," by his countryman and favorite, Tommy Moore; also a look
on Catholic art, containing illustrations from the
old masters: this was "for Reuben, with Patrick
McCue's best love," written upon the fly-leaf; then
he bought a rosary and prayer-book for Hope, and
a crucifix and prayer-book for Eva, all duly directed on the parcels, and signed "Patrick McCue,
with his respects." Then, feeling still better satisfied with himself, he wended his way back to his
little shop, where he sold wares of every sort and
description, a sort of enlarged pedler's pack, out
of which he was coining honest profits; and then
he packed the books and his presents, along with
the bookseller's receipt and the change left over,
and prolonged his delight by putting twice as
many nails in the top of the box and hammering
upon them just twice as long as was necessary, until finding there was danger of splitting it to pieces
he threw down his hammer and got the black
paint and brush to label it; and his delight was

pleasant to see, as with an indescribable flourish he wrote name and address upon the lid as if every letter meant a blessing. Then when he could do nothing more to it he closed his shop and locking the door, shouldered the box and strode down to the stage-office with it, prouder of his burden than he would have been of a field-marshal's baton. And he gave so many directions and charges about the safety of the box, that the stage-driver, bothered and exasperated, threatened not to take it at all if he "didn't hold his jaw and be off."

Then Patrick gave in, and stood off at a safe distance, watching it with jealous eyes until the stage drove off and was out of sight; then he stuffed his hands into his pockets and went homewards, whistling "The Blackbird" like a fife, and thinking he would be glad to get his dinner, having eaten nothing since six o'clock that morning—and it was then four. "Bedad!" he thought, "but it's a day of days, surely ; and the best part of it is the letter I'll get to-night from the ould mother, God bless her, that's lying waitin' for me at the post-office." And the thought of it so lightened his heart that he scarcely felt the ground under his feet as he hurried along.

CHAPTER XIX.

SORROWS ARE NOT ACCIDENTS.

As he had promised her, John Wilde came almost every evening to read " Milner's End of Controversy" with Hope, and occasionally had long, grave talks with Wolfert Flemming himself on the subject of their new belief, but as yet he had found nothing in it all to make him feel even for a moment willing to abandon his own religious principles for others which seemed to his comprehension, no better. He was, he firmly believed, a converted man, possessed of that inward light against which it was impossible for a true believer to err; " of what use would it be then "—he argued—" to be running after novelties in faith, which already perplex and disturb my mind. Simple gospel doctrines are good enough for me; and I cannot, if I would, go against my conscience, even for the sake of Hope." It is true that the man's mind had become somewhat enlightened, and the great scarecrow which Protestants call " Popery" was quite torn down and demolished in his sight, while he had nearer and better views of the True Faith; indeed, he frankly admitted that the Flemmings had good reasons to show for their change of faith; but the best and only result attained by him was that he

had come to look upon the Catholic religion as a
Christian sect—a great advance for a Puritan of
that day—and could not see why such difficulties
should be raised about the marriage of himself and
Hope. Seeing the daily life of the Flemmings,
and noting their righteous, cheerful way of life, and
how the inward peace of their souls permeated
every act and word and thought—making their religion, without any self-assertion on their part, in-
tegral with their very existence—he could not for
the life of him see the wide gulf that separated
them, and quite lost sight of his dread of all the
unhappiness which would inevitably result from a
union where there was such a wide difference of
religious belief. The more he was with them, the
more consoled he inwardly felt; and finally made
up his mind, if Hope would consent to marry him
then, just to trust to Providence, leaving all religious discussions out of the question, and yielding everything to her except his own individual belief. He told her as much, in good, manly faith,
but she gave no assent to the plan, and the little
she did say quite discouraged him. About this
time the Elders and the Deacons of his sect, led
on by old Father Ray, began to make his time uncomfortable by the way they felt moved to take his
affairs in hand. They rebuked and counseled him
in season and out of season, in private and in pub-

lic; his being so much with the Flemmings was in itself a grave offense, but when it got to be known that he was reading their Popish books and spending hours at a time in religious conversation with the banned ex-Elder, they threatened roundly to turn him out of meeting if he did not speedily mend his ways. Then John Wilde's spirit was up, and he told them plainly that "they might do as they pleased. No earthly consideration could make him a Roman Catholic; but if Hope Flemming would marry him, not all the world should prevent it. He was a staunch believer in the doctrines of the Westminster Catechism and in simple gospel teachings, and saw no prospect now or henceforth of ever having any other belief, and with that they must remain satisfied and not meddle with him or his affairs." They did not judicially meddle with him again, but they did not exactly let him alone; they made him feel in a thousand ingenious ways that he was, as it were, under a ban; their intercourse with him, once so friendly and cordial, became cold and formal; he saw himself actually shunned on certain occasions, and more than twice or thrice he had to sit in the old meeting-house and hear sermons preached at him, prayers prayed at him, and hymns sung at him, until, half beside himself, he was tempted to fling his hat on his head and march out from among

them. But conscious of his own religious integrity, these vexations, while they stung and irritated
him, did not make him waver a hair's-breadth from
his own spiritual standpoint. The hardest trial of
all to the true, tender heart of the man were the
pleadings and tears of his own mother, whose
fears, excited and exaggerated by all the things she
heard from Father Ray, Deacon Sneathen, Miss
Deborah, and others of the like sort, made her almost give up her boy as lost. Then John Wilde
realized something of Job's trials in having his
friends and kinsmen and those of his own house
stirred up against him, treating him like a sinner
and backslider, when he was never more faithful
and firm in his religious belief since his conversion
than at that time. " If I could only believe as the
Flemming's do," he said one day hotly to his
mother, "I'd stand this no longer; but I can't—
I couldn't believe those doctrines to save my life.
I almost wish I could, for the sake of peace and
my own happiness. But for all that, if Hope—
Romanist though she be—will consent, I shall
marry her, come what will." And constant to his
purpose, he went straight down to the " Old Homestead," and asking to see Hope alone, proposed to
her to marry him without any further delay. But
she, who had been thinking long and prayerfully
over the matter, weighing all that was for and

against it in her own clear mind, had come, with
many a sharp pang, to the deliberate conclusion
that it would be best for the happiness of them both
that all should be finally over between them; and
so she told him, her cheeks blanching whiter and
whiter, and her eyes overflowing with tears she
tried in vain to keep back as she spoke.

"You do not mean this, Hope; surely you do
not mean it?" he said, utterly shocked and surprised.

"I mean it; every word of it. Let us part,
John; for from this moment all that has ever been
between us must be over." The effort she made to
speak firmly imparted a sternness to her manner
and a severity to her words which gave the *coup de
grace* to the man's hopes, putting an end to all his
torture of uncertainty and conflict with himself.
Angry and grieved, thinking but little or nothing
of her sacrifice, only knowing how earnestly she
meant whatever she said, he got up to leave her without a friendly word or a clasp of the hand. Standing before her for an instant, his hat crushed in his
hand, he said in a low, harsh tone, almost choked
with emotion: "You have ruined my life, Hope
Flemming, unless God helps me. I have done all
and promised all that lay in the scope of my power
to do or promise, and you have trodden my great
love under foot, and sacrificed me to a fanaticism I

cannot understand." Then, dumb and helpless, sick at heart but strong in the will to do what was right, she did not speak; and he went away. The next that Hope Flemming heard of her lover, he was on his way to visit the far off lands beyond the ocean.

Religion does not avert grief or its sting; it shields us neither from cross or loss, or the cruci- fixions of nature, but it has a sweet distilling balm for the faithful soul who seeks strength and resig- nation in it, leading her through the fiery ordeals unscathed, where her dross and imperfections are consumed, and heals at last the deep wounds of her life which have elevated her to heights near heaven. Sorrows are not accidents; they form the very woof which is woven into the warp of life. They develop the soul's life; and every son of man who would attain the true end of his being must be baptized with fire. "It is," writes one,* "the law of our humanity, as that of Christ, that we be per- fected through suffering; and he who has not dis- cerned the divine sadness of sorrow, and the pro- found meaning which is concealed in pain, has yet to learn what life is. The Cross, manifested as the necessity of the highest life, alone interprets it."

Hope Flemming's heart was sorely tried, as we may imagine; but her new faith, upon whose altar

* Robertson.

she had laid her sacrifice, taught her where to seek
for consolation and help. And the pain of her
trial was neither light or fleeting; it paled her
cheeks, it took the brightness out of her eyes and
the elasticity from her step for many a long day,
leaving the peace of her soul undisturbed by re-
grets, and strengthened by the consciousness of a
pure intention.

Of course this sudden breaking up of Hope's
prospects added much to the cup of Mrs. Flemming's bitterness, and she said words that had
been better left unsaid; unwise, unmotherly words,
that thinking them over, almost made the girl believe that her mother's reason was temporarily unsettled by her troubles. They had all, from the
father down, been very tender with the poor little
mother, bearing all that she said and did with
sweet patience, knowing how honestly she thought
they were wrong and she right, and what good reason—in her own opinion—she had to feel sore and
troubled; in fact, what real trials and cares had
come upon her through their confession of the
Catholic Faith; but, so far, it had not appeared to
soften her; she went about her daily domestic
tasks as she had been doing all her life, never
omitting the slightest minutiæ, and attending with
scrupulous care to the individual comforts and
needs of each one of her household, and ordering

all things with care and neatness ; there was no diminution of any comforts her husband and children and servants had been accustomed to, except that she became rigidly economical in the table expenses, and they missed the old cheerful ring of her voice singing over her work, and her quiet, decisive tones heard here and there and everywhere through the house; she was very silent nowadays, and only answered them in mono-syllables when they tried to get her to talk with them.

None of them had ever known such hard, plain fare in their lives; but the Flemmings were of a strong, healthful race, and did not mind that—none of them except Nicholas, who was growling one day over his dinner when Mrs. Flemming broke out with :

" We are too poor now, Nicholas, to waste things in luxurious living. If people could only be satis-fied without running after newfangled notions, much trouble would be spared in the world. As a man makes his bed so he must lie. You've all turned Papists, and must bear the consequences."

This was more than the little woman had said for a long time, and Nicholas not knowing exactly what answer to make, took a stick, and his knife out of his pocket, and began to whittle, whistling under his breath at the same time. If he had not

finished his dinner he would have fallen to and
tried everything before him; for he dearly loved
his mother, and would have done anything in his
sturdy, awkward way to restore her peace of mind
even for a moment; but he was quite at a loss for
something to say which would not make matters
worse, but could think of nothing, and whittled
and whistled in a low sybilant undertone until the
table was cleared away, and he was left sitting in
the middle of the floor with a little heap of shavings at his feet, which his mother was about sweeping into a dust-pan, stooping over with the veins in
her forehead swollen and full, when he sprang up,
gathered her suddenly in his great arms, kissed
her lips and cheeks, and carried her to her chair,
where he sat her down all amazed and out of
breath at such doings; then, before she could
speak, he had snatched the dust-pan and brush
out of her hands, cleared up every vestige of the
litter he had made, and vanished out of the side
door down the garden path. Mrs. Flemming's
first impulse was to box Nicholas, her next was to
laugh outright; it was all so ridiculous; but she
did neither, and her face settled back into its grim,
rigid lines again, although in her heart she was
warmed and pleased with the rough caressing of
her "bear," as she sometimes in the old days used
to call him.

"It's a comfort that he at least has something to look forward to," thought his mother, looking after him as he disappeared down the garden path; "but it's all owing to Huldah's indifference to gospel truth and her determination to marry him in spite of everything. And Huldah will be very rich when her father dies. The Deacon holds only a life estate in the property, which comes to her from her mother. His control over it is absolute; she can't get a penny of it, if he chooses to keep her out of it now; but she and Nick don't mind waiting, for they'll have it all some day." And these hard, practical thoughts about her son's good prospects came now and then through the darkness that surrounded her, like sunrays through the clouds of a stormy sky, comforting and somewhat consoling the poor little woman.

Mrs. Flemming went to meeting every Sabbath, the chaise driven by Reuben, who dutifully attended public worship with her; she, with her stern, sorrowful face, intent only on the religious exercises that were going on, and trying in this her hour of trial to quench her thirst from cisterns that held no water, and receiving stones instead of bread, for which the hungry soul was starving; Reuben, indifferent to all around him, not caring a straw, in fact, where he went on Sabbath, so that he could go on dreaming out his dream unmo-

lested; and behaving so strangely, standing up
when he should have knelt, kneeling when he
should have sat, and breaking out in shrill falsetto
notes when he should have sung in solemn tune,
that Deacon Sneathen and others declared the boy
was crazy. And his absurd awkwardness to set
things right when a touch of his mother's hand,
or the astonished glance of some one near him, or
the sharp whisper of some indignant Pharisee, re-
called him to himself, did make him appear just a
little flighty; but Reuben was not crazy, and these
were only the symptoms cropping out of the mystery of his life, about which he was dreaming and
thinking all the time.

So it came to pass that while all the rest of the
Flemmings were banned and morally outlawed,
Mrs. Flemming got to be looked upon as a suffering saint, and her old friends and neighbors always
collected around her after meeting to show by their
sympathetic greetings and outspoken speeches
about her heavy trials, and their uncouth attempts
to console, which only probed and tortured instead
of comforting her, that whatever they might feel
towards the rest of her family their friendly interest in her was unchanged. But she received all
of their demonstrations with a stiff reserve which
astonished them, and had even seemed to resent
Father Ray's praying publicly for her as one under

heavy tribulation. She wanted none of their pity; whatever *she* had a right to do and think about her own flesh and blood, she couldn't stand by and see them outlawed, persecuted, and ruined in fortune and estate, and shake hands over it all with those who did it, knowing all the time in her inmost heart that there was not a man among them whose walk before God was so pure and upright as her husband's. It became clear to them all, after awhile, that she neither wanted their sympathy nor adulation, and they began to understand that she came constantly to meeting, not to keep in favor with them, but because she thought it right and consistent for her to do so. But they pitied her none the less, and said all manner of kind things of her over their tea-cups, and some of them even went so far as to go and see her to tell her how her friends felt for her; but old Lady Pendarvis herself, could she have stept out of her frame, could not have been more frigid and reticent than her Puritan descendant, Martha Flemming, and when her guests went away she did not invite them to come again. She preferred fighting out her battle alone; with the instincts of a wild animal she hid herself, wishing none to see her wounds.

Soon after John Wilde left the country George Merill came up from Boston, fired with indigna-

tion and full of great intentions. His grandfather
had written him a long letter giving him a particu-
lar account of all that had happened at the "Old
Homestead," and of the present status, moral, temporal and social, of the family, hoping that it
would put to flight forever any thought his grandson might still have of seeking Eva Flemming for
his wife. But he did not know the young fellow,
who, leaving his constant devotion for Eva out of
the question, had become during his residence at
the "Hub" a something that was half Pagan, half
Unitarian—whose strange tenets allowed a scope
of liberality towards other creeds which was
boundless; hence he did not care a twig for Eva's
being a Catholic; but he did care, and took it
sorely to heart, when he heard from his friend and
ally, Huldah Sneathen, who wrote him an astonishing letter, all the particulars of the social interdict
laid on his old friends, and how nearly they were
ruined. She told him, too, of the trap which her
father and aunt were laying for him; "but the cunning old souls might as well save their time for
something better; for you know, George, even if I
were not engaged to Nick Flemming, whose very
footprints I love, I wouldn't marry you to save
your life." George Merill burst out laughing;
then he thought of the Flemmings and swore a
little, and ended by pitching some of his city clothes

into a valise and starting right off for the hill country, where he arrived about dusk the following day, and swinging his valise in his hand he walked up towards the "Old Homestead." Near the house he met Mrs. Flemming, who had been to see her old "help," Sarah Gill, who was bedridden and had got a palsy of the head from the shock of hearing suddenly that Elder Flemming and his children had turned Papists, and spent her time relating her astounding dreams, which she called "visions," and telling of "death-watches" and mysterious tappings, and a "grief child" which appeared to her whenever she fell into a doze—"all signs and wonders," she declared— "rising out of the dretful doings down yonder," meaning the Old Homestead.

When Mrs. Flemming saw George Merill, a sudden hope took possession of her which brightened her eyes and brought a warm glow over her pale, thin face, making her look ten years younger ; but there was a little quivering of her lips as she held out her hand and said : "George, I am very glad to see you."

"I am very glad to see you, Mrs. Flemming," he said, grasping her hand warmly. "I was just on my way to your house. I only jumped out of the stage a little while ago, you see," he added, swinging his valise round.

"You haven't been up to the Minister's, then! I do wonder?" answered Mrs. Flemming.

"No. My grandfather and I are sure to quarrel when we meet; and, as I must go back to-morrow, I thought I'd see what awaited me here before I have my set-to up there. How are they all, Mrs. Flemming?"

"All well—in health," she added.

"And Eva! I have come to see her; is she at home?"

"Yes, Eva is at home."

"You see, Mrs, Flemming," said the young fellow, full of his generous, unselfish love, holding her hand in his, "I have heard all about the row there's been up here, and how the godly brethren have behaved to the Elder, and I left everything to come and ask Eva once more if she will marry me. I have to go back to-morrow; I have a case coming up in court in a few days and shall have to hurry off to be there in time."

"I can promise you nothing, George," answered Mrs. Flemming. "You know our house is divided against itself now; I am a cipher as to influence. But come in, and go into the parlor; I will send Eva to you. I wish you well, I am sure, if you don't mind her being a Pa—— a Roman Catholic."

"I shouldn't mind it if she were a Pagan; she

could never be anything but Eva to me," he replied, as they entered the house together.

"Go into the parlor. I will send Eva in," repeated Mrs. Flemming, as she went into the old part of the house in search of Eva, who was in her bedroom tacking up the clean, snowy window-curtains—just from under the iron—over the windows.

"Some one is in the parlor wishing to see you, Eva," said Mrs. Flemming, just putting her head into the door, then going directly away—almost feeling mean, for this was the first deception she had ever practiced in her life; but the hope of the good that might come of it reconciled and quieted her conscience.

Eva, who had no thought of George Merill in her mind, put in the last tack, looped back the curtains, and hastily smoothing back her curling hair and tying on a nice black silk apron, ran down stairs, her sweet face flushed and illuminated with a smile of welcome; but when she opened the parlor door and saw who her guest was, her first impulse was to draw back and go away without speaking; the smile faded out of her face, and a grave, almost a stern expression settled on her countenance; but the Flemmings, as we know, had nice ideas of hospitality, and would not have inflicted a rudeness upon their greatest enemy under the sanctuary of their own roof; so she went in, and without any word of welcome, shook hands with him, asked him how he was, and sat down in the chair he placed for her. He soon let her know what had brought him there, and she listened patiently to all he had to say. Touched by the constancy of his affection, and his generous devotion, unlike the spirit of the little world around her, Eva hesitated a moment in answering him—hesitated, because she shrunk from giving only pain in return for all that he offered; then in a sweet, womanly way put an end to his hopes, saying: "I am sorry to inflict pain, as I am conscious I shall do, but the only answer that I can give you, George, is what—"

"Before you say any more, Eva," he interrupted, "listen to all that I have to say. I know what has happened up here relative to your having become Roman Catholics, all of you, and there may be something in your mind on that score. But let no thought of the religious difference between us influence your decision, for I tell you honestly, before God, that I'd as lief my wife should be a Roman Catholic as anything else; in fact it would take but little, I think, to bring me over; but whether I am brought over or not there should not be the impediment of a straw laid in *your* path, and a portion of my fortune should go towards building and decorating churches of your faith, if it would make you any happier."

He had spoken rapidly and earnestly ; it was evident that he meant every word he uttered, and in proportion to *his* generosity so did *her* repugnance to give him pain increase ; but he must be answered, and Eva said :

" I believe all that you have said, George—every word. You are worthy of the devotion of a true and noble nature like your own; but as for me, the only answer that I can give you is what I told you before, I shall never marry—be assured of that, and some day, perhaps not far distant, you will understand much that seems heartless to you now, and your generous soul will give me full pardon. 1 shall never forget you, my brother, and shall pray that your nobleness of soul be rewarded tenfold. I thank you for coming—yes, thank you for coming in this the hour of our trial, when other friends and neighbors stand aloof—and doing that which, while it convinces me that there does exist in the world noble unselfishness and true constancy, will bring only blame and derision upon yourself. But let us part—part as friends; and if prayers will help you, mine shall abide with you as a shield and defence through life."

There was a strange, bright calm brooding over the girl's beautiful face as she held out her hand to him, and the tears that sparkled on her long eyelashes and rolled over her cheeks had a deeper significance than he could fathom then; but he knew that it was all over now, and with a sudden impulse he leaned over and kissed her forehead, saying: "Just this once, Eva; it is the seal on the sepulchre of my dearest hopes. Ours is a long farewell and it will take a tedious time to smooth away the remembrance of this—to me—bitter parting. I cannot understand you, Eva; but good-by—it is useless to defer going," he said, holding out his hand.

"Good-by, my friend and brother," she answered, as he wrung her hand and then passed away out of her sight, a saddened and disappointed man.

"Is George Merill gone, Eva?" inquired Mrs. Flemming, an hour or so later.

"Yes, mother. We parted as friends, nothing more," she answered. "He has gone back to Boston."

"I hope you won't live to repent it," replied Mrs. Flemming. "You and Hope have made a nice mess of it: such prospects as you both had."

"Try and be patient over it, dear mother. I trust that you will see it all come out right at last. You will at least keep your daughters the longer."

"Nonsense. My daughters are like other wo-men, and should be settled for life in comfortable homes of their own; and I am like other mothers, and would be glad when my last hours come, to

know that they have husbands to protect them and
their own roof to shelter them. I don't understand
all this new fangled, romantic nonsense." Having
thus delivered herself, the disappointed little woman went away to solace herself with reading a
chapter out of " Fox's Book of the Martyrs," and
thought fire and sword would be better than the
slow torture she had been enduring for months.

That night the stage left Patrick McCue's box of
books at Wolfert Flemming's door, and it was
immediately taken into the "work-room" where,
after the family had retired to rest, he opened it and
spent half the night examining its contents, rejoicing over the treasures it contained, with far
greater joy than he would have experienced had it
been filled with the costliest jewels on earth. Here
was all he wanted until he should experience the
reward of Faith in the substance of things hoped
for; until the supreme moment when, being made
outwardly as well as inwardly a member of the
true fold of Christ, he would receive the "Bread of
Life" for which his soul had been so long hungering. And how strangely had Providence favored
him even in this! It had seemed to him sometimes like a most haphazard proceeding to have
written and sent a money-letter to a man whose
business made him a very nomad, and who might
never have seen Boston since he left the hill-coun-

try; Wolfert Flemming felt at such moments as if his wife was justifiable in calling it, with some sharp remarks, not only "a foolish proceeding," but "a sinful throwing away of money." But, as we know, Patrick McCue had got the letter, and here were the books, a bill and receipt, and the right change to a fraction.

Mrs. Flemming knew that the books had come, from seeing Reuben unwrapping and examining those sent him by the pedler, who would have been somewhat astonished if he had seen the boy lay carelessly aside "The Travels of an Irish Gentleman in Search of a Religion," by "Tommy Moore," and begin to read, nay, to devour with feverish avidity, the book illustrative of "Art in Catholic Ages." Was she never to hear the last of that pedler, who had brought her such dole? Was he to be forever coming up in some shape or other to torment her? She began to think so.

The next morning Mrs. Flemming in brushing up and putting things to rights in the "work-room," a labor of love which she had always reserved to herself, and still continued, gathered up a heap of rubbish strewed over the floor, in which the books had been packed, and was going to throw it into the wood-box for kindlings, when she felt something smooth and hard strike against her hand, something heavier than the straw and shavings she held, and upon examining she discovered that it was a small leather-bound book, which she involuntarily opened, led by instinctive curiosity and a natural desire to see what it was. "The Papist Represented and Misrepresented," she read in a low voice. "Here are two sides at last, and I will read it to see if there is any reason in it." She thrust the book hastily into her pocket, determined —as it had been evidently overlooked and accidently dropped—to say nothing about it, until, having satisfied her curiosity, she would lay it among her husband's papers, leaving him to discover it the best way he could.

CHAPTER XX.

WOLFERT FLEMMING'S BIRTHDAY

Mrs. Flemming read the little book she had found among the litter of the "work-room;" she carried it about with her in her pocket, for fear some of them should accidentally see it, and took the opportunity now and then to slip up into her bedroom, after supper, and read it while her hus·band and children were reading the books sent by Patrick McCue, reading them as thirsty travellers in the desert drink from a suddenly discovered fountain beneath the shadow of broad-spreading palms. Up there alone, like "a sparrow on the house-top," she read it with alternate emotions of fierce satisfaction and uncomfortable doubts for here it represents the Catholic religion according to Protestant ideas, there represents it to the reader as it truly is, in all its wonderful simplicity and sublime truth. The first pleased her throughout her whole Puritan nature; the second she would have dismissed from her thoughts and entirely ignored if she could; but it was impossible—the antithesis left an impression upon her which she could not get rid of, and like a moral pendulum it kept her mind vibrating from side to side, wondering if, after all, the Catholic version of the question could be right. But she kept her secret bravely; and the result of it all was that she was made more bitter by her resistance to the truth and the mental disturbance that it occasioned her.

She had grown, in a measure, accustomed to the strange order of things about her; and, although silent and grave, could not altogether stand out against the patient and loving forbearance of her husband and children towards her. She had lost none of their love, and she was thankful for that; and her heart was touched to its inmost core by their constant endeavor to express it in all the varied circumstances of their daily life. She watched

with jealous eye for something on their part which
would bring a scandal on their new profession and
offer her a salient point of attack; but she watched
in vain—for not only were their lives pure and
without guile, but their unaffected cheerfulness and
their constant devotion to herself made her feel very
often that she was making herself miserable without just cause. Never before had Mrs. Flemming
seen religion more beautifully exemplified than in
the daily lives of her husband and children; never
had she seen trials borne with so sweet a patience
or with such noble courage; never had she seen in
all her life until now the active fruits of a true
spiritual life, ripening in the eternal sunshine of a
true faith. She could not understand it; and do
what she might, she could find nothing to sweeten
the bitter fact that the beings she most loved on
earth were Papists. On the other hand, without
the remotest idea of following their example, she
felt with the deepest resentment the treatment her
husband and family had met with from her brethren
—their life-long friends and neighbors. "One
would suppose," she would think to herself, after
mentally summing up her grievances, "that they
had committed murder or theft." And now that
this little waif of a book kept her constantly drifting out among doubts and fears which fevered her

very soul, the poor little woman felt that she was literally between two fires.

We don't wish the reader to suppose that Wolfert Flemming and his daughters lived in a state of ecstasy, lifted high above the reach of the trials and anxieties which had gathered and were still gathering about them, for they were human, and felt the splinters of their cross, and their spirits sometimes sunk within them.; indeed we do not know but that there were moments when they were tempted to look back into Egypt, with its fleshpots savory with garlick and sweet-smelling herbs; but their faith was strong; it was "like an anchor, sure and steadfast" to their souls, and helped them to rise when they fell; to look away from the savory messes of Egypt, with hope, towards the manna of eternal life; to bear, with their sad faces turned towards the eternal goal whose far-off lights cheered their souls, the wounds that tortured them, without complaint—and, in the name of God, "fight the good fight" which would in the end perfect them in patience. They found the Catholic religion no shield against human or spiritual trials; but it taught them how to bear the thorny passes of life, and how to sanctify their nature by submission to the Divine will, and where to find consolation and peace when the earthly reed on which they leaned broke and pierced them. Their faith, for which they suffered, did not allow the fountain from which they drank to remain always bitter, but, like the prophet of old, when they were fainting with thirst, threw in immortal leaves which sweetened the waters, giving them strength and refreshment. And they cheered and held up each other's hands, never allowing a despondent word to escape their lips, or a despondent cloud to shadow their faces.

And the weeks passed on, bringing new trials and worries. The season, which had commenced with such rare and genial mildness that the farmers, beguiled by its seductive warmth, had planted and sown, and were rubbing their hands together with delight over their prospective crops, suddenly became cold and wet. Rain fell constantly, and rotted the seed in the ground, and there was a doubt among them if they would save enough of their crops to supply their own domestic needs. The inclement, unseasonable weather brought a strange and fatal disease among the cattle, which killed off hundreds of them, to the great distress and loss of their owners. Huldah Sneathen's beautiful white heifer, around whose sleek neck she delighted to hang garlands of wild flowers, and feed with the daintiest clover and nicest morsels, died, and she was crying over it, thinking no one saw her when her Aunt Debby's sharp voice interrupted her tears, saying: "I admire to see you, Huldy! Get up, and come away from that critter; you'll be sure to catch the pison. I b'lieve the Lord has cussed the land for the sin of them down yonder" —pointing towards the "Old Homestead."

"Go away, Aunt Debby, and let me be," said Huldah, flashing round her flushed, tear-stained face upon the spinster; "and don't go on making such a fool of yourself. If anything's brought a curse on the land, it's the treatment you pharisees have given them 'down yonder;' and take care the Lord don't condemn the Pharisee and commend the poor publican, as He did once before. Go away, and let me and my heifer alone." And Miss Debby sniffed and went her way, knowing by experience that it was no use for her to say anything more, or stay looking on; but she would have relished above all things giving Huldah a sound box on her ears before she went; her fingers tingled to do it, but this was a luxury she could never hope to enjoy again, and she had to make the best of it she could.

Wolfert Flemming did not lose more than his neighbors; but the debt hanging over him and the unexpected breaking up of his business made his losses bear more heavily upon him. He was determined not to sell if he could help it; but how he was to help it he could not tell. If he could have foreseen all this, he would not have used up his ready money and gone into debt in making the improvements about his place and adding to his lands; but he never dreamed of such difficulties, and knew at the time that the profits of his business, steadily increasing, would extricate him certainly in three years from all indebtedness; but here he was stranded high and dry, without an idea of how he should get afloat once more. He would try honestly to hold by his own, and if all efforts failed he would give up everything rather than wrong any man. Some months lay before him, and if his creditors were not disposed to persecute him on account of his changing his religion, which he had good reason to fear they would, he hoped to be able to gather enough money together to pay a portion of the principal and the full interest of the debt, or rather the mortgage on his property. This man was blessed with large hope and greater faith, and, as he told his family, he "would make every exertion to stave off the breaking up of their old home; but they must prepare themselves, as he was trying to do, to submit to the will of God, however the affair might result."

He had a small, unproductive farm of a few acres, about a mile and a half away, rented to a man named Wilbur, who was in arrears for a year's rent, and out of employment. He hoped to find a purchaser for the " Mill Farm" as it was called—from the fact that there was a ruined mill there whose wheel had once been turned by a broad, bright stream of water, long since gone dry, which of course rendered the mill useless, and it had fallen to decay. If he could sell the " Mill Farm" to advantage, it would be a great help to him, and he determined to put it into the market at once ; not that he expected to be able to find a purchaser immediately, but it would give peo'le time to talk and think about it, and find out how it would be to their advantage to buy it in time for his needs. Besides this, there was a balance of three hundred dollars still due him from the firm of Sneathen & Flemming, which he had enough of the old Adam left in him to make him too proud to dun Sneathen & Co., about. But he held their acknowledgment of indebtedness in black and white, and if they did not offer payment soon he would have to come down on them for it.

We see how the earthly prosperity in which Mrs. Flemming had gloried a few months past was crumbling and fading around her ; how swiftly, like a meteor, the bright prospects of the future had been quenched, and how the shadows of adversity continued to gather around them. The wolf was at 'heir door, and it was only a question of time how soon he would enter. The bitter prejudice against their faith, the fanatical resentment of their old friends and acquaintances, closed every avenue of help against them; there would have been some human and friendly feeling left for them if they had only turned infidels, but they had become Roman Catholics, which in the eyes of these staunch Puritans was the culminating point of all that was infamous and dreadful; hence they watched afar off, with complacent self-gratulation, the approach of what they called retributive justice on the heads of these offenders, assured in their own minds that the Almighty would be satisfied with nothing short of their destruction.

Nicholas Flemming had applied for the District School, the teacher having died six months before, and the Committee being unable to get any one to supply his place; but, bless you! Nick might as well have applied for the President's chair at Washington; his application was not even considered, but returned to him with the curt remark written on the back : " The School Committee decline all communication with, or employment of, Papists."

" I'm not a Papist—yet, anyhow !"—exclaimed Nicholas hotly, " and I'd like to go and punch their stupid old heads for them."

" Have courage ! if your good act has called forth a mean and ignoble one, how can it hurt you?" said Wolfert Flemming, feeling strongly in spite of himself at the insult. "I only wish you possessed fully the faith for the sake of which they persecute you."

"I wish I did, father, and I believe that in time I shall," replied Nicholas. "There's one thing certain : if I can't believe enough to become a Catholic, I shall be nothing. I believe they'd burn us all at the stake, if they could ; I really do."

"Hush, Nicholas," said his mother, with a red spot on each cheek.

"I will, mother ; they're your friends," said Nicholas, sorry the moment after for saying it.

"Are they ?" she asked drily.

"Nicholas," said his father, glad to change the subject, "I want you to go down to Wilbur's this afternoon, and see if he can pay his rent or any part of it. Tell him I'm pressed for money, or wouldn't push him, knowing he's in a tight place himself."

"Yes, father, I'll go ; but I don't think there's any use in going ; for he's had no work for six months ; and I heard yesterday that the sheriff had distrained his goods to pay the doctor," said Nicholas.

"Well, well, ride over and see. It's hard on me to lose ; but Wilbur's an honest man."

"Why don't you do as others do ?" interrupted

Mrs. Flemming. " I don't see why you should be distressed for another's shortcoming."

" He will pay me if he can, mother," answered Flemming, gently. " He's an industrious, honest man ; but seasons of misfortune come to us all. He's out of work, and has had a sick family for months. Yes, let us bear one another's burdens, and be merciful—lest, should we be in the same case, the sting of remorse be added to our sorrows."

" I don't live in the clouds," she answered, " and the logic of common sense is all that I understand. I don't think a man has any right to distress his own family for the sake of a stranger. But I expect nothing but trouble now."

" Let us be patient, mother ; let us be patient," he replied, laying his broad hand tenderly on her head, where he noticed for the first time among the black silken hair many threads of white, which touched the man's heart, and he sighed, for he understood their significance.

" How can I be patient," she cried, " when I see all that has happened? I can't be patient. You are all killing me. You have left me, as much as if you had gone away to a far country ; you are joined to idols, and have brought poverty and disgrace upon your house, and ruined the prospects of your children."

" According to the world, mother," he answered,

in his low even tones, " according to the world,
mother, your reproaches are just, and well de-
served; but according to the divine law, things
wear a different aspect. They who serve God must
expect tribulation, and bear it for His sake; they
must love Him before and above all, giving up
their nearest and dearest—aye, all things—for the
love of Him. We are in His hands; and I am not
afraid, for He is merciful as well as just."

" You have a prospect of having your principles
well tested," she replied bitterly; then she went up
stairs, and locking herself in her room, had a good
cry, after which she read " Fox's Book of Martyrs"
until it got too dark to distinguish one letter from
another.

Nicholas came back from the " Mill " farm
empty-handed, saying that Wilbur would see his
father the next day if he was able; then he walked
off in the twilight to keep his tryst with Huldah
under the old hemlocks that shadowed the mountain side a few rods from her father's house; a spot
which had been her favorite resort since she was a
little, toddling girl, and used to seek refuge there
from the iron rule of her Aunt Deborah, to nurse
her kittens, or cry her fill over the long strips of
hemming and endless seams of felling given her
for a task in punishment for certain misdemeanors
by that inexorable woman. The Deacon had gone

up to " The Pines," on business, and Miss Debby
was taking tea with a neighbor'; and Huldah could
have received her lover at home without fear of interruption, quite like the old time, when the " course
of their true love" *did* "run smooth ;" but Nicholas
had been forbidden the house, and was too proud
and honorable to enter it clandestinely. But it
was neutral ground up there under the old hemlocks, with God's sky bending over them and the
stars glistening through the dark foliage as if listening to the whispers of the little mountian brook
that fell over the rocks not far away and rippled
down through the ferns and mosses at their feet ;
and there they occasionally met to talk over the
situation and shake their fists in the face of the
world, making light of their difficulties---and, so
long as they felt assured of each other's constancy,
hoping for the best. Huldah often declared she
" rather liked it, as it made her feel romantic, and
reminded her of the heroines she had read of in the
old novels in the garret."

But this evening, Nicholas, sobered by his
father's troubles to an unusually gravity, and still
feeling the smart of the insult he had received
from the School Committee, told her everything,
and explained the misfortunes impending over his
family ; and the warm-hearted, generous girl was
so shocked and grieved at it all, that for the first

time in her life she felt too benumbed to speak—
but not too much so to think. The forces of her
physical life seemed to be absorbed by her brain,
giving it strange power, and clearer, keener perceptions; until, uneasy at her strange silence,
Nicholas, sensitive and unreasonable, began to
think that she shrunk from him and her engagement, now that poverty, disgrace and distress had
come upon them; and said some such thing to
her, which roused her, and she exclaimed:

"Don't Nick. You are talking like a teapot.
You know that you don't, in your heart, believe a
word that you are saying. I don't. But I tell you,
Nick, I'm sorry for your good, noble father, and
the rest of them, and if I could get hold of my
money I'd make short metre of all this trouble. But
I can't, you know; and I want just to go home and
think it all over, and see what can be done. Good-
by, Nicholas, you shall hear from me soon." And
Huldah, with a strange seriousness on her face,
rose to go.

"What nonsense, Huldah!" said Nicholas, im-
petuously. "You know that you can do nothing;
and I won't have you asking favors for my family,
or bringing yourself into trouble on their account.
Sit down."

"Don't be uneasy, Nick, about my doings," she
answered. "Let me go home now; I really must

go and think all this over. I want you to go away, right off."

"Go, then," replied Nicholas, letting go her hand. "It is easy to say 'Go' to the unfortunate;" and he was striding angrily away when Huldah said:

"Nicholas Flemming! how dare you say such a thing to me who love you so?"

"Forgive me, Huldah," he answered. "These troubles of ours are making me suspicious and irrational; but where's the use of going away like this, when I see you so seldom?"

"Trust me, Nick—mind! no half trust—and let me go home," said the girl; "and remember, if it should come into your thoughts at any time that I'm mean enough to want to throw you over because you are poor, don't ever come near me again; because if you have such thoughts of me now, you are wanting in confidence in me and respect for me."

"Very well," he answered. "I don't understand your strange humor, Huldah; but I'll think over what you say, and see what I can make out of it. Depend upon one thing: I shall need no second telling to 'go,' if I have reason to think you want to get rid of me."

"Don't be proud with me, Nick. I declare it's **exactly** like a scene between Don Ferdinando and

Donna Angeletta. How nonsensical for matter-of-fact lovers like you and I!" said Huldah, with her old merry laugh. " Good night." And she offered him her hand, which he grasped; and holding up her sweet, truthful face, she kissed him; and before he could say another word she was half way down the narrow path, lost to his sight amidst the shadows; and Nicholas went homewards, half sulkily, yet not altogether miserable.

The next day poor Wilbur came up to the Old Homestead, his trembling limbs scarcely able to support him, looking so wan and heart-worn while he was telling of his misfortunes and sorrows that Mrs. Flemming's heart was touched; and, forgetting her own trials, she slipped out of the room and went up to the lumber-room, where she opened a chest filled up to the top with the shrunken and worn-out garments of the family; and selecting the best of them, such as she knew would be useful to this stricken household, she made them into a compact bundle; and when the man crept away, she, on the watch for him, slipped out of a side-door and waylaid him among the trees, placing it in his hands, while she said: " Let me know if I can do anything for you all. You know that the El——, my husband, I mean, must be in a tight place to push you, and we are too poor to give much help to others; but the little we may be able to do, you will be welcome to."

"I know it, Miss' Flemming. I know it," answered the man. astonished and overcome, while tears rolled over his thin cheeks; "and God bless you. The Elder couldn't have done more for me if I'd been his brother; he's given me leave to stay on the 'Mill-Farm' 'till it's sold; and says not a stitch of my goods shall be touched for the rent; and if God spares me to get on my legs strong agin, he shall have every cent of it with interest. And I tell you what, ma'am, I wish other people's religion 'round here would crop out accordin' to the same rule his'n does, much as they all abuse it. Thank you, Miss' Flemming, for we've nothing but rags like these," said Wilbur—taking hold of his tattered coat—"to cover us."

"There's a bottle of Elderberry wine in the bundle, for your wife," said Mrs. Flemming.

"Lord bless you, ma'am, the Elder give me bread and wine too, seeing how weak I am—and I owing him such heaps of money that I couldn't hold up my head, I was that shamed; but he shan't lose a cent—not a cent—so help me God. Thank you ma'am, for the wine for my wife."

"I won't have you stand talking any longer now," answered Mrs. Flemming. "Good-by, and let me know if I can do anything to help you."

And she shook hands with him, and watched him
as he crept slowly, with the help of a stick, down
the road. How it would have sweetened the bitter
waters of her soul to have felt that what she had
done she did for the sake and love of God; but she
did not feel this; her act was the impulse of simple
humanity—good and beautiful in itself, but un-
sanctified by that motive without which all nobility
of act or will, all grandeur of purpose, all heroic
sacrifice, all generous giving and profuse alms " are
as nothing." Mrs. Flemming looked on "works"
as superrogatory and unnecessary to salvation; but
this did not prevent her, as we have seen, from giving freely and from pure benevolence the surplus
means that she could not use herself. Not so with
her husband and daughters, to whose lives the love
of Jesus had become the animating principle and
the sweet incentive to works of mercy, and gave
them the blessed consciousness of knowing that
they ministered to Him under these poor disguises
of suffering humanity. Now that they knew the
real condition of the poverty-stricken family at
" Mill Farm," they did not let their own misfortunes stand in the way of doing all in their power
to assist them. " Silver and gold had they none;"
but what they had they gave freely, and with words
of good cheer. They gave the labor of their hands;
they watched and tended the helpless, bedridden

wife, and gave tender care to the half-starved, neglected little children. Denying themselves at their
meals, and frequently going without their supper,
Hope and Eva managed to feed these famished
beings who had almost forgotten the taste of nourishing food. They saved, with zealous care, the
cold scraps, which in their days of plenty used to
be thrown to the dogs, and cooked them up, with
onions, salt and thyme, into savory messes the very
smell of which would have excited the appetite of
an epicure, and felt more than repaid when they
saw the relish with which they were devoured to
the last morsel; and occasionally they baked a
large brown loaf for the hungry mouths. They
sewed and mended and patched the tattered garments, and cleansed the poor abode until everything in it—from the floors, to the shelves with
their scanty assortment of cracked delf—shone
again; and still found time, now and then,to sit beside
Mrs. Wilbur and read some of the soul-touching
devotions for the sick from the Catholic prayer-
book Patrick McCue had sent them; from which
the afflicted woman seemed to derive much comfort.

The time devoted by Hope and Eva to these
works of mercy was taken—not from their daily
home duties, Mrs. Flemming would have objected
to that—but from their sleep, their spare moments

when they might have read or rested, and from
their long, pleasant walks among the romantic
scenery around; and they ere long found reward
for their self-denial in seeing the pale cheeks of the
Wilburs filling out, and strength returning to their
wasted limbs. This, added to the sweet consciousness of doing good, gave them a new sense of happiness such as they had never imagined or experienced before. As to who used to fetch water
enough from the far spring to last the poor family
all through the succeeding day, chop their wood
and pile it up at the door, and feed and milk the
cow, the girls did not know, and did not like to
ask; they were sure Wilbur didn't do these chores;

he wasn't strong enough; and they very naturally
suspected their father, who used to disappear
every evening about dusk, for an hour or two, and
always come in with such a smile of content on his
countenance that it seemed to brighten up everything around him. The gratitude and thanks of
the people at "Mill Farm" were almost oppressive;
indeed, as Eva said, "they made her feel ashamed
of the poor little she had done;" but we shall see
by-and-by what a queer turn their gratitude took,
thereby giving the good Flemmings a new experience of life, and affording Mrs. Flemming an opportunity to say with unction "it is just what I ex
pected." But we must not anticipate.

One day Hope and Eva were busy over a piece of sewing in the old sitting, or "living room," as New-Englanders say. The outlook of the family affairs was gloomy, and ruin seemed inevitable. They were very quiet and thoughtful while the golden September sun shone through the vines over the windows, and fell glittering and quivering among the old Dutch silver in the beaufèt A bright little fire crackled on the tiled hearth, for there had been frost already. Mrs. Flemming was in the adjoining room—seated on the very lounge that Patrick McCue was laid on the night he was brought in out of the storm—knitting as if for life, a stitch and a tear very often together, and enough of sorrowful and bitter thoughts under every loop to give whoever wore the stocking the cramp all their days. Suddenly Wolfert Flemming came in, pranked off in his best suit of clothes, clean linen, gold studs, freshly shaved and brushed.

"Why—father!" exclaimed Eva, as she looked up.

"Father! are you going anywhere?" asked Hope, with a sudden fear. She thought perhaps his troubles had unsettled his mind.

"No, daughter. I am going to be very happy at home to-day!" he answered, with his old pleasant smile.

"You have heard good news?" said Hope, looking up eagerly.

"In one sense, yes; in another, no," he replied.

"What is it that makes you look so strangely happy, father?" asked Eva.

"Why, I have just found out something. You have heard me say, since our conversion, that in the dark years of the past my soul used to be moved, strangely moved, whenever in the Old Testament or the New I came across any prophecy or passage alluding to the Blessed Mother of Jesus. I spoke of it to no one then, for I feared it was wrong; but I could not stifle the impression; and at last in my heart of hearts I felt a deep Catholic reverence for her, without knowing what it meant or being able to define its significance. Since I have been brought to a knowledge of the True Faith, it is all plain, consoling, and blessed, and I have come to believe that SHE was caring for my soul in those days and leading me through the darkness to HER SON. And now, what do you think? This, you know, is my birthday—the 8TH OF SEPTEMBER; and I only this morning discovered, in looking over the calendar, that it is also the BIRTHDAY OF MARY—and I am going to hold high festival in her honor to-day; and every birthday of my life, henceforth, I shall devote especially to Her, my patroness and Queen!* Put aside your sewing, daughters, and all thoughts of

* Which he did, literally.

worldly care; go out and gather flowers, and bring
them up to old Massisquoi's room; and after we
have decorated the shrine of Our Lady, and
lighted the wax candle you made, Eva, in her
honor, we will say the Litany and read the Office
of the Rosary together.

"Oh, father, father!" exclaimed Eva, unable to
restrain her emotion, as she ran and threw her
arms about his neck and blessed him, "how happy
it makes me to hear this! I congratulate you,
dearest father, and I am sure that Our dear Lady
will deliver you temporally, as she has led you
spiritually."

"Dear father!" said Hope, kissing his broad
brown hand, and folding it in both of hers to her
breast, "I congratulate you too, and pray that the
Blessed Mother may obtain for you many returns
of this happy day."

"And heaven at last—" added Flemming, his
whole countenance beaming with happiness.

"And heaven, at last," repeated Hope in sweet
solemn tones. Then he went away up into old
Massisquoi's room, while the girls set to work to
gather some rich autumnal roses and scarlet
blooms for the shrine of the Virgin.

As to Mrs. Flemming, she had dropped her
knitting, and sat motionless, listening in a sort of
dumb amaze, hearing distinctly every word uttered

by her husband and daughters, unseen by them, until they went out; then the sudden silence seemed to rouse her, and she exclaimed: "They are all crazy together, to be going on with such nonsense when ruin is staring us in the face. Festival! I'd like to know where the festive part comes in?"

Poor Mrs. Flemming could not understand where the "festive part came in," because she still dwelt in the material darkness of her cold belief, fettered by human reason and full of spiritual pride, which blinded her so that she could not distinguish the deep spirituality of the Faith professed by her family. She stood on the borders of the "new earth and new heaven" they had found, but failed to see the glories thereof; her trials had blotted and blurred her religious perceptions; and, smarting under the cross, she was sometimes almost ready to "curse God and die." Above all did these usages of Catholic devotion, which now beset her on every hand, irritate and annoy her; for they were to her feet a "stumbling-block, and to her mind foolishness." But this could not cloud the happiness of the group kneeling so devoutly at the foot of MARY in the little room up stairs, calling in the simplicity of their faith on the "Star of Jacob," the "Virgin of Virgins," the "Refuge of sinners," to aid them and obtain from HER divine SON the conversion of their mother and brothers.

Wolfert Flemming said that night that he was just one year old, and this was his first birthday, one which he should remember in Eternity.

CHAPTER XXI.

MRS. FLEMMING IS GLAD OF SOMETHING AT LAST.

In the meanwhile Huldah Sneathen began to exhibit a change which not only kept Nicholas in a fever, but attracted the serious attention of her father and aunt. She grew snappish and absent-minded, reversing the order of things, as is the way with absent-minded people. and very often made them all uncomfortable by putting salt into things that required sugar, and sugaring things that should have been salted; sometimes she was very gay, at others, very silent; and once she actually patched the knee of her father's black pantaloons with yellow cloth, which he did not discover until he had got into Plymouth the next morning—having dressed by candle-light—when his attention was called to the fact by the hootings and laughter of the *gamins* of that godly town. Huldah laughed when her father scolded her about it, and said she was sorry, then asked him if he had a letter for her, which he shortly answered in the negative. Then Huldah, who had all her life been blessed with a good, wholesome appetite, and dearly loved the flesh-pots, began to grow dainty about her eating, and did very little more than peck at her food when she sat down to the table, and of course began to get pale and thin; and her aunt told the Deacon in confidence that she had heard her crying in the night, and walking about the floor when she should have been in bed asleep. He was puzzled and uneasy, for he remembered that Huldah's mother had gone off with a strange, slow sort of complaint, that nobody thought was anything worse than indolence, until one day she laid her poor head quietly back in her chair and died.

"She's fretting—that's all; fretting about Nick Flemming," said the Deacon, rubbing his head violently with his yellow silk handkerchief.

"La suz!" exclaimed Miss Debby, "I'd like to know neow! But 'taint that, Deacon; for she sees Nick Flemming every day or so. She's chipper enough as fur as that goes. She's going to turn Papist—that's what it is."

"Don't be a fool, Deborah! It's no such nonsense as that. It's Nicholas, I tell you; and I won't have her worrit into getting sick," answered the Deacon, growing purple in the face.

"Lands sakes! Deacon——," began the spin-ster.

"I don't want to see my child's property going back to them ungodly people—her mother's relations. They're hungering and thirsting for it— them Barkers are. So I won't have her worrit, and you may let Nick Flemming know that he can come whenever he wants to," answered the Deacon, looking benign.

"Suz!" exclaimed Miss Debby, with an extra sniff; "I forgot all about that Barker will; why, if Huldy was to die off to-day, like her poor mother did, all the property would go right straight to the Barkers; and you couldn't afford that. Yes, I guess mebbe that Nick Flemming has got some hand in it, and he'd better come to chirk her up."

So Nicholas was duly notified that he could visit the house again; but Nicholas had been snubbed two or three times by Huldah since the evening they met under the hemlock trees, when she sent him away and had behaved altogether so strangely that his pride was up, and he stood off.

So, whatever was the matter with Huldah, she kept it to herself in a little "ring of fire" that scorched her sometimes until she was half beside herself; but "she wouldn't tell—no, not if it killed her"—she declared to herself over and over again. Nick's coldness was almost too much for her; for she "knew that he was thinking meanly of her, misconstruing and misunderstanding her; but he was the very last one she could tell her trouble to ; and if he chose to mount his high horse and go putting on airs to her; why, let him do so to the end of the chapter ;" then Huldah had a good cry to herself, which, when it was over, seemed to do her good, for she bounced up, began to brush her curls vigorously, soused her face in a basin of cold water, and dressed herself prettily in a new maroon tabinet which she had bought from a peddler with her dairy-money, and put a frill of rich yellow lace around her throat and fastened it with a gay ribbon bow, then stuck another among her curls, singing snatches of song, and saying now and then : "It will come to-morrow. I am sure it will. I shall hear from him to-morrow ; then I shall be so happy ! But maybe Nick will be here this evening. I don't care, though, if he don't." Her hope that Nicholas Flemming would come, was the secret of her *grande toilette*, but who was it she expected to hear from ? Had the sly puss got another lover ?

But Nicholas did not come. He had gone down to Holderness and Plymouth with a great wagonload of farm and dairy produce, and his mother's beautiful carpet, just finished and taken out of the loom the day before, to sell. She counted on getting a good round sum for it, for it was almost as pretty as a store carpet; then there was a good lot of wool—the wool from their sheep was always

considered the finest and whitest in the country—
and she had taken uncommon pains in curing it
for market; besides this, were two barrels of maple
syrup, as clear as amber, and a keg of elderberry
wine, several years old, equal to any foreign wines
in the land. And the thrifty little woman watched
her wheeled argosy until it was out of sight, hoping
for quick sales and high prices; then went back to
her sad thoughts and her spinning-wheel, for she
was busy making her fine yarn, almost as fine as
the yarn brought from Shetland, for which she
always got a high price.

Everything was going on as usual in the Old
Homestead and around it. The golden sun of September shone as brightly as ever on the wide-
spreading beeches around it; the windows glittered like diamonds as its rays darted down through
the dappled foliage upon the small clear panes, and
brought out with rare bright touches the patches
of moss and lichen upon the old black roof. There,
between the lichen-covered elms that bordered the
broad gravelled walk running through the middle
of their garden and the field beyond, shone a
glimpse of the lake, and one of its gem-like islands;
farther, in the distance, the Belknap Mountains lay
like a purple wave against the sky; nearer still
arose Ossipee and the haughty Chocorua, with
stripes of crimson breaking the dark monotony of

the summer foliage upon their slopes,—with here and there, as if Indian warriors were in ambush upon their heights, flashes of orange and scarlet, like flitting plumes. All around, the ledges and boulders of the solemn picturesque hills stood out bravely in blue and purple, warmed and glorified by clusters of yellow and crimson sumachs that waved their palm-like leaves gaily in the sun. Down along the edges of the rivulets, pink and purple blossoms lifted their heads among the grass; and the sweetbriar clinging about everything was full of fragrance and thickly hung with scarlet berries, while blue and white asters dappled the meadow lands, and the great ferns began to wear a crimson tinge as they waved in the low lush dells watered by sly little brooks that only whispered in soft shy whispers as they crept along through the mosses towards the beautiful lake. Nothing was changed outwardly. The old house nestled there amidst all the early autumnal beauty, looking as it did a century before,—looking as it did when the oldest man and woman living in those parts first remembered it; looking as it did one short year before, when the very name of Flemming was a power in the land, and every one in the little world around spoke of its inmates and pointed it out with pride. But we know what a change had come upon them, and why. The Flemmings had found out that the " Kingdom of Heaven" is not of this world; and, knowing this, had entered into its portals, willing to be stripped of all things rather than relinquish the right to abide there. They had taken up the cross, and in its strength they were ready to make every sacrifice for the eternal good they had found. I think you know all this, but it is so good a thing that it bears repetition.

One day Wolfert Flemming came home from a journey he had taken to see a man who had written to him about the purchase of " Mill Farm;"—came home disappointed, for the man had changed his mind and bought other property. After caring for his tired horse—for he had a tender heart for the dumb creatures that served him—he entered his house and experienced a sort of relief when he found the old sitting-room empty; he felt for a moment that it would be hard to meet his wife's anxious, eager eyes, and he having nothing better to tell her than he had. Indeed there seemed to be no one in the house—everything was so silent; and he thought it would be a good opportunity for him to spend a half hour in " Eva's sanctuary," as Hope called it, to confide his thoughts and beg the assistance of the " Help of Christians."

Laying his hat down in the passage, he wiped the perspiration from his forehead and opened the door. Eva was there, kneeling, with eyes closed and lips softly uttering the beautiful devotion of the Rosary as she slipped bead after bead through her fingers. The last crimson rays of the setting sun shone through the window upon the white statue of MARY and her SON, clothing them as with a garment, and throwing out in strong relief the crucifix at their feet. Eva turned at the sound of her father's entrance, and, greeting him with a sweet smile of welcome, moved a little to make room for him as he knelt beside her. Here, in this spot consecrated by prayer to the Mother of God, the clamor of worldly cares and the angry mutterings of the storm that threatened him with shipwreck and ruin ebbed away from the man's weary heart; they could come "only so far;" and as a sweet calm settled on his soul, he realized the full significance of that peace which "the world cannot give, nor take away;" and grew strong. Compared with this, the affairs of this life sunk into nothingness; and he realized, perhaps more than he had yet done, the dual struggle and warfare of his being—the struggle of nature for perishable goods, the warfare of his soul for an immortal heritage; and he thought —full of faith—" Be not disquieted, Oh my soul ! for the Lord is thy helper in the day of trouble. His holy will be done." He expected no miracle to be wrought for his deliverance from his present strait : he simply referred all things to the divine

will, while doing all that justice to his family de-
manded and human prudence required—assured in
the depths of his soul that if the worst that he
dreaded should happen, the blow would be sanctified to the good of him and his household through
Him who had suffered all things for them. Thus
reposing on the will of God, without a single visionary thought or purpose, he felt that he could
bear with courage whatever befell ; what could he
not bear, sustained by the strength of his newly-
found Faith and the peace born of it? He felt
calmed, refreshed and thankful.

Their devotions over, Eva said : "I am glad you
are back, father. I hope you have had good success ?"

"No," he answered, as he drew a chair to the
window and sat down ; " Deacon Flynt had already
bought a place."

"I am sorry, father, but I can't despond. I have
been praying constantly to our Blessed Mother to
help you, and somehow I feel that she will not refuse me," said Eva, as she brought a low bench and
sat beside him.

"I hope so, daughter ; I hope so. I have great
faith in her intercession. How strange!—how
strange !" he added.

"What is strange, father?"

"That having studied the Scriptures from my

youth up, I should have remained blind so long to the claims of Christ's holy Mother ;" he answered. " It is true that I always felt a certain veneration for her above the other holy women of the Bible ; but it is only since I have become in faith a Catholic, and have read the belief of the Church concerning her, that I understand all the mysterious allusions to her, and the wonderful and indissoluble connection that there is between her and our redemption. Men may try to argue it away, to preach and write it down, to ignore it with scorn, and inveigh against it with contempt; but the fact remains : and, if they are Christians, they half reject Christ if they reject and throw discredit on His Mother!"

" Father, do you know that I sometimes think that the very personality of Christ would have faded into a myth if the Catholic Church had not preserved and cherished through past ages this tender memory and holy devotion to His holy Mother. They would have denied the Incarnation and denied His Humanity—having lost sight of her."

" It might have been so ; yes, it seems possible. I never thought of that before ;" answered her father, looking far away into the glowing depths of light now softly fading in the west.

" And I can't tell you, father, how much nearer

and more *real* the Saviour became to me when I learned to know His holy Mother," said Eva, in low fervid tones.

"And no wonder," he replied; "for in thinking of the Holy Motherhood, who can forget the Divine Humanity? In contemplating Him, is it possible to divest the mind of her who was chosen by almighty God from His whole creation to be the Mother of His Son? Full of grace, she was both prophet and apostle, in whom met the Old Law and the New, who fulfilled prophecy and interpreted the Scriptures. From her lips man learned the wonderful story of the Incarnation, which was confirmed by angel messengers and sealed by the birth of her Divine Son. Oh, my heart gets very full when I think and talk of Our Lady."

"Talk on, dear father," said Eva, folding her hands together on her knees, while her countenance glowed with devotion; "talk on; it does me good."

"It does me good too, daughter, to think and talk of this Mother of the Redemption. Eve was the mother of creatures, Mary of souls. Both were created without sin: Eve fell, entailing sin and eternal death on her offspring; Mary brought life to hers, by giving birth to the Saviour who redeemed them, and suffering with Him all the penalties of guilt, that the guilty might be pardoned. Oh, it is wonderful! From the time she was promised to our first parents, to the hour when she gave birth to her Divine Son, the Scriptures are full of her. Everything foreshadowed her. The temple, built of the purest and most precious materials; the ark of the covenant; made of costly and indestructible wood, which none but priestly hands might touch and live, typified her who was to bear in her sacred womb the Holy One. The women Sara, Rebecca, Esther, Deborah, Judith, Ruth, Jael, Lea, Anna, Abigail, Noemi, Rachael and the Sunamite woman, were imperfect types of her who, as ' fair as the moon, bright as the sun, and terrible as an army in array,' was to crush the serpent's head. She is the burning bush of Moses which was yet unconsumed; she is the ' garden enclosed,' the new Eden into which nothing defiled could enter or taint; she is the ' sealed fountain' the waters of which nothing can pollute ; she is the ' eastern gate' through which the true Light enters; she is the ' brilliant dawn' which precedes the rising Sun ; she is the rainbow, the true sign of the new Covenant and man's reconciliation with the Most High ; she is the sacerdotal rod of Aaron which blossomed in the tabernacle ; she is the fleece of Gideon, moistened with heavy dews when all else remained dry and arid around it ; she is the dove always spotless, the lily ever pure, the rose ever fresh and without thorns. And what sweet and august epithets are bestowed

on her by the Book of books: ' Queen,' ' tabernacle
of the Most High,' ' house of God,' ' blessed land
of the Lord,' ' star of Jacob,' ' strong woman,' ' the
most beautiful among women,' ' the most happy
mother of beautiful love, of faith, of wisdom, of
holy hope, and full of grace.'   She is compared in
the holy pages to the pavilion of cedar, to the fount
in the garden, to the light of the morning, to the
source of the waters of life which flows from
Libanus, to the azure of the heavens, to the cypress
of Zion, to odorous and precious perfume, to storax,
to spikenard, to galbanum!   As the heavens are
filled with stars, so are the Scriptures gemmed
with the glories of Mary brightening up that long
night of gloom from the fall to the Birth of the
Messiah!   I had read over and over again all these
names and titles without knowing to whom they
applied until the scales fell from my eyes and I beheld her crowned with them as with a precious
diadem before which the lustre of all other crowns
is eclipsed!   All the inspired writers delighted to
speak of her.   Isaias exclaims: ' Behold! a Virgin
shall conceive and bring forth a Son whose name
shall be Emmanuel.'   In another place he says:
' And there shall come forth a rod out of the root
of Jesse, and a flower shall rise up out of his root.'
Jeremias declares: ' The Lord hath created a new
thing on earth, a woman shall compass a man.'

And here," said Wolfert Flemming, taking a small
book from his breast and holding it close to catch
the light, now almost faded into night, " is what
Tertullian, St. Jerome, and St. Bernard, interpret-
ing these words, exclaim : ' This woman is Mary!
The root of Jesse signifies the race of David ; the
scion of this root is the Virgin of Israel; and the
flower born of this scion is Jesus Christ, the Son
of Mary. Most truly,' " he went on reading, in
almost exultant tones, " ' a creature promised by
God Himself to our first parents at the beginning of the world ; a creature who was to have
part in the designs of the Most High for the salvation of the world ; a creature prefigured by so many
mysterious types, represented by so many illus-
trious women ; a creature called by such beautiful
names, and on whom was bestowed such gracious
and honorable titles ; a creature predicted and announced by the prophets, could not be an ordinary
being. She must have had prerogatives above
those of common humanity !   No ! there is nothing
in all this to surprise us, for is not MARY the mar-
vel of marvels, an abyss of miracles ; the greatest
wonder the heavens or the earth ever beheld ?
From these considerations flowed the belief that
she was, by the power of the Most High, conceived
without sin ; it is from this assemblage of wonders
that the faith of all Christian ages in it was derived

—a faith which is in itself one of the strongest proofs of the fact.'"

"I believe it, father. How could I doubt it? I could not believe that Eve, who was to be the mother of mankind, was created without sin, and that Mary, who was to be the Mother of Jesus Christ our Saviour, was not. Oh, I am sorry it is growing so dark! This has been so lovely, dear father!" exclaimed Eva. Just then there came a sound from the outside of the door, like a smothered sob, and there was a rustle of garments retreating down the long dark passage; and when Eva went out she could discover nothing, and thought it might have been the rustling of the branches of the huge old trees against the windows —for she remembered how often she had heard that, and what an eerie sound they made, scraping and tapping on the glass.

"I forgot to tell you, father," she said, as they walked together along the passage, "that poor Ruby is quite ill. He fainted dead away this morning."

"My poor lad! Where is he; I'll go straight to him,' he answered.

There was no light in the boy's room. He saw the dim outline of his wife, standing against the window, looking drearily out on the gathering shadows—and he spoke cheerily, saying:

"You see I am back, mother. How is the lad."

"He's a little weak, that's all," she replied without turning her head. She would never admit that it was anything but weakness when Reuben had one of his attacks. "He has not been out to exercise in the open air for several days, but has been moping around, doing nothing, and it don't agree with him."

Wolfert Flemming groped his way to the bed, and stooping down to kiss the boy found that his face was drenched with tears; then he gathered him up in his strong arms and held the beautiful head, with its golden tangles of hair, upon his breast, and leaned his cheek upon it as tenderly as a woman. Mrs. Flemming was watching; accustomed to the gloom of the room, she saw it all, and her eyes overflowed with tears; she longed to go and lay her head beside Reuben, on her husband's shoulder; her heart was full almost to bursting with tenderness and pity; but her Puritan pride held her back silent and motionless.

"Father," whispered Reuben, "I'll be a man yet!"

"Get well, my lad; get well and strong again; that is all I ask," answered his father. "I'll sit here, mother, if you wish to go down."

"Yes, I have something to attend to. But tell me, before I go, if you made any bargain with Deacon Flynt about the farm?" she said, turning to go.

"None, I am sorry to say!" he replied, "He had bought one nearer home."

"I thought nothing would come of it," she said with a sigh.

"I shall be well enough to churn for you, 'little mammy,' in the morning," said Reuben, while he folded his father's great hand close to his breast.

"I hope so, Ruby. I'm sure I shall be glad to have you notwithstanding you make 'ducks and drakes' of my cream," she replied as she left the room.

"It is so good to be resting here on your breast," said Reuben. "Did you bring me a letter, father?"

"No, my lad; do you expect a letter?"

"Yes, sir; and I think I shall be better when it comes."

"Whom do you expect a letter from?"

"I would rather not tell you now, sir. I will show it to you when it comes."

"Very well. It can be nothing wrong, if you are willing that I should see it."

"No, father, I don't think it is wrong, what I have been doing. Maybe it is foolish," answered Reuben thoughtfully.

"I guess this letter will explain some of your little mysteries, my lad?"

"Yes, sir—all of them. Oh, I wish it would come! I do wish it would come! Father, if that

letter comes, and is what I expect, I shall be as
well and chipper as a robin."

"Perhaps it may come to-morrow. Always hope
for the best."

"I never hope for anything else, father. Why,
I feel better already, just thinking about it. These
sugs that I have are nothing. I just run down like
a Connecticut clock, and get wound up again,
ready for anything; and it has done me lots of
good to see you." And Reuben put his arms
about his father's neck, and, clinging close to him,
fell into a deep refreshing sleep, with a pleasant
smile parting his lips. Wolfert Flemming laid him
gently down upon the pillows, shaded the candle—
which some one had come in and lit—and stood
looking down at the rarely chiselled features of this
the Benjamin of his flock; at the wild curling hair
that shone like a golden aureole around his forehead, and at the long tapering hand, so small and
shapely, for all the world like the hands of his an-
cestress, Lady Pendarvis: then, laying his own
lightly upon his head, blessed him from the depths
of his heart, and went down stairs to join his
family at tea.

The next afternoon Hope and Eva thought they
would go down to "Mill Farm," to find out how
the Wilburs were getting on. They had not been
there for several days—there being no need—for

Wilbur had got work, and his wife was up and about again, thanks to their assistance and help. But they did not like to give the poor family up altogether; so, putting a fresh loaf of brown bread from the morning baking, some doughnuts and a pound of sweet butter into a basket, they started on their errand of Christian kindness. But when they got in sight of the house, they saw to their amazement that all the doors and windows were closed, and no sign of life about it.

"What in the world can be the matter?" exclaimed Eva.

"It looks as if they had flitted;" said Hope, laughing; "only I am sure they would not do such a thing without letting us know."

"No, I guess not. They are too grateful for the little we have done for them to behave like that."

"Well now, Eva, I don't think it *is* a *very* 'little' that we have done. It was the best we could do, and it proved 'much' for them, poor souls; and if they have gone off—" said Hope, whose eyes began to sparkle.

"Why, even the cow's gone!" exclaimed Eva.

Just then they heard a rustling in the myrtle bushes near them, and looking round they saw little Ned Wilbur's white head sticking up from among the purple furze that grew knee-high thereabouts.

"Why, Neddy, is that you?" said Hope, laugh
ing.

"Yes'm; it be."

"How are all your folks to-day?"

"They's right well. 'm."

"Here's a doughnut for you, Neddy." The boy
sprang out from his covert, and snatching the
doughnut from her hand, began to eat, winking
his eyes and smacking his lips with delight, while
his wild little heart grew mellow with the flavor of
the delicious morsel. The sisters laughed, and
Eva said : "Neddy, what in the world are you all
shut up so tight down there for ?"

"I'm 'fraid to tell!" he replied, munching.

"Tell me this minute, Ned, and I'll give you
another doughnut," said Hope. The bait was too
inviting, and Neddy began to nibble.

"Daddy shut the house up to keep the Papishers
out. Father Ray bid him to. Daddy's goin' away
—he is—and all of us," said Neddy with his glistening eyes fixed on the doughnut in Hope's hand.

"For what? Where ever in the world are you
all going ?"

"Why, you see, 'm, Father Ray got my daddy
some work, and he told him if he didn't stop
lettin' you all come round us he'd have it tuk away
from him and have us all sent to jail for beggars.
I 'clare he did, 'm; so mammy toult me to tell you,

when I see you, please not to come no more. Gimme my doughnut now!"

"I won't give you a crumb of it until you go and ask your mother if we may come in; I want to see her," said Hope.

"I'll go, 'm," answered Neddy, upon whose palate lingered enough of the delicious taste of the doughnut to make him ravenous for more. He crept into the house, through some loophole Hope 'and Eva could not discover, and presently they heard alternate whacks and yells sounding from within, and while they were wondering what the hubbub meant, Neddy came rushing towards them rubbing his shoulders and legs, his face looking like a harlequin's, it was so besmirched with dirt and tears—the redness of his freckled skin showing in bars across his cheeks—while he screamed between his sobs: "Go 'way; mammy says go 'long away. She don't want you to come anighst her. Father Ray's going to send us to school, and give us a house to live in; an' it'll ruin us, mammy says, if you don't go right away. Now gimme my doughnut."

"Well—I declare!" exclaimed Hope. "Eva, I have good mind to march right in and give that ungrateful woman a blowing-up."

"No, don't," answered Eva; "don't. It's all the

same, darling, if you will only remember for whose dear sake we helped them."

"After our self-denial, and working for them like negroes! I declare I can't stand it—I must go and tell her what I think of it!"

"And lose the merit of your good works, and the sweet approval of Him for whose sake you worked!" remonstrated Eva. "Come! let us go back."

"No. I intend to whip Neddy. Let him suffer vicariously for his ungrateful family," answered Hope grasping Neddy's ragged sleeve.

"No! no!—dont'ee, dont'ee—Miss Hope. I smarts all over now, mammy dinged at me so," cried the boy, dancing with fright.

"I have a mind to," said Hope, laughing. "Here—here's your doughnut, Neddy, and go take this loaf of bread and pot of fresh butter to your mammy, and tell her not to put them on her head, there might be coals of fire in them. Tell her that's the way that *Papishers* punish their enemies. Clear out with you." The urchin needed no second bidding, but scampered off as fast as his legs could carry him.

"It's as funny as exasperating!" exclaimed Hope.

"I'm glad we had a chance to help them in their need," said Eva.

"I suppose I ought to be, too, but I really am not. I should like to shake them all! such fanaticism! Why, they would have starved, if it had not been for the help they got. Why didn't Parson Ray help them then? It is true that the ways of men are past finding out."

"You don't mean half that you say, darling?"

"Yes, I do; every word."

"What did you send those things for then? Ah, I've caught you there!"

"No, you haven't. I sent them just for the satisfaction of sending that message about the coals of fire with them. The ungrateful creatures!" replied Hope.

Then they turned and walked away, strolling on until they reached the lake shore, where they sat down to watch the lights and shadows ever flitting from the clouds above over the summer ripples as they flowed around the fair islands and laved the giant feet of the Ossipee. While they sat there talking, and drinking in the loveliness of the scene, their attention was attracted by a gentleman evidently a stranger in the neighborhood, who had a small pouch hung over his shoulder which they thought at the first glimpse was a bird-bag; but as he had no gun, only a queerly constructed hammer in his hand, with which he went about cracking pieces of rock off the boulders that projected here

and there from the earth, they took it for granted
that he was no hunter; but what he was so idly
busy about, they could not imagine, and thought
he might be just a little flighty. This idea and the
lengthening shadows together, warned them that it
was time to turn their faces homeward.

It was almost dark when they got back, and their
father and mother—and Reuben, who was better—
were about sitting down to tea. Hope gave a
spirited account of the Mill Farm adventure, at
which Reuben laughed, and his father with a grave
smile said:

"It will always be a pleasant thought, daughters,
that we were able to help them a little in their extreme want. I am glad Wilbur has found work."

"It is nothing more than I expected," said Mrs.
Flemming, drily, while her handsome eyes snapped
sparkles of their old fires.

"Well! well! it was only human nature for
them to follow their worldly interests, having no
higher aim, and knowing nothing better," said
Wolfert Flemming. "The fanaticism of their
friends and advisers is more to be deplored than
the little mortification it may occasion us to feel."

"I'd like to know why Father Ray did not do
something for them when they were sick and starving; and so I shall tell him," said Mrs. Flemming.

"Let it rest, mother; discussion will do no good, and may provoke angry feelings," said her husband.

"I can't help it. I shall speak my mind," she answered.

"Hark!" exclaimed Reuben. "I think I hear the wagon bells! Yes! yes! I know the sound of the bells! Just listen, all of you!"

And, listening, true enough they heard the musical jingle of the horses' bells coming nearer and nearer, then uprose a cheery halloo, and they knew that Nicholas was almost there. Wolfert Flemming arose from the table and went out, followed by Reuben, to meet him, and the little mother bestirred herself to get ready a substantial supper for the hungry traveller, well knowing that Nick always came home from a journey with the appetite of a kite—wondering all the while if he had returned with an empty wagon and a full wallet—half fearing (she was always expecting the worst now) that he had found a poor market for his wares and brought them back. Before long he came in, hugged and blessed her as he always did, shook hands and kissed his sisters, then sat down to his supper, saying: "I'm awfully hungry. Mother, I'll tell you all about business presently. It's all right, you know. Hope, have you seen Huldah since I went away?"

"Yes, she was here yesterday. You know she is

to come whenever she pleases now, and you are to go there as you used to," answered Hope.

"Whew" said Nicholas, cutting into a cranberry pie, "I don't know when I shall go, though! I don't like being played fast-and-loose with."

"Pshaw, Nick! where's the use in minding Deacon Sneathen?" said Hope.

"I don't," answered Nick, while he thought of Huldah and her secret; "I don't mind him any more than I do an old turkey-cock."

"Then don't hurt Huldah's feelings by not going."

Reuben and his father now came in and drew up around the table with the rest.

"I was glad to find that wagon empty, Nick," said his father.

"Yes, sir! I had splendid luck; sold everything I took along, and could have sold more if I had had it. Mother, Deacon Green, at Plymouth, bought your carpet; and what do you think he said?"

"What?" inquired Mrs. Flemming sharply. "There's nothing the matter with the carpet; there's not an uneven thread in it."

"He said he'd buy the carpet, not only because it was a very handsome one and a good strong piece of work, but because it was made by one of the best women——".

Hu sh, Nick!" said Mrs. Flemming, " I don't want to hear what the Deacon said. What did he give for it ?"

"One of the best women," continued Nick, heedless of the interruption, " one of the best mothers, and one of the best wives in the world."

" That is so ; that is all true," they all exclaimed, delighted to hear their mother's praises from so good and honorable a man as Deacon Green, while her husband looked at her with a flush of pleasure on his calm handsome face. Then Nick added, as he took out his wallet and handed it to her, " He paid cash for it, mother; it's all there with the rest ; about two hundred dollars in all. The Deacon paid one dollar a yard for the carpet."

"Hand it over to your father, Nicholas," said Mrs. Flemming, a bright light in her eyes and a flush upon her cheeks. " It is his."

"Keep it, mother, until the time comes to use it," said Wolfert Flemming, lifting his heavy brows and looking at her with a heavenly tenderness in his clear truthful eyes—for the man's heart was profoundly touched.

" Very well," she answered, coldly.

Then they laughed and talked together, Nicholas telling them all that he had seen in Plymouth and Holderness, and what sharp bargains he had driven with people who wanted to take advantage of him because they thought him inexperienced in business; then they told him about the Wilburs, and after he had laughed over the comical way that Hope related their adventure at "Mill Farm," he declared that he would go there betimes the next morning and thrash the whole family; which of course he had no idea of doing, but it did the young fellow good to say it and think that he should like to do it.

Wolfert Flemming sat up late that night talking over his plans with Nicholas. "If he could not raise the money to meet the note due on the first of December he should sell the Homstead farm, rent the house and garden—he could not bear even to think of selling his house—and move his family to Ohio, where he would begin the world anew."

"But, father, how do you expect to raise the money—a thousand dollars?" asked Nicholas, gravely and sorrowfully.

"I hope to sell "Mill Farm," my lad; and there's a balance due me from Sneathen & Flemming—a balance of three hundred dollars. I hope to raise the money," said the man, lifting up his head and drawing a long breath; and his upward look and deeply-drawn sigh seemed like a prayer, it was so full of trust and pathos.

"And I want you to go up to 'The Pines,'" he

said, presently, "as soon as you get rested, my lad."

"I'm not tired, sir. I'd like nothing better than to start to-morrow," said Nick, glad of an excuse not to go near Huldah, while he was longing in his very heart to see her; but she had a secret which she kept from him, and as long as she with-held her confidence he didn't care to meet her, for that secret had made a coldness between them which rendered their interviews anything but pleasant.

"Very well; thank you, my lad. Be ready to start early in the morning. Good night."

"Good night, father," said the young man. Then, instead of going to bed as he should have done, he put on his hat and went out into the clear frosty night, and walked about a mile up to the turn in the road, whence he could see afar off the light shining from Huldah's window; and there he stood—foolish fellow—watching it, and imagining he saw her shadow flitting back and forth, when it was suddenly extinguished; then he went home and tumbled into bed, and had no sooner stretched himself upon it than he was sound asleep—for Nick was no Romeo.

He was away two or three days, and came back without the money. "Deacon Sneathen"—he told his father—"was up to 'The Pines,' and seemed to be in a dreadful fuss. I tell you what it is, father —if there's not trouble brewing there, my name's not Nicholas. The Deacon told me, when I let him know what I had come after, that it was one of the things that had brought him up there, to examine the books and settle your claim; 'but,' says he, 'I can't do it now, Nick. I can't do it until the middle of October, no how. My pardner hesn't put nothing into the business, and he's drawed five thousand dollars out of it to build that dratted steam saw-mill with;' and if you'll believe me, sir," continued Nicholas, "they haven't got above the foundation yet. Jones, the foreman— you remember Jones, father—he told me up and down that he believed things were all going to smash; and said it was awful, the prayer-meetings that the new partner keeps up. The fellows up there don't care much about prayer-meetings, you know, sir; they like, when their day's work is over, to go to each other's huts and smoke their pipes, and drink a little, and tell yarns; but the new man wants to break up all their old habits, and make them come to prayer-meeting; and those who won't come he dismisses. There'll be a row up there before long. The Deacon's at his wits' end."

"I'm glad of it; I am heartily glad he is," snapped Mrs. Flemming, from her corner, where she sat reeling her fine yarn into hanks.

"Mother!" said Wolfert Flemming, looking up in surprise.

"I am heartily glad of it," she repeated; "and it serves him right."

"And father"—Nicholas continued, after a quiet little laugh in his sleeve at his mother's outbreak—"what do you think the Deacon said?"

"What, my lad?"

"He said, sir, that he had never had any trouble about his accounts or his affairs while you managed them; that everything went on fair and square, and there was no muss of any sort but now everything was in a 'dratted tangle and confusion.'"

"Serves him right!" exclaimed Mrs. Flemming.

"And he didn't know at which end to begin putting things to rights," continued Nicholas.

"I'm glad of it," repeated Mrs. Flemming, making her reel fly round; "I never was so glad of anything in my life."

"Let us pray for our enemies, and bless those who despitefully use us," said Wolfert Flemming, in his grave, sonorous tones—for his great, forgiving heart was really pained to learn how his old associate's affairs were going to the bad.

"You can do it, father; I can't. I should be a hypocrite to say I could. To throw you over like he did, for a 'man gifted in prayer!' But I think the gifted creature will be a little more than he

bargained for. I am honestly glad to hear it all "
replied Mrs. Flemming.

CHAPTER XXII.

THE MAN WITH THE HAMMER—THE LAST BITTER DROP.

Golden September had melted into crisp, ruddy
October. The autumnal fruits and the poor har-
vests of the summer were gathered in, made the
most of, and stored away in granaries and barns.
People were thankful when they found there would
be enough to subsist their own families and stock
on during the coming winter; it was more than
they had expected. Looking down from one of the
peaks of Prospect Hill, the beautiful valley of the
Pernigewasset appeared like a kaleidescope; it
was so dappled and checkered and striped with
crimson, russet, orange, scarlet and rich winter-
green; it was so gay with flashing waters, so spangled with peaks of glittering quartz, so beautified
by mountain ranges, melting off into the distance
in exquisite shades of blue and purple!

Apple-parings, singing-classes and quilting bees,
with all the other gatherings in which these thrifty
people blended the *utile* and *dulce* at this season of
the year, began to make the neighberhood lively;

but our friends at the Old Homestead—who were, you know, morally outlawed—remained quietly at home, receiving no invitations, and too busy over their own domestic affairs to take the slight much to heart. There were moments when they all felt the mortification of being so utterly neglected; they would have been more than human had they not; but, thinking over the cause, they were straightway consoled, and offered themselves anew to Him who said: "Blessed are they that suffer persecution for justice sake, for theirs is the kingdom of heaven. Blessed are ye when men shall revile you . . . . and speak all manner of evil against you, untruly, for MY sake; be glad and rejoice, for your reward is very great in heaven."

And what did all they had suffered, and still expected to suffer, weigh against this magnificent promise? Nothing; and in their souls they were glad and rejoiced, even as the sun shines behind the cloud, even as the rainbow crowns the brow of the storm!

Deacon Sneathen had sent Wolfert Flemming a check for the three hundred dollars, and Nicholas had been down to Plymouth again with his loaded wagon, and came back with a hundred more; this, with the two hundred on hand, left a balance of four hundred to make up the needed amount; but where or how it was to be raised none of them could imagine. The outlook was discouraging. No one seemed to want to buy " Mill Farm ;" this was the last resource, except selling out altogether But they did not make each other miserable by desponding and worrying over the situation, and went on exactly as if nothing had happened, full of grave thoughts, it is true, and often wondering how it would end, but trying cheerfully to bear each other's burdens. Nicholas was the most gloomy and unhappy of them all, except his mother. Coldness had grown up between him and Huldah : he was too proud to ask, she too proud to offer an explanation, consequently he had not availed himself of the Deacon's permission to visit the house again. Poor Huldah! her secret had been productive of nothing but trouble to her. If her little mystery had turned out as she had hoped, it would have explained itself and exonerated her fully ; but the letter she had been so long expecting had not come yet, and "never would," she thought. Neither had Reuben's letter come. But the two letters had nothing to do with each other.

Things were in this way, when one bright morning as Reuben was creeping slowly along in the sunshine towards the Old Mill, everything looked so lovely that he sat down on a moss-covered rock to enjoy the scene of which his poet's heart never grew weary. The little rivulet—all that was left of

the big brawling stream that used to turn the great
mill-wheel—was dancing and flashing over the
pebbles at his feet, making a low murmur as sweet
as the tinkling of silver bells. Reuben was soothed
by the sound into a reverie half pleasant, half sad;
a dreamy mist arose out of his mental life, through
which he caught glimpses of a promised land. He
abandoned himself to his dreams, and believing
that he was alone with nature, yielded himself entirely to their sweet entrancement.

"A fine day!" said a loud, harsh voice, somewhere over him; and starting round, Reuben saw
the man with the hammer. "A very fine, wholesome day."

"Yes, sir," replied the lad, touching his hat.
The blood had all gone in an instant from his delicate face at the sudden address and sight of the
stranger, and as swiftly returned, flushing his
cheeks like roses.

"I beg your pardon. I started you considerably,
I reckon; but I'm a rough sort of a fellow," he said,
good-naturedly. "The truth is, I live so much
alone among the woods and rocks that I'm afraid I
sometimes forget the customs of civilization."

"I'm glad to see you, sir," replied Reuben, at a
loss what else to say. "I've been sick, you see,
and any little thing makes me jump. Are you a
stranger up here?"

"I was, a month or so ago; but I have trudged over every inch of ground, mountain and valley, within ten miles round, and know them all like old friends. In fact, I shall hate to go away, for the scenery is the grandest I ever saw."

"Hadn't you better stay, sir? You'll lose a great deal if you miss seeing the winter up here."

"No; I can't stay. I'm writing a book, a history of New Hampshire, and shall have to hurry home in a week or two to get the first part of it in type!" Reuben's heart began to go out to the man; and when he found out that he was an author, he felt as if he had met one of the genii of his dreams, and regarded him with a strange mixture of awe and delight. "How grand that mountain bluff, with the scarlet sumachs waving from its crevices, looks with the sunlight shining upon its bald brow! What do you call that?"

"That is Chocorua, sir!"

"An Indian name?"

"Yes, sir."

"I hope it has a legend?"

"It has a true, veritable history, sir," replied Reuben, whose eyes kindled and whose interest in the man increased.

"I should be very glad to hear it, if it is not too long. I dote on these Indian legends."

"It is not very long," replied Reuben, now in his

glory; "and I shall be glad to relate it. Many years ago," he began, "a colony of hardy, intelligent pioneers settled at the foot of the mountains, and the chief man among them was named Cornelius Campbell, whose gigantic stature impressed the Indians with awe, and whose superior intellect threw a spell over his companions, who felt that although he was among them he was not of them. He had the bold, quick tread of one who had often wandered fearlessly among the terrible hiding-places of nature; and while his voice was harsh, his countenance, sometimes under the gentle influences of his home, unveiled a deep tenderness of expression which lit up his hard features like the sunlight on a rugged headland. His wife was a beautiful, high born lady, who had displeased her father by rejecting some splendid offers of marriage for the sake of Cornelius Campbell, who had been a zealous and active enemy of the Stuarts, and whose hopes were finally crushed by the restoration of Charles II. He and his beautiful bride fled to America, and accompanied the party who formed the little colony which settled in this place, which was so remote from all intercourse with civilization that they endured great hardships and sufferings. From the Indians they received neither injury nor insult. No cause of offence had ever arisen; and although their visits were frequent and troublesome to the white settlers, they never exhibited the least jealousy or malice.

"In the tribe there was a prophet named Chocorua, who was to his people an object of peculiar veneration. He had a mind which education and motive would have nerved with giant strength; but growing up in savage freedom, it wasted itself in dark, fierce, ungovernable passions. There was something fearful in the quiet haughtiness of his lips; it seemed so like slumbering power—too proud to be lightly roused, too implacable to sleep again. In his small, black, fiery eye, expression lay coiled up like a beautiful snake. The whites knew that his hatred would be terrible; but they never provoked it; and even the children became too much accustomed to him to fear him.

"Chocorua had a son ten years old, to whom Caroline Campbell had occasionally made such gaudy presents as were likely to attract his savage fancy. This won the boy's affections, and he became almost an inmate of their dwelling; and being unrestrained by the courtesies of civilized life, he would inspect everything and taste everything which came in his way. One day he discovered some poison which had been prepared for a mischievous fox which had long troubled the little settlement, and drank it, then went home to his father to sicken and die. From that moment hatred and vengeance took possession of Chocorua's soul. He did not speak of his suspicions, but brooded over them in secret, to nourish the deadly revenge he contemplated against Cornelius Campbell. One bright, balmy morning in June, Campbell left his dwelling for the fields. Still a lover, though ten years a husband, his last look was towards his wife, answering her parting smile; his last act a kiss for each of his children. When he returned to dinner they were all dead, and their disfigured bodies too cruelly showed that an Indian's hand had done the work.

"In such a mind, grief, like every other emotion, was stormy. His home had been to him the only green spot in life. In his wife and children he had garnered up all his heart; and now they were so terribly torn from him, the remembrance of their love clung to him like the death-grapple of a drowning man, sinking him down into darkness and death. Then followed a calm a thousand times more terrible. Those who knew and reverenced him feared that his reason was forever extinguished. But it kindled again, and with it came a wild demoniac spirit of revenge. The death-groan of Chocorua would make him smile in his dreams; and, when he awaked, death seemed too pitiful a vengeance for the anguish that was eating into his soul.

" At the time of the murder, Chocorua's brethren were absent on a hunting expedition, and those who watched his movements observed that he frequently climbed the high precipice which afterwards took his name, looking out probably for their return. Here Campbell resolved to effect his deadly purpose. A party was formed under his guidance to cut off all chances of retreat, and the dusky prophet was to be hunted like a wild beast to his lair.

" The morning sun had scarce cleared away the fogs, when Chocorua was startled by a loud voice from beneath the precipice, commanding him to throw himself into the abyss below : ' The Great Spirit gave life to Chocorua, and Chocorua will not throw it away at the command of the white man," he answered.

" ' Then hear the Great Spirit speak in the white man's thunder,' exclaimed Campbell, as he pointed his gun at the precipice. Chocorua, though as fierce and fearless as a panther, had never overcome his dread of fire-arms. He placed his hands upon his ears to shut out the report ; the next moment the blood spirted from his neck, and he reeled fearfully on the edge of the precipice. But he recovered himself ; and, raising himself on his hand, he shouted in a voice that grew more terrific as its harshness increased : ' A curse upon ye, white men ! May the Great Spirit curse ye, when

He speaks in the clouds and His words are fire! Chocorua had a son, and ye killed him while the sky looked bright. May the lightnings blast your crops!—winds and fire destroy your houses!—the evil spirit breathe upon your cattle!—your graves lie in the red man's war-path!—panthers howl and wolves fatten on your bones! Chocorua goes to the Great Spirit!—his curse stays with the white man.' Still uttering inaudible curses, he died, and they left his bones to whiten in the sun. But his curse rested on those settlers. The tomahawk and scalping-knife were busy among them; the winds tore up trees and hurled them at their dwellings; their crops were blasted, their cattle died, and sickness came upon their strongest men. At last the remnant of them left the fatal spot, to mingle with more prosperous colonies, while Cornelius Campbell became a hermit, seldom seeing his fellow-men, and two years after he was found dead in his hut,[*] And to this day the cattle in Burtontown, over there, die off with a strange disease, and the people believe it is owing to Chocorua's dying curse."

"Muriate of lime, I guess, in the springs," said the stranger, as Reuben ended the legend. "What you have been telling me is very interesting. I have been making notes, you see, and shall put it into my book. Really, I am much obliged to you.

* Abridged from Mrs. Child's account.

And you told it with spirit, too! You must be a poet! Yes, that is beyond doubt the most picturesque feature in the landscape."

"There is a finer glimpse of it, sir, from the upper windows of the Old Mill over there, if you care to see it," said Reuben, flushed with excitement.

"I'd go anywhere to look at a fine view,'· replied the stranger, picking up his hammer and carpet-bag, as he rose up from the mossy bank upon which he had been half lying. They crossed the brook and entered the ruinous building, and climbed up the crazy, dilapidated stairs to the long room under the roof, which had formerly been used by the miller to store away his finest grain in. They looked from the window northward, and the stranger was enthusiastic, as well he might be, for nothing could surpass the grandeur of the view—Chocorua towering in the midst, like a steel-hooded giant! At last there was nothing more to be seen, and the stranger turned away from the windows and stood scanning the black rafters overhead—then, looking up and down, walked quietly towards a rough table at the lower end of the room, upon which lay several rudely-hewn blocks of stone and something covered with a coarse cloth.

"I shall have to go now," said Reuben, uneasily.

"What have we here? Wait one moment!" answered his companion, as with the restless curiosity of a tourist he pulled aside the cloth and discovered a finely sculptured head of a woman, the bust unfinished. There was a wistful, despairing expression in the face, a sorrowful appeal in every faultless feature, and the effect was heightened by the color of the material out of which it was chiselled—a bluish gray stone, which gave it the appearance of an antique. Uttering an exclamation of surprise, the stranger turned to Reuben, and asked him "whose work it was, and what it meant?"

"I had nothing to do, sir, and I have been experimenting a little with the chisel," answered the lad, modestly. "I spend my mornings here, reading and chipping; and that is a face I tried to make like Hagar's when her child was dying of thirst."

"And you have succeeded! The effect is admirable! But the stone—where did you get the stone?" asked the man, cracking a fragment off one of the blocks with his hammer, and examining it closely through a magnifying glass.

"I found it a few rods from here," answered Reuben.

"Is it possible? I have seen no specimens like it anywhere before. Who owns the land?"

"My father—Mr. Flemming."

"Ah!—does there seem to be much of it—the stone, I mean."

"Yes. I found it by accident, while I was looking for something that I could work easily. It is very soft and smooth. I think there's a good lot of it."

"What does your father intend doing with it?" inquired the man, looking keenly at Reuben.

"I don't think he knows anything about it. At least he wants to sell the place," answered guileless Reuben.

"Hasn't he seen this?" said the stranger, pointing to Hagar.

"No. They don't know how I spend my time here; and I haven't told them, because I was afraid they would think it all nonsense," replied Reuben.

"It's not nonsense, certainly. What a situation this would be for a summer cottage. I should like to buy the place myself, but I fear that I am not rich enough."

"My father only expects to get two thousand dollars for it," said Reuben, full of zeal.

"That's moderate. The scenery around is almost worth the money. The land don't seem to be much, though."

"Good crops have been got out of it sometimes; but this has been a bad year, and the man who lives on it has been too sick to work it," answered

Reuben, standing up bravely for the reputation of the land.

" I should like to see your father. Where is he to be found ?"

" I am going home now, and if you like you can come with me, sir," replied Reuben. " I know that father will be glad to see you; he is anxious to sell as soon as he can."

" Thank you ; I'll go."

" How shall I introduce you to my father, sir?" asked Reuben in some embarrassment.

" My name is Cutter—Ethan Cutter," replied the man-with-the-hammer.

Mr. Ethan Cutter had a long interview with Wolfert Flemming, who received and treated him with kind hospitality ; and when he took leave he had as good as promised to buy Mill Farm and pay two thousand dollars cash for it. This was great news for Mrs. Flemming and the girls ; and they all praised Reuben, and were so thankful that their father's troubles seemed to be coming so nearly to an end that every one was glad, and so cheerful that it seemed quite like the old times again. No more anxiety about that dreadful note, no more fear of breaking up and leaving their dear old home—" and," said Wolfert Flemming, " since Almighty God has been so good to us, we will go to Boston to receive baptism, and be received into the Church. This is the first wish of my heart."

"That will be a great happiness, father," said Eva in a low voice.

"It will indeed," added Hope earnestly.

"To think of really receiving those august Sacraments! Oh, my God!" exclaimed Wolfert Flemming, folding his hands together and looking up with an expression none had ever seen on his face before, "it is like the thought of entering into Thy very presence." None of them had ever seen him betray emotion like this before; it was as if the man's soul were suddenly unveiled and he transfigured before them. No one spoke; an awe had fallen upon them, and to at least some of them his words had a deep and sublime significance which thrilled their hearts, almost making them still. Mrs. Flemming grew very white, and her hands dropped into her lap while she sat as if in expectation of something; but nothing more happened; her husband got up quietly and left them, and Eva, listening to his retreating footsteps, knew that he had gone up stairs into the little sanctuary to pour out his full soul at the feet of Jesus and Mary.

They expected every day to hear from or see Ethan Cutter, but were disappointed. Wolfert Flemming could not account for his silence; he had seemed so eager to buy "Mill Farm," and said

so positively that he would return in about ten days
with the money and take possession ; but the days
had run into weeks, and he had neither come or
written!   What could it mean?   Had the man
changed his mind? or was he a sharper?   He
might be dead ; he was always scrambling among
the rocks,—perhaps he had fallen and broken his
neck ; perhaps he had been waylaid and murdered
for the money he had about him !   This surmising
and expecting, was a weary and unprofitable business, and at last they gave it up, feeling blind and
tired ; but knowing well whose right hand was
leading them, and having done all that humanly
speaking they could do, they gravely awaited God's
will, praying for submission to it whatever it
might be.   The   bright prospects were clouded
over, and Wolfert Flemming resigned himself to
the worst.

In this strait a strange thing happened.   One
evening late, as he was coming from the stables
with the lantern still alight in his hand, a man approached him, gave him a letter, and hurried away
without speaking, before he could even get a
glimpse of his face. Thinking it was a strange proceeding, he however set the lantern on a barrel and
opening the letter, read it; his heavy eyebrows
lowering and every vestige of color fading out of
his face the while.   It ran,

" WOLFERT FLEMMING,"

" I know that the waters are rising around you, and that certain ruin threatens you. Abjure your Papistical errors ; place your candlestick once more upon the altar of Gospel truth ; return at once to the pure, simple doctrines which you have abandoned, and I will advance whatever money you may need.   ELISHA RAY."

Wolfert Flemming strode into the house, straight to his work-room, and placing the stable lantern upon his desk, he wrote :

" I write immediately, lest you fall into the error of thinking that I give your offer one moment's consideration. I have this instant received it, and suppose it is meant in kindness ; but I call my God to witness that nothing which this world contains of riches, honors, ease or fame, could induce me to deny my faith in the doctrines of the Holy, Apostolic, Catholic Church, which is the only true Church, and founded by Jesus Christ Himself.

Yours in Chrisian Charity,

WOLFERT FLEMMING."

Having folded and directed the letter, he took the lantern and went back to the stables, where he saddled his horse, and mounting him he galloped out into the road, never drawing rein until he got to Father Ray's door, where he dismounted, and knocked in a way that brought the old minister's housekeeper quickly to open it.

"Give that to the minister!" he said, handing her the letter; "and lose no time."

"Land sakes!" she almost screamed, peering over her spectacles; "if it ain't Elder Flemming!"

But he had mounted his horse again, and was off; and the woman stood gaping out into the night, listening to the tramp of the horse's hoofs with as frightened a look as if she had seen the evil one himself; indeed she believed to the day of her death that she had seen him in the likeness of the backsliding Elder.

"Why! where have you been?" inquired Mrs. Flemming as her husband came into the sitting-room, where they were waiting supper for him.

"I had a little business to attend to, mother, which was unexpected, and gave me no time to speak to any of you," he answered, speaking slowly and gently, for his spirit was still ruffled and he had need to restrain himself under this crowning, humiliating insult. To seek to take advantage of his misfortunes by offerng him money to abandon his faith—it was almost too much for the man's patience.

"Have you heard from that man?" asked Mrs. Flemming eagerly, hoping that the business was connected with the sale of Mill Farm.

"No indeed, mother. I think we may give up all expectation of seeing or hearing anything of Mr. Cutter again," he replied. "It seems hard, I know; but let us trust in God; we are in His hands, and His ways are not as our ways."

"I suppose that He knows best," she answered in a tone so softened and subdued, so unlike herself, that each one's heart was touched and went out in great pity and tenderness towards her.

Wolfert Flemming said nothing about the old minister's letter, and no further questions were asked concerning the business which had taken him away in such hot haste from home; but as they all sat around him that night in the bright ruddy light of the fire, which lit up every nook and cranny of the old room—the china and pewter on the shelves; the quaint *buffet* in the corner, with its treasures of silver all glittering and crinkling and flashing just as they did the first time we saw them—he talked over his plans with them about going to Ohio. It seemed so certain now that their home here must be broken up, he deemed it most wise and kind to repress any lingering hope they might entertain of remaining, by speaking unreservedly of their future, so as to accustom them to the thought of their approaching trial. A grave, chastened sadness fell upon them, and their tears flowed in silence and unchecked; the very idea of

leaving the spot so dear to them was like tearing
something away which had taken root in their
hearts; but they thought of each other, and of
Him who had borne the cross unto death for them;
and they resolved with His help to bear their
heavy trial with courage and patience and utter no
complaint or murmur.

"As there are no chances or accidents in God's
universe," said Wolfert Flemming, "let us console
ourselves with the assurance that there are none in
the affairs of men. If the hairs of our head are
numbered, and even the fall of the sparrow noted
by our Father in heaven, can we believe that He is
blind to the misfortunes and struggles of His creatures whom He so loved that He gave His only-
begotten Son to die for them. No, dear wife and
children, depend upon it that He is working out
His own designs for our salvation; and if the ways
by which He leads us are not pleasant ways, and
are repugnant to our nature, let us not repine, but
resign ourselves submissively to His providence,
looking beyond this transitory life to the exceeding
great and eternal reward that awaits us if we are
faithful and patient to the end.

There was a deep and solemn pathos in his voice
which fell with almost sacramental power upon
their souls, calming, consoling and strengthening
them with the simple, hopeful words he uttered.

Mrs. Flemming, contrary to her usual habit of late, did not go away when the hour of family prayer came, but remained listening patiently to the evening devotions—which her husband read with more than ordinary impressiveness—to the responses, to the Litany of Loretto, to the *Confiteor* and all, so new and strange to her Puritan ears. No one could tell what was passing in her soul as she listened ; but she was there. She had stayed of her own will, and the man's heart was gladdened in the midst of his sorrows by the sweet hope that she, too, would at last seek refuge and consolation in the bosom of the One True Faith.

The next day Eva went into the little Sanctuary of Our Lady, her arms full of vines and clusters of richly-tinted leaves, to beautify the spot dedicated to her ; to hang garlands upon her shrine, and offer her the last bright hues of the faded summer. While engaged in her pious occupation, saying a " Hail Mary " for every golden-tinted leaf, and an " Our Father" for the scarlet ones, as she arranged them here and there among the trailing vines, her mother came to the door to ask some question about certain winter garments which she was anxious to get out, the weather having grown very cold.

"Yes, mother, they are in the red chest; I packed them there myself," she answered.

"And that is the very one I didn't open," replied Mrs. Flemming, as she lingered a moment to admire the beautiful effect produced by the vines—which Eva had trained by means of a wire framework, over the image of the Blessed Virgin—and wonder if her child was indeed an idolator—when suddenly there was a terrific crash; a black, suffocating cloud filled the room, and she could see nothing. With a loud shriek which ran through the house, and thinking only of Eva's safety, she rushed blindly in to seek her.

Wolfert Flemming, who happened to be in his work-room at the moment, heard the crash overhead—heard his wife's terrified shriek, and ran up. In an instant he stood appalled upon the threshold of the door! The whole ceiling was down, he judged from the crash, but he could distinguish nothing through the thick cloud of suffocating dust; he could only hear his wife calling wildly on Eva, and with a terrible dread of, he scarcely knew what, he went in, and groping his way to the window threw it wide open; and as the dust, finding an outlet, began to float swiftly out, he saw Eva kneeling with her arms thrown around the image of the Blessed Virgin and the crucifix, as if to protect them—her head resting on her arm, her eyes closed, her face very white, and a sweet smile upon her lips, as if she were asleep dreaming pleasant dreams. Her mother stood over her in speechless woe, wringing her hands.

Wolfert Flemming stooped to lift his child in his arms, thinking she was dead, when a gentle sigh escaped her lips; the strong current of air from the window had revived her—and lifting up her head, she said: "Mother, I am not hurt."

"Oh, Eva!—oh, my child!—I thought you were dead!" exclaimed Mrs. Flemming, kneeling down to embrace her.

"I fainted, I believe," said Eva. "I couldn't think what it was, and was frightened."

"You have been saved from a sudden and terrible death by the interposition of the Blessed Virgin, my child," said her father, kneeling beside them; "let us thank her."

Eva was not only unhurt, but untouched by the fallen mortar. Neither had the fragile plaster image of the Blessed Virgin Mary received the slightest injury; not a leaf was disarranged, not a vine displaced; and the white linen cover of the table remained spotless and unlittered by the fragments!* Everything was in the same beautiful order upon it, just as it was when Mrs. Flemming stood admiring it at the moment of the accident. The ceiling must have parted in the middle, just over the table, and fallen away on either side; they could not tell exactly how Eva was preserved, and

* This incident actually occurred as related.

were very willing to ascribe it to the gracious protection of her whose devout client she was, and were deeply thankful for her deliverance.

After the excitement of the accident was over, and the *debris* cleared away and things placed in order once more, Mrs. Flemming, who had scarcely spoken since, but who looked very much flushed, and frequently pressed her hands upon her temples, suddenly staggered as she was crossing the room, and cried out : " Hope! Father! I can't see. Help me! help—" and fell fainting in Hope's arms. When she recovered she was in a raving delirium ; and when the doctor, who was quickly summoned, told them that he feared the worst, the afflicted family thought that the last bitter drop had been added to the cup of their sorrows.

CHAPTER XXIII.

LIGHT BEHIND THE CLOUD.

And now the shadow of death fell heavily over the Old Homestead, and there was a noiseless sorrow within, sorrow for the body and soul of her who lay there unconscious of it all ; grief for the wife and mother, in whom centered the deep love of the afflicted family. All the trials which had come surging around them of late—the loss of prosperity, the contempt of the world, the rending asunder of strong ties, the prospect of giving up the home that they loved with an indescribable affection, and going into exile amongst strangers ; were all nothing to this. In all the rest there was something human to grapple with, while they strove with a heroic spirit of sacrifice for submission to God's holy will ; but here they were helpless ; her life was in the hands of Him who gave it, and they could only watch each quick, panting breath, endeavor to soothe the wild outbreaks of her delirium, administer the remedies prescribed, and pray that if it were His holy will this bitter cup might pass from them. They tried to be resigned to the dreadful issue which appeared inevitable : and the honest endeavor was much, but it was not submission ; and they felt as if their Father in heaven were hiding His face from them. Then, as she seemed to draw nearer and nearer to the " Dark River," and all hopes of her recovery were fading and going out in their hearts, the cry of their souls arose far above human fears, or hopes, that Almighty God would pity her and grant her the gift of faith before she passed into His presence. And they offered up the great sorrow—they could do no more —in union with the bitter sorrows of Him who sweat great drops of blood in the Garden of Gethsemane.

Mrs. Flemming was very near unto death. She lay day after day in alternate lethargy and delirium. Sometimes she would start up, shrieking, "I see that woman! Not old Massisquoi—no! no! but a woman terrible in her brightness! Hide me from her; hide, oh hide me!" One day she exclaimed, her eyes luminous with fever, and staring out before her—"She saved Eva! I saw her! It's no use to waste your breath talking, Father Ray. What I see I believe! You are all a set of hard-hearted, canting Pharisees! I've been watching ye all, and comparing your ways with his, and they are not alike; ha! ha! ha! they're as far apart as the east is from the west. Ye have the word, but not the spirit—whitewashed sepulchres that ye are! Tearing, tearing like vultures at the tender flesh of the pure in heart! nagging, like bloodhounds, at the life, and limbs of the innocent! Go away, and let me sail over the dark, lonely sea! Is it the 'May Flower,' captain? How strange! there's the 'May Flower' sure enough, rolling and breaking up against Plymouth Rock! Oh, I'm afraid to go— the waters look so black—and there's the woman! —hide me from her!" And so she raved—sometimes coherently, as if she saw visions; sometimes wildly, as if horrible dreams were torturing her brain; and they could do nothing but weep and lave the burning forehead and hands, and look

lovingly, while they prayed, into the wild fever-
bright eyes which were so unconscious of their
presence, and kiss the quivering lips upon which
the short breath fluttered as if every moment it
might pass away forever.

It was almost too much for Wolfert Flemming,
who walked silently in and out, and watched beside her through the long nights, upon his knees,
holding her thin burning hand in his while he besought Almighty God to pity them and spare her,
ever adding: "But help me to say 'Thy will be
done,' for of myself I can do nothing."

The news of Mrs. Flemming's illness had gone
abroad; and many and kind were the inquiries
daily made by former friends and old neighbors;
many were their offers of service "It was their
duty," they thought, "she being one of themselves;" and out of human pity for the great grief
which had fallen upon the backsliding family, they
sincerely wished to do something kind and neigh-
borly, although they did not hesitate to say to one
another, that "it was only the just retribution of
heaven on the Flemmings for their apostacy," and
looked upon Mrs. Flemming as the victim of their
sin. Mrs. Wilde came from her distant home, prepared to stay several days; even the old minister
rode over, braving all that might be unpleasant in
the visit, to pray with and endeavor to console this

suffering member of his flock. But he was told that she was utterly unconscious and the doctor had ordered perfect quiet; and he went away with wrath in his heart. Wolfert Flemming thanked all who came, but added : "There is no need, friends. We are enough." And they turned homewards, wondering, while they shook their heads, "if they were going to let the woman die without Christian help?"

Huldah was there every day, coming in so quietly, with such a sorrowful look in her face, and speaking so gently, that Hope and Eva were comforted by her presence ; and many were the little tasks of love deftly done by her swift fingers, which, had she not been there, would have taken them away from their mother's bedside. It was a sweet labor of love to the girl to anticipate what was wanting and go and do it without a fuss. She took the neglected dairy under her charge, doing everything there just as she knew Mrs. Flemming would like to have it done; and, moving quietly to and fro through the house, restored all things to perfect order and cleanliness, thinking : "If she gets well, she shall have no worry." For, even a few days illness in a family throws the best-ordered domestic affairs into confusion ; and if the illness is prolonged, nothing is more forlorn than the look of neglect that reigns throughout the household. But although there under his roof, and facing with him the great sorrow which wrung his heart until he wished he might die, Huldah and Nicholas rarely exchanged a word with each other—seldom meeting, indeed, except at the table, where each one was so occupied with the subject of Mrs. Flemming's illness that nothing else was thought or spoken of.

Once he found her in the old sitting-room, looking out into the twilight very quiet and very sad, her forehead pressed against the window-pane, upon which the first snow-flakes of the season were drifting and melting, trickling down like tears. He watched her for a little while, then walked over and stood beside her, and laying his hand upon her shoulder, said: "Have you nothing to say to me, Huldah?"

"Nothing," she answered, starting round half frightened, for she did not know that a soul was near her until he spoke. "Less now than ever. I shall never tell you now."

"Not for the sake of my dying mother?" he asked.

"For her sake—no," she replied with quivering lips.

"I shall never ask you again," he said harshly—"remember that;" and he strode out of the room, leaving her where she stood weeping silently.

But at last there came a day when Hope and Eva observed that their mother's attacks of deli: rium were fewer and less violent, and she appeared to sleep more quietly. Wolfert Flemming and his boys had been out about the place much of the day, attending to some matters which could be no longer neglected without great loss, and their heavy hearts were much lightened when Huldah met them with the good news; but alas! the doctor came and told them that " these apparently favorable symptoms were the result of increasing weakness; the fever was abating, but he had not the slightest hope that she had vitality enough left to tide over the crisis." Implicit confidence in medical opinion was not a weakness of these strong-headed, healthy people, and somehow they hoped against hope and the doctor, and renewed their patient loving watch, noting every breath and counting every flutter of the weary pulse of their mother, feeling that their yearning hearts and firm faith *must* bring her back to them, *must* stay her feet on the very marge of the Dark River!

I have now got to a part of my story which, to those who have not followed attentively every thread, may appear incredible; but what I am going to relate is simply the result of natural causes, developed by individuals and circumstances, undoubtedly governed by Divine Providence for the good of those who were willing to sacrifice every earthly thing for conscience sake. The working out of the order of God's providence upon earth is one endless miracle and attestation of His watchfulness over the affairs of His children; let us not be surprised, then, at any manifestation of His goodness, be it great or small, but with thankful and humble hearts recognize His Almighty hand—nothing doubting—and give all glory to Him " who hath so loved us."

That evening, late, Wolfert Flemming left his wife's bedside, his heart lifted up with thankfulness, for he saw much hope in the fact that she lay quietly on her pillow in a deep and apparently natural sleep. He was alone in the quaint old sitting-room, half dozing, for in truth he was worn out for sleep, and was only kept awake by the disagreeable thought which would force itself upon him that in ten more days the note, which it was impossible for him to meet, would fall due. And how then? Well! he was going over it all again, when there came a quick rap at the door. Thinking that it might be some one to inquire after the health of the poor invalid upstairs, he stepped to the door and opened it, and there stood the man with the hammer—carpet-bag and all—smiling and holding out his hand like an old friend assured of a warm welcome. The men shook hands, said "How d'ye do" to each other and Wolfert Flemming invited him in: an invitation he was not slow to avail himself of.

"I guess," he said, "you thought I'd gone off for good and all, Mr. Flemming; but I had some trouble to scrape that money together, you see—."

"Speak lower, friend, if you please; my wife is very ill, and a strange voice might disturb her. In fact, Mr. Cutter, I am in no mood for business to-night. Some other time—." Then he stopped, remembering how much depended on the sale of 'Mill Farm,' and what happiness it would be to *her*, if she was spared, to find that the note was paid, and they were to stay in the old home; and he added: "But, as you please. Just as well now, I guess, as any other time."

"Well, Mr. Flemming, I sympathize heartily with you. I had a trial of the same sort once, and know all about it, but business is business, and, like time and tide, it waits for no man. I come up to-night to conclude the purchase of that place down yonder—'Mill Farm,' I have brought the money with me, and should like to settle the matter now."

Just at that moment one of those prolonged piercing shrieks, which his wife had uttered from time to time all through her illness, rang through the silent house—and Wolfert Flemming started

up, saying : " I can do nothing about it to-night,
Mr. Cutter. I must go to my wife. Come up in
the morning, about ten o'clock, and we'll have the
affair settled."

" Very well, Mr. Flemming. That will do ; that
is, if there's no one ahead of me offering you
more ; in which case I'd like to know. For I've
taken a fancy to the place, you see, and won't be
out-bid," he added, looking keenly out of his ferret
eyes into the pale honest face of Wolfert Flemming.

" I have no other bid for the farm, Mr. Cutter,
he answered, " and consider your offer quite
liberal."

" All right. Good-by. I shall be up here at
ten, sharp," said Mr. Cutter, going away with a
well-satisfied look, for he was on the eve of a great
speculation which would eventually make his fortune—that is, if nothing happened to interrupt his
plans.

When Flemming entered the sick room, his wife
was composed, and sleeping quietly again. " Oh,
father !" whispered Eva, " she looked at me as if
she knew me ; she did indeed !"

Later on, while he sat reading the Book of books,
in the silence and half-gloom of the old room down
stairs, Hope ran down to tell him that her mother
had swallowed a wine-glass full of beef tea, and

was sleeping and breathing naturally. Once more he went up, and stood at the bedside looking at her. There was a change—he saw that at once. The scarlet flush had faded out of her face, leav· ing it very white; she breathed softly and regular- ly, and the wrung, agonized expression had gone from her forehead. Tears rushed to his eyes; the strong man gave way—and covering his face with his hand, he turned and noiselessly left the room, and going into Eva's oratory knelt before the images of JESUS and MARY to pour out the emotions of his grateful soul and implore their gracious assistance. The full moon was shining through the leafless vines that covered the window, and lighted up with a peaceful radiance the sacred images and pure *immortelles*, that were garlanded with evergreens around the shrine; and, as he prayed, a blessed calm, of which this scene was only the type, fell upon his soul, resting and con- soling him. His devotions over, he went to the window, and softly opening it, he stood gazing up into the " limitless realms of the air," knowing that somewhere in the blue spangled distance its noise- less waves laved the land of the living, the abode of God and His saints; and winged by faith, his spirit soared beyond the stars and stood upon the glorious shores, listening to the far-off anthems of the blest. He felt strenghtened and comforted,

and felt for the first time that he could say in spirit
and in truth : " God's will is my will.   Yea ! though
he slay me, yet will I trust Him."

As he lingered a moment after closing the window,
he was startled by the sound of a man's footsteps
on the flagged walk below ; and looking down he
saw a stooping figure crouched behind the trunk of
one of the old elms, as if for the purpose of con-
cealment.   Who could it be ?   Nicholas was in his
mother's room, Reuben was abed.   He went down
—and noiselessly opening the side door, treading
softly and lightly, he stepped out upon the flags ;
and walking swiftly towards the crouching object,
said : " Who are you, and what do you want,
friend ?"

" I don't want nothin' ; but don't'ee be mad with
me, Elder, I got suthin' to say that ought to be
said," answered the man from under his slouched
hat.

" Who are you?" inquired Wolfert Flemming,
amazed.

" Wal, you see, my name's Wilbur," he replied
in great confusion ;—"Wilbur, down there at the
" Mill Farm."

" What have you to say, my friend ?   Speak
quickly.   Can I do anything for you?"

" Nothin', Elder, nothing but to hear what I
come to say," replied Wilbur in quavering tones,

for Wolfert Flemming's kindness of manner touched him to the quick.

"Of course I am willing to hear whatever you may wish to say; but let us walk a little further away from the house; step on the grass—I fear to disturb my wife, who is ill. Now, what is it?"

"Elder!" said Wilbur, still calling him by his old title, with an idea that it was respectful and polite to do so; "Elder, was that man with the hammer up here to-night?"

"Yes; why?"

"'Cause," answered Wilbur, coming so close to him that their faces almost touched, and speaking in a sharp whisper, "'cause he's a big rascal, Elder, and is tryin' to cheat you. Now, you see, if it was knowed that I came up here on any arrand whatsomever, Father Ray he'd have my work took away from me right off; but I can't forgit, Elder, all that you and yourn done for me and mine; and—dang it—I don't want to, nuther! Only, you know, I must look out for the main chance—havin' all them young 'uns to see arter and feed. So, you see, I waited until I thought everybody from the Lake clean up to Mount Washington was abed and sound asleep, before I started. I knowed Miss' Flemming was sick, and knowed that some of the family'd be up along with her all night; and I thought I'd run my chance of getting speech with you afore to-morrow—for then it would be too late. I'd have come before sundown, but I was afeard on account of my work, you know. How's Miss' Flemming?"

" A little better, we hope," replied Wolfert Flemming, who began to think that the man was certainly intoxicated.

" Bully for her! Now, you never fear, Elder;— things'll come straight yet! I tell you what!—them that wears broad phylacteries, and prays aloud in public places, and goes in for crammin' the Scripture down a fellow's throat, thinks they've got the world in a sling; but when God begins to fight agin' 'em they cave in pretty quick. Look here, Elder, have you sold " Mill Farm" yet?"

" As good as sold it, Wilbur," he answered, wondering more and more at the man's manner.

" For how much?"

" Two thousand dollars."

" Gosh! Look here, Elder Flemming, that 'ere place down yonder is worth two hundred thousand dollars, if it's worth a cent!" said Wilbur, emphatically.

Thinking more than ever that the man was either crazy or drunk, Wolfert Flemming determined to get rid of him as soon as possible, and said— " Wilbur, my wife is ill, and I can stand here no longer. Thank you for risking so much to come up here to inquire after her. But you'd better go home and go to bed;" and was about leaving him, when Wilbur laid his hand upon his arm to detain him, and whispered:

"Just one minit, Elder. I tell you what it is: them two smart Boston fellows didn't know I was listening to every word they said. I was down yonder this afternoon, creepin' in and out amongst the bushes to watch where our turkey-hen laid, when here the two come, measurin' and proddin' and turnin' up the land, and crackin' away at the stuns—why, bless you, they've been at that these three days!"

"Who?—what men, Wilbur?"

"That fellow with the hammer, and another he brung up from Boston town. And look here, Elder: while I laid there in the furze, flat o' my face, watching which way the turkey-hen went, I heard the man with the hammer tell the other how he found out the soapstun kerry."*

"Soapstone!—What soapstone, Wilbur?"

"The soapstun down yonder at Mill Farm. Bless your soul, Elder, there's hull lots of it there; and the way the man with the hammer found it out was from seeing suthin' your boy Reuben had cut out of a piece—a woman's head, I believe;—then he ups and asks Reuben where he found that sort

* Quarry.

of stun ; and the boy he tells him, innocent like
where he got it, and what lots of it was where that
came from ; and, not thinking anything wrong, tells
him the place was for sale. With that he—oh, he's
a sharp one, Elder !—whips up here to see you;
and, sayin' nothin' to nobody about the kerry,
offers to buy the place. Then he goes off, you
know, and jest came back three days ago, bringin'
the other fellow with him ; and such a proddin' and
measurin' and chippin' away at the rocks and stuns
was a sight for sore eyes. I heard it all, as I tell
you, this afternoon, while I was watchin' my turkey-hen ; and I heard that man with the hammer
say as how you ' was a green one, not to know the
value of your own land ; and that it would be wuth
nigh a million of dollars that kerry.' Then says I
to myself:the Elder's folks saved my wife and young
'uns from starvation, and if I can do it without
bein' found out I'll do 'em this good turn as sure as
I live ; and here I am—and, dang it, I'm thankful
that you've heard it ! '

Wolfert Flemming's heart almost stood still as he
listened to the man's strange recital. He knew full
well the high commercial value of soapstone ; and,
if it was true that there was a soapstone quarry
down there at the farm, what a risk he had run of
losing all the advantages which a merciful Providence had furnished to extricate him from present

difficulties and make his children independent for life; how nearly he had been ruined by a sharp and dishonourable man! There was no reason why he should doubt Wilbur's story, but he determined not to act hastily; he would question Reuben; and if his wife got no worse, he would go, as soon as the sun arose, to examine into the matter himself. These were his thoughts as he stood there with his great eyebrows lowering over his eyes . while Wilbur, who was shivering with cold, watched him, wondering if he was going to be so stupid as to let that man with the hammer have 'Mill Farm' for two thousand dollars, " with the soapstun kerry thrown in for nothin'." "See here, Elder," he said, unable to contain himself any longer, "I'm afeard you don't b'lieve me, anyhow?"

" Yes I do, Wilbur, and thank you for your friendly act. Depend upon it, if that quarry turns out well, you shall never suffer for work again," he answered, while he grasped the man's hand.

" 'Nough said, Elder; I'd risk my life for any of your folks—be sure of that," said Wilbur. " You look out sharp for that fellow; and I hope Miss' Flemming'll be on the mend soon. Good night."

"Good night, my friend. You shall hear something from me to-morrow."

When Wolfert Flemming went back to the sitting-room he found Nicholas there, ready to relieve

him and watch the rest of the night. Reuben was
with him, cuddled up close to the fire, with a
sleepy, happy, dreamy look in his face. They told
him that their mother was still sleeping, and had
not started once since he left the room. This was
good news; then, instead of going to bed, he sat
down with them and told them all that had happened.

"It's true, father. I did find this nice soft stone
early in the summer; don't you remember how my
little mammy laughed at me, and scolded when I
told her I was hunting for soft stone? But I found
it; and I've been chipping away down yonder at
the Old Mill these three months, making things out
of it; and didn't tell anybody, because I was afraid
you'd say it was nonsense, and be worried with me
for idling away my time. There's lots and lots of
it there, father?"

"How did Cutter happen to find it out?"

"We met, one day, down there at the brook; and
he began asking me questions about the scenery,
and got me to tell him the story of Chocorua; then
I took him up into the mill, to show him the view
from the north window; and—and—well, father,
after that he began to spy 'round, and went and
uncovered something I was making, and asked me
right off where I got that stone. I told him, and
then I let him know that the place was for sale,

and thought I was doing great things," said Reuben, his arms folded on his father's knees—and his beautiful face, lit up by the ruddy fire, uplifted and beaming.

"And so you did, Ruby, as it turns out," answered his father, smoothing back the golden tangles from the boy's forehead ; then he leaned down and kissed it; then telling Nicholas to call him at six o'clock, went into the next room to lie down. And Nicholas made Reuben go over it all again, and tell him exactly where the quarry lay, and what he had been about all summer at the Old Mill ; and what *he* said, and what the *man* with the hammer said; until the boy's patience began to give out; then sturdy Nick said, looking with wide-open eyes at him, as if he discovered something about him he'd never seen before, "It's a funny thing altogether, Ruby, that you, idling around all the time, should be of more use after all than any of the rest of us, who have worked from sunrise to sunset, until our hands are like iron, while yours are like velvet. I don't know how it is ; it seems as if there's a chink in the world for everybody, and that nobody but the right one will fit in it. But I'm mighty glad, old fellow ! I never was so glad of anything in my life, and never expect to be again, until I see mother sitting there in her old ' May-Flower chair,' knitting stockings." Here the great, tender-hearted fellow twinkled a tear off his eyelashes, and pretended to use his handkerchief. "And I tell you what I'm going to do, Ruby, if mother is better to-morrow."

"What?" asked Reuben.

"I'm going to punch Cutter's head against the biggest block of soapstone I can find, for trying to come such a swindle over my father. Why, just think of it! If it hadn't been for you and Wilbur —of all people on earth—father would have been cheated and ruined, and everything gone to smash!"

"*She'll* be so glad—poor little mammy!—to find everything straight again when she's better," murmured Reuben. "Won't she, Nick?"

"I guess she will. And I tell you what! it'll make them stare who have been trying to grind my father to powder—because he loved God better than the world—when they find out that he has gained more than he lost. Whew!" said Nicholas, snapping his fingers while he indulged in a little pardonable exultation, "won't old Daddy Ray preach a sermon about Dives, though! and declare that God has punished father with riches, that in the end he may share that miserable cove's bed of flame, and call upon him and Deacon Sneathen in vain for a drop of water to cool his tongue!"

"What nonsense you are talking, Nick. Lie

down there on the settle, and keep quiet—I'm sleepy," said Reuben, amused at Nick's outburst, so human and so natural; adding, "you know I have to go with father, to show him where the quarry is; so be quiet, and let me nod a little. I guess, Nick, mother'll have a good time now, stuffing her pillows with soft stone—won't she?" And he laughed a quiet little laugh, as he sat looking down into the glowing coals.

Mrs. Flemming's condition grew no worse, and towards sunrise Reuben and his father were on their way towards the Old Mill. When Hagar was unveiled, and the red light of the golden sunrise streamed in upon her, Wolfert Flemming started back, forgetting for an instant what had brought him there. "It's the image of your mother, Reuben!" he said.

"Yes, father; I've seen her look so very often of late. I call it Hagar, because I think Hagar must have looked so when Ishmael was dying of thirst!"

"And this is your little mystery, my lad?"

"Not quite all, father. I'll tell you the rest of it sometime," replied the boy, with a troubled look.

"I'll trust you, my son; and promise you here, in all the sacred faith of a father's dear love, that, should prosperity result from your discovery, you shall go to Rome to study, and cultivate this wonderful talent which God has given you."

"O, father! father! I shall ask for nothing more or better on earth!" exclaimed the boy, clasping his hands. Then, almost beside himself with excitement, he showed his father the blocks of soapstone which he had dug up and hewn out himself with such labor and exertion that many a time he had fallen fainting to the earth while he worked; and Wolfert Flemming, on examining them, found them to be genuine *steatite* of the finest quality. Hurrying out, they walked swiftly down to the quarry, where Reuben pointed out the valuable stone cropping out amongst the furze and undergrowth in every direction. He was satisfied—more than satisfied—his full heart overflowing with gratitude to Almighty God and adoring the ways of His providence, as he walked homewards, thinking of *her*, ever of her, and the great happiness that prosperity would bring her, after the sharp, sudden reverses and anxieties of the past. And he thought too of the great power that riches would give him, for good; if Almighty God prospered him he should regard himself as his steward and nothing more, and labor justly in the service of the poor and suffering; so that when the end came, he should hear the blessed sentence : " Well done, good and faithful servant, enter thou into the joy of the Lord!" For this aim, he would indeed make friends of the mammon of unrighteousness. Full of such thoughts as these, Wolfert Flemming scarcely felt the earth under his feet until he reached his own door. Going in, he found Hope busy preparing fresh nourishment for her mother, and learned that she still slept quietly and peacefully.

By-and-by, Martha Flemming awoke once more to life and consciousness, knowing the dear faces bending over her; but so weak—oh, so weak—that she could only look slowly from one to another without speaking. The fever was gone. "But," said the doctor, croaking like an old raven, "the worst is to come. She is very feeble, and may not have strength enough left to rally; but feed her up with beef tea and brandy; keep everything quiet and she *may*—mind! I don't say she will—get well." But they felt, somehow, that Almighty God, in answer to their fervent prayers, was going to spare her to them; so what the doctor said did not trouble them much; full of hope and thankfulness, they only thought of following out his sensible directions. Hovering around their mother as noiselessly as sun-bright shadows, they watched her countenance and watched her pulse, and on the slightest indication of increased weakness administered the warm nourishing beef tea and the life-giving stimulant. She was too weak to utter a word; she was as pallid as death, and wasted to a shadow; but alive, and conscious, and calm!

Truly, they lifted up their hearts and were glad. Nothing should trouble them now. They would joyfully bear all things since she was saved.

Ethan Cutter came that morning at the hour appointed: with a confident, beaming, and well-satisfied expression of countenance; his pocket-book gorged with crisp hundred dollar bills, papers made out ready for signing, and jubilant over the near termination of his dishonest plans. His disappointment and fury can be better imagined than described when Wolfert Flemming told him in grave, firm tones, and few simple words, that "he had changed his mind about 'Mill Farm,' and should not sell it.'

He insisted on knowing the reasons, in a voice of suppressed fury; and although he had no right to know, Wolfert Flemming, in his quiet level tones, his grave handsome face unruffled in the least of its lines, told him that a "recent discovery of a valuable soapstone quarry upon the place, by his son, which he had only learned last night, had decided him, very naturally, not to dispose of the property." Then the man's fury broke loose. His dishonest schemes, his dreams of wealth, his glittering castles in the air, were suddenly crumbled, and came tumbling about his ears like the burnt, blackened sticks of brilliant firework; and he raved and threatened and beat the table with his hammer at

such a rate, that Nicholas seized him by his
shoulders and turned him neck and crop out of the
house, never relaxing his hold until he had run him
like a wheelbarrow, a full quarter of a mile; then
he gave him a kick which sent him whirling down
the steep hill at a speed which brought him flat on
his face when he reached the bottom. I don't
know how I can excuse Nicholas, unless you will
take into consideration that he knew the least excitement might prove fatal to his mother, for the
fellow was making himself heard all over the house
—and that he could no more have stood there and
heard his father insulted again than he could have
caught a streak of lightning and tied it up in a
bow-knot. He certainly felt better after it; and
when his father reproved him for his violence, his
only reply was: "I couldn't help it, sir. I intended to punch his head against the quarry, and
I'm thankful I didn't. Not that he don't deserve
it, for trying to swindle you: then coming up here
putting my mother's life in danger, and insulting
you before your children! Jehosaphat!"

"Let us forget it, Nick—and forgive. God has
been very good to us—too good for us to soil the
gratitude we owe Him by thoughts of uncharita-
bleness and violence," said Wolfert Flemming, in
that grave musical undertone of his that sounded
like one of the minor keys of an organ. Then

Nicholas said no more about the matter. But he felt very well satisfied, and laughed in his sleeve whenever he thought of Ethan Cutter's absurd appearance while engaged in that involuntary race which terminated so ignominiously, and he could not to save his life, feel sorry for having been the cause of it.

Presently he began to ask his father some questions about working the quarry. Sanguine and full of expectation of immediate results, Nicholas had not given the subject a single practical thought; his mind was full of chaotic ideas of wealth to be made suddenly available, which would place them all far beyond the reach of every earthly care; consequently his father's words almost took away the young man's breath.

"The discovery is a valuable one," he answerd slowly; "but to work the quarry will require some capital, which I do not possess; and I can think of nothing now, Nick, except that note which will be due in a few days, and which I cannot meet. I may be able to raise the balance on a fresh mortgage, or even by selling an interest in the quarry; but I don't know! I am in God's holy keeping; and, having done all that I can, I shall await His divine will, trusting Him to the end."

Nicholas had not thought of all this—and it came down upon his warm, glowing visions, and proud, fond anticipations like a *douche* of ice-water, "It was too hard," he thought, "that with all this untold wealth lying in the earth at their very feet, his father could not raise a few paltry hundreds to save his credit and his honor. Of course the note would be protested at the old bank down there at Plymouth; there seemed to be no help for it." The young man gnashed his teeth; he would have sold himself into slavery to have saved his father —he would have died for him—but nobody up there bought slaves, and there was no one who would have thought it worth while to set a price on his life; and the fact forced itself upon his mind, that however great and humiliating the trial, he would have to wait and bear it when it came. Then Nicholas Flemming wished in his soul that he was a Christian in deed and in truth, with the courage and resignation to bear nobly for God's sake whatever troubles He might send.

"But I am not a Christian," thought Nick; "I've never been baptized, and know nothing about it; but I'll try to bear it like a man, come what may; and, if God spares me, I'll help my father with a will, and never rest until he gets on his feet again." Then Nicholas went out to take a smoke, and wonder at things which no philosopher, or prophet, or theologian, or sage has ever been able to explain satisfactorily, and never will—for He who holds the balance only knows why this is put into one scale, and that in the other; why the innocent suffer and the guilty triumph and prosper; why His Church bears the stigmata while the world is crowned with a diadem and arrayed in purple.

CHAPTER XXIV.

HOW THE CLOUD PASSED AWAY AND THE LIGHT SHONE.

"Yes, Hope, your mother is quite out of danger. Give her some broiled chicken to-day, and a slice of toast with her tea. But she mustn't eat too much at a time—mind that! People who are getting over a low fever never know when they have enough," said the doctor, one morning as he was going away.

"I'll feed her like a motherless bird," answered Hope, laughing. "Indeed, doctor, I am so happy and thankful I don't know what to do with myself. Under God, your skill and attention have saved my mother's life."

"Well, I don't know about that. Your mother has a pretty tough constitution of her own to begin with. But I had no hope of her at one time, I assure you; she was pretty nigh gone, and *I* did nothing but come and look at her, and feel her pulse for three days. It was her tough constitution brought her through."

" And," thought Hope, " the compassion of God, in answer to our prayers." But she kept her thoughts to herself, for the old doctor, who had got his diploma in Paris, was very atheistical in his notions, and would not have understood her.

" And see here, Hope," he said, with one foot in the stirrup, " I think you might fix some pillows and blankets on that lounge in your mother's room, and let your father and Nick lift her very gently and lay her upon it. It will rest and refresh her. And remember : she's not to be excited about anything at all. Good day."

It was a happy day for the Flemmings, and fervent were the thanks which they offered Almighty God for the restoration of the beloved one. They gathered around her, as she lay upon the lounge, as white as the pillows on which she reposed, and so feeble that she could only speak in whispers, and thought that she was the loveliest and most precious sight on earth. A bright fire crackled and blazed merrily on the red hearth, and the sun shone warmly through the white curtains, making arabesque shadows of the leafless boughs of the old elms upon them. Reuben, in a quiet transport, had cuddled himself upon the floor close beside his

mother, his head resting against the lounge, his
hand clasping hers, which every now and then he
softly kissed, looking supremely happy. Her eyes
full of patient love followed her dear ones as they
moved to and fro about the room, watching their
incomings and outgoings; glad when they came,
and looking after them with wistful, tender glances
when they went. There was a look of deep, placid
content in her face, a sort of spiritualized expression, which seemed to come from some higher
cause than the healthful reaction of the vital forces.
Hope and Eva had noticed, since their mother had
recovered her consciousness, that she would sometimes lay with her eyes closed, her hands folded on
her breast, and her lips moving as if in prayer.
There had been no hour of the day or night while
she lay helpless and unconscious, that prayers, with
the silent appeal of tears, were not offered to
heaven for her; there was not an hour of the day
or night now that they did not offer thanks, and
pray for her conversion to the True Faith.

One evening Wolfert Flemming sat alone with
her. The night shadows had crept into the room,
and the firelight played upon the wall in grotesque
forms, flickering up and down like the figures in an
elfin dance. He thought she was sleeping—she
lay so quiet; but when he closed his book and
looked towards her, he observed her lips moving

and her hands folded in an attitude of prayer. Presently she opened her eyes—and seeing him standing there, smiled and held out her hand.

"Mother," he said very gently, as he drew his chair close to her bedside and held her attenuated hand in his, "would it be a comfort to you to see the minister? If it will, I will go for him now."

"No," she answered, after a pause, in which it was evident that a struggle was going on in her mind ; "no, I am going to tell you something that will surprise you."

"Had you not better wait until you get stronger?" he asked.

"No ; it will do me good to relieve my mind. I shall never get stronger with this weighing on me as it does," she replied.

"I hope I may be able to help you, dear wife," he answered. "What is it that you wish to tell me ?"

"You know, father," she began, "what a bitter trial your change of religion was to me, and how deeply grieved I was that Eva and Hope should have followed your example—how angry and disappointed when they ruined their earthly prospects for the sake of a religion which I thought worse than idolatrous."

"Yes, mother. You should have been spared it all, if the issue had been a merely earthly one there's no sacrifice that I and your children would not have made to spare you a single unnecessary pang; but this was an affair upon which the salvation of our souls depended—an affair which lay between Almighty God and our own souls for all eternity," he answered in low earnest tones.

"I know it; I know it now," replied Mrs. Flemming with quivering lips. "It caused me such suffering of mind as I had never imagined, and the unchristian treatment you received at the hands of those who had been your friends and brethren was like gall and wormwood added to it. Then I began to contrast the patient firmness, the cheerful humility and deep faith of you Catholics, with the fierce, unrelenting, persecuting spirit of the people of my own sect. And through it all I was troubled about our Saviour's words concerning the Bread of Life. I tried to stop thinking about it—but could not. Having got thus far, I began to read your Catholic books by stealth, and my mind got so torn and tossed between my pride and my conscience, that I used to think sometimes that I was going stark crazy. Then one night I was going past that room—Eva's room—and heard you, as I thought, praying. I stood at the door and listened, and heard every word you and Eva said about the Mother of Jesus; and oh, husband, it never left me an instant, but kept going on, and on, and on,

in my mind, day and night, waking and sleeping.
I had been more than usually exercised the day
the ceiling fell. You know I was at the door,
speaking to Eva, when it gave way; and as it
came crashing down I thought I saw the image
suddenly grow large and bright, and stretch out its
arms to save her. But that was owing, I guess, to
the excited state of my mind, and the terrible, terrible fright! An hour or two afterwards I fell ill,
and began to dream of her, and I kept on dreaming and dreaming constantly about her. It seemed
to me that she was always standing by me, and
told me that she had promised Eva to take care of
me. But I was afraid of her: she was 'as bright
as the sun, as fair as the moon, and as terrible as
an army in array.' The books I have read, and
your example—oh, husband!—I am vanquished! I
give up! All that you believe I believe. Take
me with you into the fold of Faith, for I have been
like one lost in the wilderness."

" Oh, my God!" murmured the man, almost overcome, "how can I thank Thee for this?" This
answer to his prayers for her was so unexpected,
full and complete, that he was filled with a joy akin
to awe! He covered his face with his hands and
bowed his head, and what passed in his soul was
known only to Him by whose grace salvation had
come to him and his household.

"Wife, this is good news; the very best I ever heard in my life," he said at last.

" Help me, and pray for me," said Mrs. Flemming. I have been wishing to tell you, but was too weak."

" Truly are we united now, in one faith and one hope ; together, dear wife, we will work out our salvation; and together, I hope ere long, we, with our children, will be received into the One True Fold, and partake of the Bread of Eternal Life. Oh, wife! this moment foreshadows heaven!" exclaimed Wolfert Flemming, full of a profound emotion in which adoration and thanksgiving were so blended that earthly language could not express it.

I will leave it to you to imagine the joy of Mrs. Flemming's children when their father related to them what I have related to you. Truly did they realize upon earth the joy of the angels in heaven over a rescued soul!

One day, the very day before the note fell due. Nicholas Flemming came home from Wier's Landing, where he had been on an unsuccessful errand to raise money on the quarry, and brought in two letters from the post-office—one for his father, and one for Reuben. Eva was up stairs with her mother; Hope and Huldah Sneathen were sitting together, talking and sewing by the bright firelight; Wolfert Flemming was reading in his old

Lutheran Bible the psalms of David, while Reuben, at his side, was poring over the less exalted strains of "Tommy Moore."

"Here's a letter for you, father, and here's one for you, Ruby, from your friend, Patrick McCue. How do you do, Huldah? I'd like some supper, Hope; I'm half famished." It was clear that Nick was in a disagreeable humor, and Hope bestirred herself to make him comfortable as quickly as possible. Huldah looked frightened, but not at Nick's grimness; she was watching Wolfert Flemming as he turned the letter over, held it up to the candle-light to examine the superscription, and finally broke the seal and unfolded it. Something, several somethings, slipped out and fluttered down upon the pages of the old Bible; very crisp and clean they were, with a great deal of figuring and printing over them; but he did not heed them, and went on reading the letter to the end, while a strange paleness overspread his face, and his hands trembled as he held it near the light.

"Come here, Hope," he said, "and read this aloud. I don't know: perhaps I have made a mistake;" and he passed his hand over his forehead, still heedless of what had fallen out of the letter. And Hope, in a sort of dumb surprise, took the letter and read aloud:

"DEAR FRIEND:

"I have been wishing to write to you for the last

six weeks, but had to wait for something I wanted to send. Yesterday I got it : twenty-five thousand dollars, which the city of Boston has paid for a lot of land they're going to build the new State House on ; and I send you five thousand on loan, and ask you, as a favor, to apply it to that mortgage business of yours. You can pay me the interest until I ask you for the principal. It will be no use to send it back, because when you are reading this I shall be half way to Europe. I intend to throw away the balance in having a good time while I'm abroad ; so if you don't take care of the five thousand for me, I shan't have a cent to begin with when I get back, which won't be for three years. Give my love to all the family, and ask them to think of the wanderer sometimes. When you see Huldah—bless her soul !—tell her I thank her for having written, and didn't answer her letter for the same reasons given above. I have written to Ruby. With affection and respect, dear Mr. Flemming.

"I am sincerely your friend,

GEORGE MERILL."

"Was that your secret, Huldah ?" asked Nicholas, whispering over her shoulder.

"Yes," she replied almost inaudibly.

"Forgive me, Huldah ?" he asked humbly.

"Yes," she whispered. All this was in a moment, while Hope was gathering up the five bank bills, of a thousand dollars each, which were scattered over the pages of the old Bible. One had fallen on the floor, and the cat was playing with it.

"It is really true, then," said Wolfert Flemming, rousing himself as from a dream. "Thanks be to God! thanks be to God!"

"It's just like George Merill!" said Hope, laughing and crying.

"Here's more," said Reuben, holding up two bank bills towards his father, while his beautiful face glowed with delight. "Here, father! I told you I'd show you my letter when it came. Read it out; I don't care who hears it now. Here's the money! Mr. Adams paid two hundred dollars for my Peri."

It was true. Reuben had sculptured the "disconsolate Peri waiting at heaven's gate;" designed and sculptured it, and packed it and sent it two months before to George Merill to sell for him; and George Merill not only sold it, but wrote the most distracting things that had been said about it; and sent him several highly favorable art criticisms, which he had cut from the Boston papers, in which it was pronounced to be the most wonderful attempt of untaught genius that had ever been seen this side of the Atlantic. I can't tell one-half of all the kind and appreciative things that were said about it; but Ruby was filled with new life;

he knew now that he had not been idling his life away, but had been blindly working out his vocation, and making much of the talent Almighty God had given him.

"I must go up and tell my little mammy!" said the boy, so delighted and exhausted that he felt as if he trod upon air. "I guess she won't want me to knit stockings and churn now."

"Reuben, my lad," said his father, while an indescribable expression of peace lit up his noble face, " not to night. Mother is feeble, and all this joy might make her ill again. God is very good to us, my children. Huldah, dear child, I thank you for all that you have done. I could not have asked this favor of George myself; but coming in this way, through you and him, I cannot refuse it, particularly since I know how easy it will be for me to repay him when I begin to work the quarry. I will go up and send Eva to you. Tell her—," and Wolfert Flemming left the room, his heart very full. Huldah was crying softly, her head on Nick's shoulder and his arm about her waist, ready to thump his own head for ever having doubted her; but before they separated that night Huldah was herself again, and threatened to marry her father's partner the next day if he didn't walk very straight—which he did. Eva was speechless when she heard the news. Nicholas thought she would be enthusiastic, and write a gushing letter that night to George Merill to come home and marry her; "it was nothing more," he said "than she ought to do;" but she didn't; she only looked around on them all with a pleased, happy smile, kissed Reuben, and went up to the little Sanctuary of Our Lady, where she spent half the night in sweet thanksgiving and communions with her, offering herself, soul and body, as her handmaid and servant, to be presented as a holocaust to her Divine Son.

That night Wolfert Flemming read the Psalm *Confitemini Domino*,* at prayer time; nothing could have expressed better all that he felt; nothing could have been more appropriate; and the exalted words fell from his lips in deep musical tones, each heart responding to them in humble thanksgiving.

" Hope," said Nicholas that night, as they lingered in the quaint old sitting-room, after the others had gone to bed; "even the old rafters look bright to-night. I believe those things in the *buffet* are dancing a jig; just see how the light from the fire darts around them. It looks as if rainbows were hanging about the room. I never was so happy in my life. How jolly it will be to-morrow, when mother knows what has happened. Forgive me, dear Hope—I had forgotten about John Wilde," said Nick, kissing her.

*Psalm cvi.

"I have not forgotten John," answered Hope, while Nick tenderly wiped the tears from her cheeks. "I shall never forget him. But I am very happy. I am content. It is a very sweet thing to live for others." And it did, indeed, seem so to her; and no one ever heard her speak of John Wilde again; until—but I won't anticipate the sequel.

The next day, Mrs. Flemming, freshly dressed and looking much better than she had done since her illness, was sitting propped up by pillows in her bed, trying to knit—her fingers not much larger than jack-straws as she slowly took up the stitches and threw the fine yarn over the glittering needles —when her husband came, and by arrangement found her alone.

"You feel strong to-day, mother?" he said, as he stationed himself upon the rug, and with an amused expression watched her indefatigable efforts to slip back into her old industrious habits.

"I feel as chipper as that robin whistling out there by the window," she answered, cheerfully. "I tell you, father, that I feel like one risen from the dead, in a two-fold sense. What day of the month is it?'

"The first of December!" he replied, watching her keenly, for he almost dreaded the effects of what he had to tell her, upon her nerves.

"Ah! have I been ill so long? And this is— Well, father, let the past be with the past; it would seem ungrateful to fret and repine, since God has been so good and merciful to us. I shall be ready very soon now to go to Ohio," she added, hesitating a little at first, then speaking more blithely.

"I don't think we shall go to Ohio just yet," he replied.

"I should like to know! I thought it was all settled, if that money—"

"Wife," he said, "are you strong enough to hear some good news?"

"I guess I am. It will do me good," she replied with an expectant look.

"Well, then, we shall not go to Ohio. We shall not be compelled to break up our old home, or even to sell "Mill Farm."

"Why! the land's-sake!" she exclaimed, dropping her hands upon the coverlid, and fixing her eyes upon him with an eager alert expression in them which half frightened him. "That *is* good news. I feel it through me! Why, father! how did it come about?"

"First through Ruby."

"Ruby, Ruby—my baby!" she murmured softly, while a happy smile lit up her pale, thin face. "Go on."

"Yes, indeed! Your boy took to sculpturing images; and while looking round for some soft kind of stone to work in, he discovered a valuable quarry of soapstone at Mill farm!"

"He did! And to think how provoked I was at him that day, when he told me he had been searching for soft stone! I thought he was crazy."

"Well, he found it, but said nothing, as he was ignorant of its great value; and it was only after Cutter came the other day, to pay for the farm, that I heard a word about it."

"You have seen Cutter, then?" she inquired anxiously.

"Yes, mother, he came back a few days ago, and brought the money to pay for it; but you were ill, and I told him to come the next morning; for I knew—or I thought I knew—how much depended on my getting the money for it."

"And you didn't let him have it? Don't tell me that he got it!"

"No, I heard about the quarry that night."

"How in the land—?"

"Wilbur came up here at midnight, and told me about it."

"Wilbur!" repeated Mrs. Flemming, as if scarcely comprehending how, by any chance upon earth, that shiftless, ungrateful man had got to be **mixed** up in their affairs. Then Wolfert Flemming sat down by her side and told everything that had happened, from Wilbur's midnight visit to George Merill's letter; he dwelt with softened voice on Huldah's kindness, informed her of Reuben's success, not omitting the smallest detail as he went on. When she heard how her great bear, Nick, had served the-man-with-the-hammer, she laughed out, and said "it served him right." Then he gave her George Merill's letters to read, and showed her the new crisp bank bills he had sent, and asked her how she felt?

"I feel well. There's no cordial could have done me half the good that your news has. Oh, husband! help me to thank God; He has been so patient and merciful." And kneeling down beside her, he lifted up his voice and poured out the adoration and gratitude of his soul to God for all His mercies, for all the trials wherewith they had been chastened, and, above all, he thanked Him for the gift of faith which had been vouchsafed to him and his household, and for giving new life, spiritually and corporally, to her who, not yet risen from her bed of sickness, lifted up her soul with his in genuine faith, true humility and fervent gratitude unto the Giver of every good and perfect gift. The prayer tranquillized and composed Mrs. Flemming; and the soft, happy tears she shed seemed brightened with the bow of a new covenant, and refreshed her body as chrism refreshes and strengthens the soul.

"Now, wife, God bless you," he said, as he leant over and kissed her; "it is nearly eight o'clock, and I must gallop down to Plymouth to pay that note, and attend to some other business."

"Be careful of your wallet, father. You might drop it," she said, as she gathered up her knitting once more; "and send Huldah to me if she is not gone."

"I'll be careful—depend upon that, mother," he answered, thinking how natural it was to hear the cautious, thrifty nature of the little woman cropping out once more. He took it as one of the best symptoms of a healthy recovery, and went on his way rejoicing.

Long and sweet was the interview between Mrs. Flemming and Huldah Sneathen; not that there was the least sentimental nonsense about it, but there was genuine gratitude on one hand, and a sincere, reverent affection upon the other, which, fused together on that occasion, in a simple, natural way, produced a confidence between the two which continued and ripened until death separated them—many, many years afterwards. Huldah's modest account of her management of the dairy and other domestic matters which must have been utterly neglected but for her, did Mrs. Flemming's thrifty heart good, and brought her many healthy steps forward into the old busy ways of life When there were no more questions to answer and Huldah had related every little detail which she thought would please her, she said : " Huldah, I don't know how to thank you. You'll make my boy a good wife—I know that—and be a comfort to father and me in our old days ; and I pray that God may bless and reward you as you deserve. As it has turned out, it was a good thing that you wrote to George Merill—poor, dear George! I always loved the boy. None of us could have done that, you know, even if we had thought of it ; we would have felt a sort of pride about asking such a favor even of our own kin, if we had any. But I am very thankful to you, my child, and don't know how the house would have got on without you." And Mrs. Flemming drew Huldah's fresh young face down to her, and placing her hands upon each of the girl's blooming cheeks she kissed her tenderly. " God has been good to me, child, in bringing me out of the darkness of error into the light of faith," she said, as she held Huldah in that soft motherly embrace ; "I am now, like my husband and children, a Catholic. Child! child! I am very happy and thankful ! Go now; I want to be quiet for a little. I must rest an hour; then you must all come up and spend the rest of the day here, when we will talk over everything." And when Huldah lifted up her face from the motherly bosom, to go away, her cheeks were wet with the first happy tears she had ever shed.

Truly, indeed, was Mrs. Flemming a little worn out by all this excitement ; but it was very pleasant to lie there in her bright, quiet room, knowing that everything was going on well and happily, and think of the wonderful ways of Divine Providence, which had turned their sadness into joy, put a new song on their lips, and delivered them from misfortune when all human aid seemed hopeless, and from the bitter struggles of poverty amongst strangers. And yet everything appeared to have happened in the natural order of things—even the coming of Patrick McCue on the night of the storm, his leaving that book as a testimonial of his gratitude—and the conversion of her husband ; each event taken by itself was simple and natural ; there was nothing miraculous, and yet how wonderfully had the mercy and love of Almighty God towards His creatures been illustrated in their regard. How truly, "she thought, 'do all things work together for the good of them who love and serve Him !" Mrs. Flemming could make nothing of it all, humanly speaking, but to feel a sweet, humble, utter dependance upon her Father in heaven, and wonder in speechless surprise at her past blindness, and His infinite, unspeakable patience and mercy. It was like " deep calling unto deep ;" it was truly a new birth into a life full of consolation and hope.

When her children came in to her that day, they found her with a look of quiet content upon her face, and a softened light in her eyes which tempered their natural brightness with unwonted gentleness, and which, interpreted aright, indicated the new-born humility which had had its birth in her soul. They were very happy sitting around her, each one relating his or her personal experience during the dark sorrowful days just past; in the midst of which Reuben, who had been engaged busily with his mother's lap-board, turned it round towards them, exposing to view a spirited charcoal sketch of Nick running off the-man-with-the-hammer, which made them all laugh very heartily.

" Ruby, what did you serve my board in that way for ? It will have to be planed to get that thing off," said Mrs. Flemming.

" I'll scrub it, little mammy, as white as your hands. And as soon as ever you get strong enough I'm going to fetch up loads of that soft stone for you to stuff your pillows with !" he answered, giving his sketch a few additional touches to complete it. Then he kissed his mother, who had been watching him fondly, and set the board upon her bureau for his father to see when he got back.

"I can't understand Ruby," said Mrs. Flemming after he went out; "he is a perfect riddle to me, and will be as long as he lives. But I admire to see him looking so bright and well. I shouldn't wonder if it was the cool, bracing weather that has made him strong again." It was not the cold, bracing weather that had improved Reuben's health, but the fact that his genius was acknowledged and approved; that his vocation was decided upon; that he had made a successful beginning, and that a career was before him which he determined, if life were spared him, should fulfill all his most ambitious aspirations. This it was which gave elasticity to his steps, which made the young blood leap with the strong impetus of hope through his veins, and imparted new life and strength to his being. Mrs. Flemming did not comprehend this; it was not in her nature to understand or appreciate the utility of any profession which had not for its aim some practical advantage or use; but she did not oppose him, later, when with his father's consent and generous assistance he went away, to be gone for years, to study and work in Rome. She only said "it was a pity, and a great waste of time, in her opinion. He might have chosen some more useful occupation; and she couldn't see how it would end." Then she hung about his neck, smoothed back his wild golden hair for the last time, kissed him, blessed him, and let him go, sad to think he was so glad to be gone.

*   *   *   *   *   *

As soon as ever Mrs. Flemming was strong enough to travel, the Old Homestead was closed, and the farm matters left in care of the man who had been working there many years, and his sister, who took charge of the dairy and other affairs belonging to the feminine department of the establishment—and all the family went to Boston. Wolfert Flemming had written to Patrick McCue of his intention; and the first object they saw when the stage drew up in front of the office was the gaunt figure of the good Irishman, his face beaming with delight, and his big hands outstretched to welcome them and help them down. He had a carriage waiting for them, and when they were all packed in it he mounted the box with the driver and conducted them to a nice boarding-house near the cathedral, where he had engaged rooms for them; and having introduced them to the landlady and seen them comfortably settled, he drove back to the stage-office for their baggage. His joy and delight at meeting with his friends defies description, and I leave it to your imagination. I should be glad to tell you of some of the remarkable things he said and did, which were so full of deep earnest feeling, of fun

and devotion and pathos all mixed together, that
the Flemmings, though not given to such emotions
laughed and cried at the same time. His last acts
of love that night were to go and inform the Bishop
of the arrival of the converts, and to spend an hour
in the cathedral before, the Altar of Our Lady to
implore her favor and patronage for them. He was
with them betimes the next morning, to show them
the way to the cathedral to assist at the Bishop's
Mass, and afterwards conduct them into his presence.

The good Bishop received Wolfert Flemming and
his family with friendly welcome and great emotion;
and, after a long conversation with them, was consoled as well as astonished to find that these people, who until then had never seen a Catholic priest
in all their lives, were so thoroughly instructed in
Catholic doctrine and dogma as to be perfectly prepared even then to receive the Sacraments.*   On
that day they went to confession, or rather began
their confession; after which they were condition-
ally baptized—that is, Wolfert Flemming and his
wife; their children never having received the rite,
now received it in all its sacramental fulness. It
would be simply impossible to describe the solemn
joy, the blissful content, the deep humility and fervent faith that animated the souls of our converts;

* A literal fact.

they seemed to enter a new life, on a new earth and under a new heaven!

It appeared so natural—and yet how strange—this actual beginning of the chief business of their souls! To place themselves in the presence of Almighty God and examine the records of their conscience, to "search Jerusalem with lamps," to hunt the "little foxes that destroy the vines," to enter the tribunal of penance and confess their sins; to receive absolution, in the firm faith that what was "loosed upon earth was also loosed in heaven," was a grave, practical, *real* affair to them, in comparison with which all temporal business seemed to sink into utter nothingness. It was the immortal grasping the eternal; their initiation into Christ's kingdom; the beginning of the means by which they were to work out their salvation. And these clear-headed, simple-minded, intelligent people felt and understood the full significance of that which they were doing, in all its broad spiritual meaning. Their reason was satisfied; they comprehended the meaning of faith in their own experience, and the necessity of good works as the fruits of faith; they accepted with joy all the ceaseless responsibilities of a spiritual life, courageously determined, with God's help, to "work out their salvation with fear and trembling;" and placing themselves under the protection of the Mother of Jesus, they implored her aid, and humbly rejoiced in the faith whose consolations were " full measure, pressed together and running over." There was nothing left for them to desire, nothing incomplete, nothing imperfect or meaningless in this holy religion into whose fold they were led ; and, if they had the grace and courage to persevere to the end, then—then heaven itself would be their eternal reward.

Midnight, Christmas eve, and the Bishop in his rich pontifical robes at the altar! Innumerable lights glittered among the fair, fragrant hot-house flowers and luxuriant evergreens that covered it. Around the shrine of the " Blessed amongst women and her Divine Babe," clustered spotless lilies, and roses as lovely as the roses of Sharon: spangled between, wherever one could be placed, with twinkling lights! Fair image of peace and holiness! well may thy children, with simple, loving hearts, decorate thy shrine with all that is lovely, to celebrate that wonderful night when, through thee, God was reconciled with man by the birth of His only-begotten Son! Neither gems from the sea, nor gold from the mine, nor frankincense nor myrrh, could make a memorial worthy of thee, who reignest in heaven, thy home and reward ; but thou acceptest the intention of thy children, whom thou lovest and pitiest with a mother's tender affection ; thy ears are attentive to their lowest whispers ; and for the

honor which they pay thee for the sake of thy beloved Son, thou bestowest upon them blessings and
graces exceeding their timid requests!—ever ready,
ever swift to obtain from Him the fruits of His Passion for those for whom He suffered!

But this is the glorious night on which thou didst
heal the deadly wound inflicted by Eve upon mankind, by giving birth to the Saviour, God's only-begotten Son!—and thy children have not forgotten
thee! They are poor and humble, but they have
tried to make thee some slight amends for the
poverty and needs of that bitter night in the stable
at Bethlehem, by offering their hearts in which to
cradle thy Divine Son; by offering their service to
thee, as thy handmaids and servants, by doing all
now that they would have done then, had they been
with thee beside the manger! The world can never
forget thee, O sinless Mother! and in looking upon
this spectacle so long and faithfully celebrated by
the Church, it halts in its headlong career to gaze
upon thy beauty and think of thy wonderful Son,
the Man-God, who was crucified for its salvation ;
and, half believing, turns away with softened heart,
and bears in its hidden thoughts the memory of
thee, O sweet Maid of Nazareth!—a memory,
which, times without number, brings the sinful and
erring in humble penitence to the feet of thy Beloved, whose face thou beholdest forever!

The cathedral was crowded with the humble poor ; there were none of any other class in those days in Boston who were members of the One True Fold. The congregation was like that which adored Jesus in the arms of His Mother in the stable at Bethlehem, bidden thither from the hills by angel messengers ! Their faith was the same, and they had also for their consolation JESUS and MARY.

In a pew in front of the sanctuary knelt the Flemming's, their souls clothed in the newness and brightness of baptismal innocence, and as fair as the angels who guarded the tabernacle where the Lord, under the veil of bread, reposed. They awaited in almost rapt expectation for the moment when He would come to them their food and their guest.

The *Gloria in excelsis* pealed from the organ in notes of solemn joy, the words borne upwards by voices of strange power and sweetness ; the *Credo* was chanted in loud sonorous tones, as if inviting all the world to listen ; then followed the Offertory, when the Bishop, in a low voice, offered the bread and wine, which by the power of Almight God, and the words of consecration, would soon be changed into the real body and blood of His Son. In low, sweet, tremulous notes, the organ breathed its music as the unbloody Sacrifice went on ; then it burst forth again in stately melody at the Preface, increasing in power and sweetness until it poured out all of its harmony at the grand and tremendous moment of consecration, when bread was no longer bread, but the true, real, living Body, Humanity and Divinity of Jesus Christ : which all present, with lively faith, adored as the Bishop elevated the host which veiled His glory, as His Humanity once veiled His divinity upon earth.

I dare not attempt to describe what passed in the souls of our converts on this occasion ; the pen of an angel only could portray the sweet and heavenly consolations vouchsafed to their faith ! The long hoped for moment at length came ; and they went forward as they saw others do, and knelt at the sanctuary railing—father, mother, daughters and sons together. When the good Bishop approached where they knelt, he recognized them, and tears of consolation rolled over his cheeks and glittered among the golden embroidery of his vestments, as he administered to them the Bread of Eternal Life.

Patrick McCue was of the greatest assistance to Wolfert Flemming, in making inquiries, and finding out and introducing him to persons who were able to give him information as to the best method of working his quarry. He hired laborers and bought machinery to take back with him ; but by this time the soapstone quarry got to be talked about, and at last written about in the daily papers ; for this

soft magnesian stone, for which there was an un-
limited demand, was scarce—and the prospect of a
supply which would be able to meet it created quite
an excitement, which brought Wolfert Flemming
into personal intercourse with a rich capitalist who
made him such fair and equitable offers that they
entered into partnership, which continued during
their lifetime to their mutual satisfaction.

Every morning found the Flemmings at the Bishop's Mass ; their afternoons were devoted to seeing all that was of interest to intelligent minds like
theirs ; sunset found them again in the cathedral,
resting their souls in sweet contemplation and humble prayers. These moments were very precious to
them ; in them they realized all the spiritual depths
and sweetness of that holy religion which even the
most liberal-minded of the sects regard as a cold,
senseless formula! Contrasted with their former
narrow belief, how grand, how sublime, how holy
was this faith into which they had been thus providentially led! It supplied every need of their
souls ; it had a consolation for every fear ; it was,
indeed and in truth, the " substance of things hoped
for" unto them.

They went back to the Old Homestead full of the
joy of a new life, united in faith as they had ever
been in affection, and looked back on their past,
with its trials and sorrows, as the traveller standing

upon the verdant flowery glades of Goshen gazes
out into the parched arid desert he has just passed
—the desert where the sirocco blasts, and the false,
fleeting mirage; deludes the unwary with its bright
mockery.

*　　*　　*　　*　　*　　*　　*　　*

Rome, and sunset on the Pincian hill. Two
young men—Americans—are wandering—in different directions, about the beautiful gardens, listening now to the music, now pausing to watch the
dancers, now following a picturesque group of *con-
tadina ;* one of them stopped to admire the dia-
mond sparkles of a fountain which tossed its spray
like a libation into the golden, rose-tinted haze of
evening; the other paused upon the terrace which
overhangs the Piazza del Popolo, and looked down
with sad, thoughtful eyes on the obelisk and foun-
tains below ; then his gaze wandered out beyond
the purple masses of domes and cupolas, beyond
the shadow-wrapped Mausoleum of Hadrian, beyond
the pearl-white mists rising from the Tiber, towards
the golden West. About the same moment they
both started to leave the gardens. The gay crowds
were going ; why should they remain ? Walking
quickly from opposite directions, they came against
each other with such impetus that they were near
falling to the ground.

"I beg your pardon!" said the younger, with a light, merry laugh.

"Hilloa!" exclaimed the other, emerging from the cloud of dust their collision had raised.

"Hilloa, too!" shouted the first, holding out both hands, which his companion grasped and shook heartily.

"John Wilde!—where in the mischief—"

"George Merill!—where in the world—"

"What brought you here, John?"

"Where have you been, George? You look like a Bedouin?"

"I feel like one. Come let us go and sit under the laurels by the fountain and have a good, sensible New-England talk."

"Now, tell me when you left home?" said John Wilde, as they settled themselves upon a stone seat under the laurels, where the misty spray of the fountain was occasionally blown against their cheeks.

"Two years ago. For the last six months I have been exploring the Nile, and trying my best to un-riddle the Sphynx; but she made no sign, and I got sick of it and came to Rome to rest. I arrived only this morning, little expecting to find an old friend before night."

Then they fell to talking over their travels and adventures; and as the twilight deepened around them, and the stars looked down out of the purple heavens, thoughts of their far-off home in the western world came fluttering into their hearts like doves flying home to their cotes; and they questioned each other as to the latest news.

"I got a letter some months ago from my mother," said John Wilde, dropping his voice; "a letter full of strange news about the Flemmings. I suppose you have heard all about their good fortune. I was heartily glad."

"Yes, I heard about that streak of good luck, or rather I read of it in a Boston paper which my agent sent me. I get nothing but papers from home; nobody writes to me that I care to hear from. My grandfather writes, but his letters are such doleful sermons on the subject of my unconverted state and total depravity that I don't take the trouble to read them. I should have committed suicide long ago, if I had been foolish enough to have taken them to heart. I got one letter from Huldah Sneathen about the time you speak of."

Both were silent for a little while; busy memories were crowding into their minds, fraught with sadness and full of the ghosts of their love's young dreams.

"My mother wrote me word that Hope Flemming had gone to be a nun," said John Wilde at last.

"That's a mistake, John. Huldah told me all about it. She ought to have known, for she was with them in Boston, when—well—it was Eva who went to be a nun or a Sister of Charity, or something of that sort," answered George Merill.

"George, are you certain? are you quite sure?" asked John Wilde, eager and excited.

"Of course I am sure. I remember the very name she has taken. She is now Sister Monica. There's no mistake in its being Eva. I should remember,; for you know, John, how I loved Eva Flemming, and it's not likely that I should forget anything concerning her," replied George Merill sadly.

"When my mother wrote, the family were in Boston, and the news came to her through Miss Debby Wyatt, who no doubt had it second hand from some one else who was misinformed," answered John Wilde, whose heart was beating quickly and joyfully.

It was growing dark, and the young men rose to go. Arm-in-arm, they walked slowly down the steep road, talking as if they had not another day to live. Crossing the Piazza del Popolo, they strolled on, scarcely knowing or caring whither, when they suddenly heard the musical tinkling of a little bell, and saw a procession bearing lighted candles coming towards them. From every window on each side the street was held lighted candles those who held them kneeling devoutly. On the sidewalks, all uncovered and knelt; and upon the air arose, with the faint odor of incense, the solemn *Tantum ergo*, in grave musical numbers.

" Let us get out of the way of that," said George Merill.

" Rather let us keep in the way of it," answered John Wilde, as the procession drew nearer. He uncovered his head and knelt, while George Merill hid himself under the shadow of a deep, arched doorway until it got past. " What is it all, and what does it mean ?" he inquired.

" The priest is carrying the Holy Viaticum to a dying person," replied John Wilde ; " and if you'll excuse me, George, I'll go with them. Later I'll come to your lodgings."

"John, tell me one thing ; are you a Roman Catholic ?" asked George Merill, standing before his friend and looking fixedly at him.

" I am, thank God," was the reply.

" Well! I suppose it's a good thing, old fellow. I'd as lief be a Catholic as anything else, I guess ; but I don't much believe in anything, except my actual existence. I'm at the English hotel in the Piazza di Spagna, and shall wait up for you," And George Merill, light-hearted, careless, and looking upon all religions, irrespective of creed or dogma, as systems good enough in their way for bettering the moral condition of mankind, made a *detour* and wended his way towards his lodgings; while John Wilde, hastily purchasing a wax candle from a shop near by, lighted it and fell into the procession, and accompanied it to the house of the dying, whose soul, trembling on the borders of time, was only waiting to be strengthened with the "life-giving Bread," as it passed through the shadow of death into the presence of Him who declared that "whoever eat of this Bread should have eternal life."

* * * * * * * *

" Now tell me, John, if you please, how it happens that you are a Catholic?" asked George Merill that night, as they both sat in the balcony overlooking the old deserted piazza, talking, and smoking cigars of so choice a brand that the air was fragrant around them. This was one of George Merill's special and dearly-prized luxuries, which John Wilde felt no compunction in sharing.

" Don't expect to hear anything marvellous, George. My conversion was a very gradual and simple business. Before I left home I read ' Milner's End of Controversy,' and other Catholic books, solely to find out Hope's reasons for becoming a Catholic. I was impressed more than I would own up to ; but I wasn't prepared to believe all that I read, or sacrifice my worldly in-

terests either; and so I told Hope; and, as you
know, she thought it best for the happiness of both,
differing so widely in religious belief as we did, to
break off our engagement, almost on the very eve
of our wedding day. I tell you, George, it came
near ruining me, body and soul; it was the bitterest trial I ever had, or ever expect to have; and my
faith in God was shaken to its foundations. Then
I determined to go abroad, and endeavor to forget
my hopeless love, in foreign travel among strange
scenes. But it was no use. The violence of my
emotions simply died out—nothing more; and as a
sort of calm succeeded, I begin to think over the
books I had read, and the conversations I had had
with Hope and her father. You see; *the seed was
planted*, and I all unconscious of it! About this time
I formed the acquaintance of a young Englishman,
on board a steamer, on his way to Rome. He was
of noble birth and large estate—I learned that afterwards from another—but after his conversion he
resigned his rank and fortune, except so much,
which was to be annually expended for the poor,
and determined to enter the Society of Jesus and
devote his life to the service of God. I knew nothing of his history then; but it happened one day
that I was able to do him a little service when he
was quite ill, for which he was very grateful, and
his reserve melted away like frost under the sun-

shine. He was very fragile, and often reminded
me of Reuben Flemming. His intellect was highly
cultivated, and his natural gifts were wonderful.
As we grew more and more attached to each other,
I found out his religion : then we began to discuss
the subject, and at last we talked of nothing else.
We journeyed to Rome together ; he entered the
novitiate at the Gesù, then I saw him only occasionally. One day, towards the close of Lent, on Fri-
day, I went to the Coliseum to see the " stations."
He, with other scholastics from the Gesù, was
there. I got as near him as I could, hoping to ex-
change a few words with him on our way back; when
I saw him suddenly grow very white, a stream of
blood gushed from his lips and he fell into my arms
unconscious. I got permission to visit him every
day while he lived ; he lived long enough, George,
to prevail with me, by God's grace ; and the day
on which he received the Holy Viaticum, I received
at the same time, in his presence, the Bread of
Life. Independent of the profound joy I experienced in this, my first Communion, it was something
very like heaven to see the angelic smile that irra-
diated his dying countenance as he watched me ; to
feel the faint, loving clasp of his cold fingers, and
hear him whisper as he kissed me : " Well done !
well done !" They were his last words ; in another
moment my friend and brother was at rest. I

staid on in Rome. Somehow I could not bear to leave the spot where I had been so blessed: where I had found a balm which consecrated my trials, and gave me strength to look out into life with a firm, healthful purpose. I could not bear to leave the hallowed grave of my friend, out of whose death my soul had risen into a new life. It was a sacred tie which bound me to the earth where he reposed. Since I had heard the news about Hope Flemming there seemed to be nothing to take me home ; and after my conversion I had still less desire to return. Until to-night, I believed that she had consecrated herself to Almighty God in a religious life."

"No ; it was Eva, John. Be sure of that," said George Merill sadly.

"To-morrow I shall start for home," continued John Wilde. "There is no obstacle now to prevent Hope's fulfilling her engagement with me, unless she has changed her mind."

"She hasn't changed her mind, John ; depend upon that. I congratulate you, old fellow ; upon my soul, I do," exclaimed George Merill, with hearty sincerity. "Here you are settled in the matter of religion, which is a good thing to begin with ; and you will go back and more than realize the hopes which you thought were dead and buried. You are a lucky fellow !" he said, with a sigh, which he tried to smother under a laugh.

"Thank you, George. I am not so sure about Hope Flemming; but I shall go back and see what awaits me," answered John Wilde, rising to go.

Then they parted, with a warm, friendly grasping of the hands, kind, brave words, and promises to write to each other frequently; John Wilde thanking God in his heart of hearts for the fair promise of the future; George Merill sorrowful and lonely, and half believing in Fate.

* * * * * * * *

I have, really, but little more to tell; but my narrative will be incomplete unless I tell that little. If you remember the last time Nick Flemming came back from "The Pines," he told his father that "he believed everything was going to smash up there, through the mismanagement of the Deacon's partner and too much praying." He was not mistaken in his prediction; for soon afterwards there was a strike among the lumbermen, which the "man gifted in prayer" felt to some purpose; for, enraged at his petty tyrannies and disgusting hypocrisy, furious at an effort he made to curtail their wages and still further restrict their privileges, they fell upon him one night and gave him a beating which bruised every bone in his body. The next morning he had vanished—gone off with the Deacon's money—some eight thousand dollars, which he had drawn from time to time under the pretext of using it to buy machinery and materials for the construction of the steam saw-mill, which up to this time had not risen more than two feet above the foundation. Everything was found to be in a terrible snarl at " The Pines," and the business seemed ruined forever. The Deacon took it very hard. Altogether, the loss, the mortification and the worry agitated him and put his blood in such a ferment, that by the time he managed to get all the details of the affair into his head with a clear idea of the situation, he found it more than he could stand, and had an attack of apoplexy, which terminated fatally.

Huldah and Nicholas were soon afterwards married by a young clergyman whom the Flemmings were honored in having for their guest. The young man—just ordained—had fallen into such a precarious state of health, that with the Bishop's consent, and by the advice of his medical man, he accepted the invitation of Wolfert Flemming, who was in Boston at the time, to return home with him to spend the summer months in the bracing, life-restoring air of the New Hampshire hills. The wedding was a very quiet one, and the young couple went to house-keeping in the old brown cottage under the elms where Huldah was born. She became a convert to the Catholic faith, which shed

such a halo of pure happiness throughout her whole
being that she was more cheerful and blithe than
ever; this, with her thrifty, industrious habits, and
real intelligence, made her husband's home a very
happy and attractive one. Miss Debby lived on
with them—Huldah's cross, which she bore with
sweet patience and pity for the lonely, dependent
woman, who let her know without reserve "that
she felt herself disgraced and demeaned by being
obliged to live with Papists." Nothing softened
her : no attention or kindness could sweeten her
bitter nature, and she grumbled and fretted and
found fault to the end of the chapter, affording
Huldah daily, and sometimes hourly, occasions of
merit which were not lost to her. The business at
" The Pines," under Nicholâs Flemming's management, became gradually more prosperous than ever.
Spiritually and temporally, they were blessed beyond all their imaginings, and never ceased giving
thanks to Almighty God, whose providence had
directed all things so mercifully for them.

It was not long after Nick's marriage when
John Wilde came home, nor many days after his
arrival that Hope Flemming had occasion to un-
lock the old cedar chest, in which three years before she had folded away her bridal *trousseau*, her
tears dropping heavily upon the white, transparent,

beautiful garments, as if she had laid a dearly loved face, on which she was never to look upon again, in its coffin. But now I can say no more than that there was great happiness and soon a Catholic wedding in the Old Homestead.

Do you remember the quaint old Puritan room which I described so particularly in the first chapter, its rafters black with age and the breath of Puritan generations who had lived and prayed under them, its floors dark and polished beneath the tread of their feet? Can you imagine the stern prayers that used to be uttered there to be defended against the Pope and idolatry; and the councils that used to be held there over the fate of unfortunate Catholics who had the temerity to trust themselves to their mercy; and the righteous " amen " uttered, when " hanging" or " branding," was determined on.

Now behold! At one end of the room, in front of the tiled fireplace, which was concealed by boughs of cedar, stood a temporary altar decorated with lights and flowers. There was a costly crucifix upon it, which John Wilde brought from abroad— a genuine Benvenuto Cellini, the dealer had assured him; and at the foot of the crucifix a quaint old chalice, which Father H—— had found among the antique treasures of silver and gold in the *buffet* which the Dutch ancestors of the Flemmings had taken, with other rich spoils, from some Spanish galleon which they afterwards sunk. It was a sacramental cup; the inscription and the devices upon it were unmistakable, and now it was to be put once more to the holy use for which it was fashioned. Father —— celebrated the bridal Mass; all the family—and Patrick McCue, an honored guest—being present; also the Wilburs, who thought it the finest show they had ever seen. Truly was that feast of the Bread of Eternal Life, which the Flemmings and Patrick McCue partook of that fair summer morning with John Wilde and his bride, a holy and happy one! Eva, far away in her novitiate in the beautiful valley of St. Joseph's, offered her Communion in spirit with theirs, and prayed for the happiness, temporal and eternal, of her dear ones at home. Mrs. Wilde's heart was half broken at her son's conversion, and she declined being present at the wedding; indeed, it was more than a year before she consented to see him or his wife. But a little girl was born to them, which they named for her; and that vanquished her, then she was very happy, and ashamed of herself. One day John was unpacking a box which George Merill had sent him from China. He took out a rich silk robe, such as are worn by mandarins of the first class, and he and Hope were examining it, when Mrs. Wild came in with her chubby namesake in her arms.

"Goodsakes, John!" she exclaimed, "is that the dress you wear when you go to Mass?"* It was the first reference she had ever made to his religion, and it was too much for him; he shouted with laughter, and was tempted to tell her "yes," but didn't. But it broke the ice; and from time to time after that they had many talks about the Catholic religion and its doctrines. Mrs. Wilde, now very old, and waiting any hour for the coming of death, is prepared with the best dispositions to be received into the Church as soon as Father H——, who is expected from Boston, arrives.

Soon after Hope's wedding, she noticed one day that the portrait of old Lady Pendarvis was hanging in the "best room," with a wreath of evergreen and *immortelles* around it.

" Why, mother, who did this?" she asked in surprise.

"I did, Hope. Lady Pendarvis was a Catholic."

"And you knew it all the time?"

"Yes, and I should have been glad to burn it up any day, once, for that very reason; but she looked too much like Ruby."

* This question was really asked.

"Dear Ruby!" said Hope, looking dreamily at the picture, while her thoughts were far away in the atelier of the now famous artist. Dear Ruby! how glad I shall be to see him! Why, mother, the papers say that some of the things he has made are equal to the antiques, and he has more orders than he can execute; and honors are conferred upon him constantly by royal personages. I'm very proud of him."

"Well! it seems a very useless sort of a business to me. I can't see the good of it; and never could. But he's happy; and I try to be content," said Mrs. Flemming, brushing a tear from her cheeks.

*　　*　　*　　*　　*　　*

The Wilburs staid on at Mill farm : and Wilbur is now Wolfert Flemming's factor, and one of the thriving men of the neighborhood. The Flemmings live among themselves, still avoided, and their prosperity envied by their Puritan friends. The old Puritan bitterness is not dead ; but it is more feeble, and slowly dying out in staunch, brave New England; and it is safe to believe that upon the soil where men have suffered for the faith in the old Puritan times—where in our own day a convent has been burnt* to the ground, and a holy

---

* Ursuline Convent at Charlestown.

priest* tarred and feathered and almost murdered by fanatical mobs—the Church will grow and flourish—nay, even now in some parts it is growing and flourishing, " like a tree hard by living waters."

* Father Bapst, S. J.

THE END

THE AMERICAN
CATHOLIC TRADITION

An Arno Press Collection

Callahan, Nelson J., editor. **The Diary of Richard L. Burtsell, Priest of New York.** 1978

Curran, Robert Emmett. **Michael Augustine Corrigan and the Shaping of Conservative Catholicism in America, 1878-1902.** 1978

Ewens, Mary. **The Role of the Nun in Nineteenth-Century America** (Doctoral Thesis, The University of Minnesota, 1971). 1978

McNeal, Patricia F. **The American Catholic Peace Movement 1928-1972** (Doctoral Dissertation, Temple University, 1974). 1978

Meiring, Bernard Julius. **Educational Aspects of the Legislation of the Councils of Baltimore, 1829-1884** (Doctoral Dissertation, University of California, Berkeley, 1963). 1978

Murnion, Philip J., **The Catholic Priest and the Changing Structure of Pastoral Ministry, New York, 1920-1970** (Doctoral Dissertation, Columbia University, 1972). 1978

White, James A., **The Era of Good Intentions: A Survey of American Catholics' Writing Between the Years 1880-1915** (Doctoral Thesis, University of Notre Dame, 1957). 1978

Dyrud, Keith P., Michael Novak and Rudolph J. Vecoli, editors. **The Other Catholics.** 1978

Gleason, Philip, editor. **Documentary Reports on Early American Catholicism.** 1978

Bugg, Lelia Hardin, editor. **The People of Our Parish.** 1900

Cadden, John Paul. **The Historiography of the American Catholic Church: 1785-1943.** 1944

Caruso, Joseph. **The Priest.** 1956

Congress of Colored Catholics of the United States. **Three Catholic Afro-American Congresses.** [1893]

Day, Dorothy. **From Union Square to Rome.** 1940

Deshon, George. **Guide for Catholic Young Women.** 1897

Dorsey, Anna H[anson]. **The Flemmings.** [1869]

Egan, Maurice Francis. **The Disappearance of John Longworthy.** 1890

Ellard, Gerald. **Christian Life and Worship.** 1948

England, John. **The Works of the Right Rev. John England, First Bishop of Charleston.** 1849. 5 vols.

Fichter, Joseph H. **Dynamics of a City Church.** 1951

Furfey, Paul Hanly. **Fire on the Earth.** 1936

Garraghan, Gilbert J. **The Jesuits of the Middle United States.** 1938. 3 vols.

Gibbons, James. **The Faith of Our Fathers.** 1877

Hecker, I[saac] T[homas]. **Questions of the Soul.** 1855

Houtart, François. **Aspects Sociologiques Du Catholicisme Américain.** 1957

[Hughes, William H.] **Souvenir Volume. Three Great Events in the History of the Catholic Church in the United States.** 1889

[Huntington, Jedediah Vincent]. **Alban: A Tale of the New World.** 1851

Kelley, Francis C., editor. The First American Catholic Missionary Congress. 1909

Labbé, Dolores Egger. **Jim Crow Comes to Church.** 1971

LaFarge, John. **Interracial Justice.** 1937

Malone, Sylvester L. **Dr. Edward McGlynn.** 1918

The Mission-Book of the Congregation of the Most Holy Redeemer. 1862

O'Hara, Edwin V. **The Church and the Country Community.** 1927

Pise, Charles Constantine. **Father Rowland.** 1829

Ryan, Alvan S., editor. **The Brownson Reader.** 1955

Ryan, John A., **Distributive Justice.** 1916

Sadlier, [Mary Anne]. **Confessions of an Apostate.** 1903

Sermons Preached at the Church of St. Paul the Apostle, New York, During the Year 1863. 1864

Shea, John Gilmary. **A History of the Catholic Church Within the Limits of the United States.** 1886/1888/1890/1892. 4 Vols.

Shuster, George N. **The Catholic Spirit in America.** 1928

Spalding, J[ohn] L[ancaster]. **The Religious Mission of the Irish People and Catholic Colonization.** 1880

Sullivan, Richard. **Summer After Summer.** 1942

[Sullivan, William L.] **The Priest.** 1911

Thorp, Willard. **Catholic Novelists in Defense of Their Faith, 1829-1865.** 1968

Tincker, Mary Agnes. **San Salvador.** 1892

Weninger, Franz Xaver. **Die Heilige Mission** *and* **Praktische Winke Für Missionare.** 1885. 2 Vols. in 1

Wissel, Joseph. **The Redemptorist on the American Missions.** 1920. 3 Vols. in 2

The World's Columbian Catholic Congresses and Educational Exhibit. 1893

Zahm, J[ohn] A[ugustine]. **Evolution and Dogma.** 1896